NIETZSCHE

The Key Concepts

Peter R. Sedgwick

Routledge
Taylor & Francis Group

LONDON AND NEW YORK

First published 2009
by Routledge
2 Park Square, Milton Park, Abingdon, Oxon, OX14 4RN

Simultaneously published in the USA and Canada
by Routledge
270 Madison Avenue, New York, NY 10016

Routledge is an imprint of the Taylor & Francis Group, an informa business

© 2009 Peter R. Sedgwick

Typeset in Bembo by Taylor & Francis Books
Printed and bound in Great Britain by TJ International Ltd, Padstow, Cornwall

British Library Cataloguing in Publication Data
A catalogue record for this book is available from the British Library

Library of Congress Cataloging in Publication Data
Sedgwick, Peter R.
Nietzsche: the key concepts / Peter Sedgwick.
p. cm. – (Routledge key guides)
1. Nietzsche, Friedrich Wilhelm, 1844–1900. I. Title.
B3317.S49 2009
193–dc22
2008048205

ISBN 10: 0-415-26376-X (hbk)
ISBN 10: 0-415-26377-8 (pbk)
ISBN 10: 0-203-87851-5 (ebk)

ISBN 13: 978-0-415-26376-4 (hbk)
ISBN 13: 978-0-415-26377-1 (pbk)
ISBN 13: 978-0-203-87851-4 (ebk)

For my mother

CONTENTS

LIST OF CONCEPTS

Platonism/Socratism
politics
postmodernism/deconstruction
prehistory
promise
psychology

reason
revaluation of values

science
self

self-overcoming
slave morality
sovereign individual
State, the

truth

will to power
will to truth
woman/women

Zarathustra

ABBREVIATIONS

Antichrist   *Twilight of the Idols* and *The Antichrist*, trans. R. J. Hollingdale, Harmondsworth: Penguin, 1968. First published 1889.

Beyond Good and Evil   *Beyond Good and Evil*, trans. R. J. Hollingdale, Harmondsworth: Penguin, 1973. First published 1885.

Birth of Tragedy   *The Birth of Tragedy* in *Basic Writings of Nietzsche*, ed. and trans. Walter Kaufmann, New York: Basic Books, 1968. First published 1872.

Daybreak   *Daybreak*, trans. R. J. Hollingdale, Cambridge: Cambridge University Press, 1982. First published 1881.

Ecce Homo   *Ecce Homo*, trans. R. J. Hollingdale, Harmondsworth: Penguin, 1992. First published 1908.

Gay Science   *The Gay Science*, trans. Walter Kaufmann, New York: Vintage, 1974. First published 1882/1887.

Genealogy   *On the Genealogy of Morality*, ed. K. Ansell-Pearson, trans. C. Diethe, Cambridge: Cambridge University Press, 1994. First published 1887.

Human, All Too Human   *Human, All Too Human*, trans. R. J. Hollingdale, Cambridge: Cambridge University Press, 1986. First published 1878–80. Also includes: *Assorted Opinions and Maxims* and *The Wanderer and his Shadow*.

Twilight   *Twilight of the Idols* and *The Antichrist*, trans. R. J. Hollingdale, Harmondsworth: Penguin, 1968. First published 1889.

Untimely Meditations   *Untimely Meditations*, trans. R. J. Hollingdale, Cambridge: Cambridge University Press, 1983. First published 1873–6.

Will to Power   *The Will to Power*, trans. Walter Kaufmann and R. J. Hollingdale, New York: Viking, 1968. First published 1901.

Zarathustra   *Thus Spoke Zarathustra* in *The Portable Nietzsche*, ed. and trans. Walter Kaufmann, New York: Penguin, 1995. First published 1883–92.

PREFACE

Friedrich Nietzsche was born near the city of Leipzig in 1844. In his youth, he attended the well-known Pforta School and then the universities of Bonn and Leipzig. At university he read the philosophy of Schopenhauer and studied classical Greek philosophy. Nietzsche specialised in classical Greek texts, which bore fruit in the form of his appointment at the age of twenty-four to a post at the University of Basel. After a year, Nietzsche was made a professor. After another nine years, he was forced to retire due to ill health. The university granted him a pension which supported him for the rest of his life. For near on a decade, Nietzsche wrote, travelling through Europe as he did so. In January 1889, he suffered a mental collapse from which he was never to recover. He died in 1900. The brevity of Nietzsche's creative life, 1872–88, stands in stark contrast to the books he wrote and the transformations of perspective they bear witness to.

Nietzsche is a thinker at once approachable and provocative, a writer by turns endearing, irritating, and challenging. He is nearly always complex: often when writing in terms that appear straightforward he turns out to be at his most subtle: 'I did say I would speak crudely: which does not in any way signify a desire for it to be heard crudely, understood crudely' (Genealogy, III, 16). He is a philosopher of stunning originality, which is not by any means to say that everything he has to say is to be agreed with. Since not long after his tragic mental collapse at the age of forty-four, Nietzsche has also been written about in industrial proportions – a fact that, given his views about mass culture, may well have amused and horrified him in equal measure. Indeed, so much Nietzsche literature exists that it would be impossible to summarise it in ten books. Much of what has been claimed of him, for him, and against him, has usually been contested elsewhere. Faced with this problem, this volume takes a rather direct approach. It seeks to offer the student reader of Nietzsche who is (as any informed reader of him ought to be, too) sometimes nonplussed by what they encounter, straightforward discussions of notions central to the Nietzschean oeuvre. Some things are pretty obvious; some are less so. Suggested reading, in all but a few cases, has been relegated to the appropriate place at the end of an entry. Each entry should be read as no more than a signpost, something that directs the reader to go beyond it both into the rich endowment of Nietzsche literature and, above all, into the often rich terrain of his thought.

NIETZSCHE

The Key Concepts

AMOR FATI

Amor fati is love of fate. This attitude, Nietzsche tells us in *Ecce Homo* ('The Wagner Case', §4), characterises his 'innermost nature'. The phrase initially occurs in *The Gay Science* (§276), where it is expressed in terms of Nietzsche's desire to be a 'Yes-sayer', i.e. to be one that does not negate existence but affirms it, even in criticism: '*Looking away* shall be my only negation'. In this regard, love of fate is an essential constituent of the mature Nietzsche's Dionysian aesthetic, for the deep desire to embrace existence and endow one's life with a sense of justification requires that *everything* in life be affirmed – the key feature of the notion of eternal recurrence. *Amor fati* is Nietzsche's formula for all that is great in humanity. It means not wishing anything at all to be different about one's life: neither forwards nor backwards, nor in all eternity. To love fate means to love what happens because this is how it *must* happen: one cannot avoid this necessity without *denying oneself* and by implication condemning existence. One must therefore love what is even terrible about one's life. Love of fate means, in effect, love of the inherent plurality of life, of the fact that every moment of joy brings with it the potential for loss and suffering. Nietzsche's view is well illustrated by the following passage:

> no one *gives* a human being his qualities: not God, not society, not his parents or ancestors, not *he himself* [...]. *No one* is accountable for existing at all, or for being constituted as he is, or for living in the circumstances and surroundings in which he lives [...]. One is necessary, one is a piece of fate, one belongs to the whole, one *is* in the whole – there exists nothing which could judge, measure, compare, condemn our being, for that would be to judge, measure, compare, condemn the whole...*But nothing exists apart from the whole!*
> (*Twilight of the Idols,* 'The Four Great Errors', §8)

Fate suspends the possibility of criticism and the only viable attitude that remains is love of existence. Such love, according to Nietzsche, is the prerequisite of all great creative achievement.

Further reading: Thiele 1990; Yovel 1986.

APOLLO/APOLLINIAN

The Apollinian is a notion that Nietzsche deploys in his first book, *The Birth of Tragedy*. Apollo is the sun god of the Ancient Greeks, he is 'the shining one', the god of light and 'of all plastic energies' (*Birth of Tragedy,* §1), a figure who rules over the inner world of self-consciousness. The Apollinian aesthetic principle, whose first manifestation is in Homeric myth, presents an art world characterised in terms of dreams. It encapsulates a formalised aesthetic of constraint that channels and thus structures in such a way that artistic expression of the most formalised kind is rendered possible. The Apollinian is thus best expressed in terms of order and form, as the form-endowing force. It is strongly associated with the 'principle of individuation' in so far as by way of its formalistic aspect the individual is differentiated from the rest of reality to the extent that he or she can regard it with some degree of detachment and hence objectivity. The individuated element is most manifest in the Apollinian plastic art of sculpture. In contrast to the Apollinian stands the Dionysian. According to *The Birth of Tragedy,* the fusion of these two antagonistic principles underlies the great achievement of Ancient Greek tragedy. The Apollinian provided a structural condition wherein the Dionysian could be given its fullest expression in artistic form.

See also: **art.**

Further reading: Del Caro 1981; Gillespie and Strong 1988; Kaufmann 1974; Kemal et al. 1998; Schacht 1983; Tejera 1987.

ART

From the early, metaphysical speculations enshrined in *The Birth of Tragedy* to the final outpouring of his very last works (*The Antichrist, Ecce Homo*), the path of Nietzsche's thought is patterned by a concern with the nature of art and the creative artist. Consistently this concern is also accompanied by an interest in the wider significance of the aesthetically conceived principles of the Dionysian and Apollinian, first elucidated in *The Birth of Tragedy.* Writing in a note of 1888, Nietzsche states that these two principles can be comprehended in the following manner:

> The word 'Dionysian' means: an urge to unity, a reaching out beyond personality [...] the great pantheistic sharing of joy and sorrow that sanctifies and calls good even the most terrible and questionable qualities of life [...] the feeling of the necessary unity of creation and destruction. The word 'Apollinian' means:

the urge to perfect self-sufficiency, to the typical 'individual', to all that simplifies, distinguishes, makes strong, clear, unambiguous, typical: freedom under the law. The further development of art is necessarily tied to the antagonism between these two natural artistic powers [...].

(*Will to Power*, §1050)

The development in question is exemplified by the 'monological' conception of art Nietzsche discusses in Book 5, §367, of *The Gay Science*. This is a form of art that is authentic because it is the consequence of an act of creation that is bound by the internal logic of the artwork rather than exterior considerations. The concept of monological art is best illustrated by considering initially Nietzsche's earlier claim in his first book, *The Birth of Tragedy*, that the Dionysian and Apollinian principles form the condition for the emergence of Greek tragedy. This is because the mature Nietzsche's assertion that there is such a thing as an authentic, monological mode of artistic creation is a later recapitulation of the ideas first developed in the earlier book.

In *The Birth of Tragedy*, both culture and human nature are envisaged as attaining their greatest possible expression through art: 'art represents the highest task and the truly metaphysical activity of this life' (*Birth of Tragedy*, 'Preface'). Nietzsche seeks to answer the question as to what might be the highest form of human activity that can serve as the goal of culture by way of the redemptive capabilities of art. Primarily, this involves focusing upon the Greek tragic form as the means of providing a clue to the way in which art can redeem humanity from the pain of individuated existence identified by Schopenhauerian pessimism as the cause of all human suffering. On the one hand, Nietzsche argues, we are presented with the Dionysian aspect of art. The Dionysian artist achieves a state of self-identification with a 'primal unity' (*Birth of Tragedy*, §5) which signifies a state of 'oneness of man with nature' (*Birth of Tragedy*, §3). This sense of oneness overthrows established social boundaries separating individuals. In the Greek Dionysian festivals, 'nature for the first time attains her artistic jubilee; it is with them that the destruction of the *principuum individuationis* for the first time becomes an artistic phenomenon' (*Birth of Tragedy*, §2). Under the sway of Dionysian ecstasy, Nietzsche argues, humanity experienced itself and its relationship with nature *symbolically*. In order for such symbolic experience to be possible, however, the ability to think symbolically must already be in place. The symbolic order that the Dionysian uses to achieve its expression is, in fact, the product of its apparent opposite: the Apollinian, the 'symbolical analogue of the soothsaying faculty and of the arts generally, which make life possible and worth living' (*Birth of Tragedy,* §1). Apollo is the 'form-giving force, which reached its consummation in Greek sculpture' (Kaufmann 1974, p. 128). The Apollinian is an artistic expression of the proportion and harmony of the human form. The Apollinian art of sculpture inhabits a world of images, with which may be contrasted the 'nonimagistic, Dionysian art of music' (*Birth of Tragedy,* §1). The Apollinian is 'the principle of individuation' which, through sculpture, presents an individuated human identity. In opposition to the Dionysian principle (a state analogous to that of '*intoxication*'), the Apollinian inhabits a symbolic world of '*dreams*' (*Birth of Tragedy,* §1). Whereas the Dionysian engenders a state of 'self-forgetfulness', the Apollinian 'dream experience' consists (at the symbolic level) in that which is itself forgotten in Dionysian rapture. This is because what is forgotten in the Dionysian state, Nietzsche claims, is both the individuated existence of the self and the life-enhancing illusion which art is able to bestow upon life. This is why Dionysus needs Apollo: the Apollinian provides the Dionysian with the symbolic language that is used both to conceal the sublime Dionysian terror of existence and yet, in moments of Dionysian rapture, is simultaneously called upon in order to reveal it. For this reason, the harmonious, Apollinian consciousness of the Ancient Greek finds itself mirrored in the Dionysian state. Hence, the Apollinian individual's response to the spectacle of the collective release of Dionysian festivity:

> With what astonishment must the Apollinian Greek have beheld him [the Dionysian reveller]! With an astonishment that was all the greater the more it was mingled with the shuddering suspicion that all this was actually not so very alien to him after all, in fact, that it was only his Apollinian consciousness which, like a veil, hid this Dionysian world from his vision.
>
> (*Birth of Tragedy,* §2)

In the Attic tragedy these two elements become reconciled in 'an equally Dionysian and Apollinian form of art' (*Birth of Tragedy,* §1). In the tragic form we have, on the one hand, the tragic chorus, 'the symbol of the whole exited Dionysian throng' (*Birth of Tragedy,* §1). Through the Dionysian state engendered by the chorus, the spectator's individuality is sundered, so that he or she becomes an active participator within the tragedy. The dialogue of the tragedy, on the other hand, is Apollinian. Nietzsche notes that Sophocles' language is remarkable precisely for its 'Apollinian precision and lucidity' (*Birth of Tragedy*, §1). This language is a mask, a veil which is a necessary consequence of seeing into the 'terrors of nature' (*Birth of Tragedy*, §9). The Dionysian excitement engendered by the chorus is 'transferred [...] to that masked figure', which becomes an instantiated symbol of Dionysus: 'now Dionysus no longer speaks through forces but as an epic hero' (*Birth of Tragedy*, §8). In short, the tragic hero speaks symbolically *through* the language of Apollo, but speaks of the Dionysian terrors of existence. However, it would be incorrect to assert, in the light of this, that, for Nietzsche, the Apollinian grounds the Dionysian. The 'bright image projections of the Sophoclean hero' reveal the opposite of a linguistic, 'optical phenomenon' dependent upon images (*Birth of Tragedy*, §9). The imagery and language of the figures within the drama point us toward something of which they themselves can only be said to be its effects. Apollinian language is a mask that serves to conceal and reveal the Dionysian terror of existence at one and the same time (*Birth of Tragedy*, §10). The Dionysian and the Apollinian are thereby locked together inexorably. These two aspects need each other to such an extent that neither could be said to be primary: the communication of the non-imagistic reality of the world of nature must take place within the images of language, just as language must negate itself at the very moment it succeeds in presenting the Dionysian reality. It is for this reason that when the later dramatist Euripides spurned the Dionysian he also lost touch with the Apollinian. The greatness of the Attic tragedy, according to Nietzsche, lies in the equilibrium achieved within it of the Dionysian and Apollinian elements, in the constant interplay of the tension which exists between the two. But in what way does Euripides actually abandon Dionysus? The answer to this question leads directly to the monological aesthetics of the later Nietzsche, for it is in the role of the spectator that the key to Nietzsche's view of art is to be found.

In the same way as the spectator in the theatre is able to 'overlook' those about him (both in the sense of to ignore and survey them) so, too, the tragic chorus both addresses and ignores its audience. This is because the 'chorus is, first of all, a vision of the Dionysian mass of spectators' (*Birth of Tragedy*, §8). This vision engenders in the spectator a state in which their sense of 'reality', in so far as this word refers to the social world comprising fellow spectators sitting there with them, is suspended. As such, the chorus is not actually addressing 'spectators' as an audience composed of civilised individuals engaged in a night out at the theatre. As a 'Dionysian mass', the chorus itself constitutes the audience of the play: the chorus is the servant of Dionysus and only addresses the individual spectator in so far as it excites the listeners' mood to such a degree that with the appearance of the tragic hero they perceive 'a visionary figure, born as it were from their own rapture' (*Birth of Tragedy*, §8). The spectator is thereby invited to abandon his or her individuated identity and become a member of the chorus, a servant of Dionysus. Euripides, in contrast, commits the ultimate act of sacrilege against the Dionysian by introducing 'the *spectator* onto the stage' (*Birth of Tragedy*, §11). In this way, the spectator is invited to pass judgement on proceedings rather than becoming fused with them. In fact, this spectator is not to be found amongst the 'masses in general' but takes two forms: first, that of 'Euripides himself, Euripides *as thinker*, not as poet'; second, the enemy of Dionysus and the inventor of dialectic, Socrates (*Birth of Tragedy*, §12). The poetic force of Dionysian art is in this fashion sundered by the demands placed upon it by logical thought. Socrates, a figure of 'tremendous intellect' in which 'instinct becomes the critic and consciousness […] the creator' (*Birth of Tragedy*, §13), marks a turning point in Greek culture whereby, through his pupil Plato, '*philosophic thought* overgrows art and compels it to cling close to the trunk of dialectic' (*Birth of Tragedy*, §14). The rationalist demand that the world conform to the prescriptions of logical discourse thereby sunders the poetic vision of Dionysian tragedy. The individuated spectator, in other words, takes control of the aesthetic realm and demands that it serve the interests of 'the *theoretical man*' (*Birth of Tragedy*, §15). The theoretical man is the individuated being *par excellence*, and this individuated nature justifies itself through the theoretical dissolution of masks and illusions. It is for this reason that it must break with the Dionysian (which engenders loss of self) and must likewise be abandoned by the Apollinian, whose masked illusions and symbols operate in the service of Dionysus.

Nietzsche himself is a theoretical man, i.e. a thinker who dissolves illusions through analysis. But he also considers himself an advocate of the Dionysian. This engenders a tension that requires resolution, and the already-mentioned monological view of art outlined in §367 of *The Gay Science* represents an attempt to overcome theoretical traits, or at least render them irrelevant when it comes to the question of the meaning of art conceived of as a creative act. Through this one gets a clear view both of the mature Nietzsche's conception of the nature of art and of the close relationship this view bears to his earlier writing. There is, Nietzsche argues, a distinction to be drawn between all works of art (and, indeed, attitudes of thought, too): 'All thought, poetry, painting, compositions, even buildings and sculptures, belong either to monological art or to art before witnesses' (*Gay Science*,

§367). Whereas the latter gains its value from the spectator, the former presupposes 'solitude'. In fact, what we are presented with here is an aesthetics which can be opposed to Kant's, for, as Nietzsche argues in *On the Genealogy of Morality*, Kantian aesthetics depends upon an unconscious introduction of a spectator as the subject of moral judgement into the concept of the beautiful. As Laurence Lampert notes, the view of art presented here is rooted in the death of God; it is the aesthetics of a solitary, for whom God is no longer a possibility, and is hence an aesthetics which is 'impossible in religion' (Lampert 1993, p. 396). Significantly, however, there is perhaps one god before whom Nietzsche's monological art can be practised, and that is Dionysus. Dionysian art is required by 'those who suffer from the *over-fullness of life* – they want a Dionysian art and likewise a tragic view of life, a tragic insight' (*Gay Science*, §370). The difference between those who want Dionysian art and those impoverished souls who require art as a palliative to life resides not only in the latter's requirement that art redeem them from themselves. Those who suffer from life also embrace 'logic, the conceptual understandability of existence – for logic calms and gives confidence – in short, a certain warm narrowness that keeps away fear and encloses one in optimistic horizons' (*Gay Science*, §370). In short, those who suffer from life are akin to Socrates, the worshipper of individuated logic and rationality (see *Twilight of the Idols*, 'The Problem of Socrates') and the culprit singled out as the destroyer of the tragic in *The Birth of Tragedy*. The parallels between the early and the later Nietzsche do not stop here. The creative, monological aesthetic also embraces a moment of forgetting which has its analogue in the forgetting of self experienced by the Dionysian worshipper. Thus, Nietzsche asserts that he cannot think

> of any more profound difference in the whole orientation of an artist than this, whether he looks at his work in progress (at 'himself') from the point of view of the witness, or whether he 'has forgotten the world,' which is the essential feature of all monological art; it is based on *forgetting*, it is the music of forgetting.
>
> (*Gay Science*, §367)

In other words, the creative act engenders the suspension of the social realm, of others. In the same way as the spectator of the Attic tragedy becomes a member of the chorus and servant of Dionysus so, too, the monological artist is dissolved into the creative act itself. Thus, through art, the self has become 'the work in progress', an Apollinian mask that simultaneously conceals and expresses Dionysian creative rapture. In Attic tragedy, the role of language is conceived in terms of its ability to engender within an audience a state of forgetting of self. In this state, the individuated subject loses its sense of identity and the 'rational', normative constraints of social life are abandoned along with it. In *The Birth of Tragedy,* the Apollinian language of tragedy thereby achieves the aesthetic effect of taking its audience beyond language into a realm of immediate aesthetic awareness of the violent, exhilarating world of becoming, where the individuated self is lost in a moment of reidentification with the natural world from which humanity sprung. Likewise, for the later Nietzsche, the monological artist creates in a manner that can only be conceived from the perspective of this state of abandonment of self, where the self becomes subsumed within the 'music of forgetting' (*Gay Science,* §367). The symbolic order of language and image is merely the product of this state, an Apollinian residue or mask that, in Dionysian works of art, points beyond itself. It is no coincidence, then, that Nietzsche describes one of his own pivotal experiences of artistic creation, that of writing *Thus Spoke Zarathustra,* in parallel terms: 'You hear, you don't search; you take, you don't ask who is giving; like a flash of lightning a thought flares up, with necessity, with no hesitation as to its form – I never had any choice' (*Ecce Homo, 'Thus Spoke Zarathustra',* §3).

Art, for Nietzsche, is consistently regarded as being replete with the potential for challenging the tyranny of unthinking adherence to norms. Equally, art is to be grasped in terms of its relation to both suffering and life. In this regard, as in others, art and philosophy are one. All art and philosophy can be regarded in terms of their ability to serve 'struggling and growing life; they always presuppose suffering and sufferers' (*Gay Science,* §370). However, sufferers come in two forms. There is the Dionysian sufferer, the being who suffers from 'the *over-fullness of life*', who desires tragic Dionysian art because through it this over-fullness can be affirmed. Then there is the person who suffers from '*impoverishment of life*', who seeks rest and comfort, 'anaesthesia' from art (*Gay Science,* §370). Romanticism in art and philosophy is an expression of this impoverished sensibility. Wagnerian music and Schopenhauerian pessimistic philosophy epitomise it. The key artistic question, in turn, poses the problem of whether an artwork is an expression of a lack that needs negating or an excess of creative energy. Dionysian art, as fulfilling the last of these demands, is 'an expression of an overflowing energy that is pregnant with future' (*Gay Science,* §370). It remains a kind of pessimism, in so far as the Dionysian being lives in a world without hope of redemption by way of a 'beyond', but it is a 'pessimism of the future', a 'Dionysian pessimism' (*Gay Science,* §370).

The significance of the arts of tragedy and music as conceived of in *The Birth of Tragedy* is rethought by the later Nietzsche. Nevertheless, tragedy remains open to being reinterpreted as an expression of cultural need. For example, Nietzsche comments that the Greeks of the time of that other earlier exemplar of tragedy worthy to rank alongside Sophocles, Aeschylus, were beings whose moods were resistant to being easily swayed (*Daybreak*, §172). Tragedy served them because it allowed an encounter with the feeling of pity and the suffering this engenders in a manner that provokes even the most hardened soul. Art becomes a mirror. Thus, modernity, in contrast, is an era of oversensitivity where, consequently, tragedy is no longer possible as a means to the creation of such feeling. The same goes for music. Modern music, too, Nietzsche notes, must appeal to people all too easily moved. Perhaps, he ponders, there may come a time when things are better, when 'artists have to make it appeal to the strong men in themselves, severe, dominated by the dark seriousness of their own passions' (*Daybreak*, §172). Already evident here is the presaging of the mature Nietzsche's view of the monological Dionysian aesthetic. Such an aesthetic stands opposed most clearly to what Nietzsche comes to regard as the narcotic temptation represented by decadent Wagnerian music drama (see *The Case of Wagner* – memorable not least for Nietzsche's description of his forcing himself to 'enjoy' Bizet's opera *Carmen* for the twentieth time – §1).

Further reading: Kaufmann 1974; Kemal et al. 1998; Liebert 2004; Magnus et al. 1993; Pothen 2002; Rampley 2000; Winchester 1994; Young 1992.

ASCETICISM/ASCETIC PRIEST

Nietzsche's interest in the ascetic, the denier of bodily pleasures, is linked most notably to his discussions of the ascetic priest and philosophy. In *On the Genealogy of Morality,* the priest is discussed as the creature of *ressentiment* (rancour or resentment – Nietzsche resorts to the French word because there is no precise equivalent in German)without equal and promulgator of slave morality (see the first essay). However, beings of this kind are not as easily dismissed in negative terms as this initial portrait might suggest. For one thing, the priestly type is responsible for the development of our intellectual and spiritual abilities (*Genealogy*, Essay I, §7). Without such people there would, indeed, be no human history worth talking about. Asceticism has its origins in human prehistory. When the primitive predecessors of humanity first became communal beings, Nietzsche argues, they were obliged by the need to survive to police themselves by way of norms. The individual, initially a creature dominated by the drives and the whim of the moment, is by degrees transformed into a being of culture, one able to make and keep promises. The moral memory that characterises and differentiates humankind from the rest of the animals was therefore quite literally, battered, burnt and stamped into existence by way of force being exerted over the body. Promises, in their original form, inspired dread, and the solemnity of a promise today is still a reminder of this (*Genealogy*, Essay II, §3). Suffering and pain lie at the heart of the emergence of humanity and human psychology.

> When man decided to make a memory for himself, it never happened without blood, torments and sacrifices: the most horrifying sacrifices and forfeits (the sacrifice of the first born belongs here), the most disgusting mutilations (for example, castration), the cruellest rituals of all religious cults (and all religions are, at their most fundamental, systems of cruelty) – all this has its origin in that particular instinct which discovered that pain was the most powerful aid to mnemonics. The whole of asceticism belongs here as well: a few ideas have to be made ineradicable, ubiquitous, unforgettable, 'fixed', in order to hypnotize the whole nervous and intellectual system through these 'fixed ideas'.
>
> (*Genealogy*, Essay II, §3)

Thus, asceticism pays testimony to the prehistoric conditions that gave rise to deepest psychological impulses of the human being. The question of the significance of ascetic ideals is the subject of the third essay of the *Genealogy*. At one level, Nietzsche comments, asking what asceticism means will provoke different answers depending upon what or who you ask it of. The artist, for example, finds it useful as a tool and disguise wherein their own glorification is rendered possible (Nietzsche is thinking especially of Wagner here). The philosopher, on the other hand, esteems asceticism because it is one of the necessary conditions of his or her existence. Indeed, philosophy only emerged dressed in, and thereby protected by, the garb of the ascetic. Asceticism is a good training for independent thought. Yet, this does not answer the initial question Nietzsche poses about the meaning of ascetic ideals, and especially the role of the ascetic priest in history.

The priest is 'the actual representative of *seriousness*' (*Genealogy*, Essay III, §11). What can such seriousness mean? As with the philosopher, the power and interest of the priestly type is served by asceticism. The identity of the priest, however, is different: the priest represents a different *type*. Whereas asceticism served philosophy as no more than a means and mask to the greater end of developing the will to truth, the priest has another, more essential kind of relation to it. For one thing, 'His *right* to exist stands and falls with ideal'. The ascetic priest values life in a specific manner. The ascetic ideal as the priest exemplifies it is, Nietzsche tells us, one that envisages a timeless and pure metaphysical reality. This ideal is pitted against the world of becoming, change, appearance, the senses, sensuality. Life is taken as 'a bridge to that other existence': 'The ascetic treats life as a wrong path which he has walked along backwards, till he reaches the point where he starts' and demands that others follow him. In this way, the ascetic priest 'imposes his valuation on existence' (*Genealogy*, Essay III, §11). More to the point, this mode of valuation is no weird distortion present in some aspects and periods of human history, but the rule. The ascetic priest is to be found in all times, all societies, and all classes. Why? 'It must be a necessity of the first rank that which makes this species continually grow and prosper when it is *hostile to life, — life itself must have an interest* in preserving such a self-contradictory type' (*Genealogy*, Essay III, §11). Life, for the ascetic priest, is 'a self-contradiction' (*Genealogy*, Essay III, §11). It must thus be mastered. The ascetic priest therefore expresses a deep desire to control the 'most profound conditions' of life itself rather than merely to control and master things in life (*Genealogy*, Essay III, §11). The ascetic priest is also a being of 'unparalleled *ressentiment*' and through them this *ressentiment* wishes to master life (*Genealogy*, Essay III, §11).

Imagine that such a 'will to contradiction and counter-nature can be made to *philosophize*: on what will it vent its inner arbitrariness?' (*Genealogy*, Essay III, §12). The answer is that it will seek '*error* precisely where the actual instinct of life most unconditionally judges there to be truth' (*Genealogy*, Essay III, §12). Thus, the physical world will be dismissed as an illusion (as it is with 'Vendanta philosophy'). The embodied self will hence be denied by priestly asceticism, as will 'reason' in its self-critical reflexive form. This is not wholly bad, since philosophy has learnt from this. The wish to see the world in different ways gives rise to the possibility that the one-sided view of the world that the ascetic priest exemplifies can be overcome using resources gleaned from him. In other words, we can come to realise that all knowledge is embodied and dependent upon perspective as a consequence of being schooled in the rigour that follows from the opposite contention. The ascetic priest himself, however, is a living paradox, an embodied instance of life standing in contradiction to itself (*Genealogy*, Essay III, §13). Nietzsche then offers a surprising answer to his question concerning the meaning and need for the ascetic ideal. The ascetic ideal springs from a need that erupted as a consequence of a wild and untamed proto-humanity being enclosed within the bounds of the social world, replete with its normative constraints. Although civilised, although essentially creatures of culture, we also suffer the price of having been moulded in such terms. The human animal is a creature of the passions, yet the raw material of its passions has been contained, directed, reshaped, reinvented, transformed, and interpreted anew by the social forces to which it must succumb in order to be what it is. Another way of putting this is to say that to be a person is to suffer from simply being here. The human animal is, above all, a sufferer. And what it suffers from most is a tension that arises from within its own as yet 'undetermined' nature (see *Beyond Good and Evil*, §62). Quite simply, we do not know who or what we are, and this troubles us. The effect of civilisation itself (the 'taming of man') has been to create a type of humanity that suffers from an attitude of 'disgust at life' (*Genealogy*, Essay III, §13). The ascetic priest provides a means of applying salve to this sense of self-revulsion. Thus, '*the ascetic ideal springs from the protective and healing instincts of a degenerating life* which uses every means to maintain itself and struggles for its existence' (*Genealogy*, Essay III, §13; see also in this connection the discussion of Socrates in *Twilight of the Idols*, 'The Problem of Socrates'). The ascetic priest is an embodiment of the desire to be elsewhere, in the realm of a 'beyond' that pertains to heavenly perfection, but this desire is the very thing that traps him in existence and renders him a 'tool, who now has to work to create more favourable circumstances for our being here and being man' (*Genealogy*, Essay III, §13). In this way, and in typical fashion, Nietzsche flips an argument on its head. What *seemed* to be a dreadful and contemptible manifestation of human culture now reveals itself in much more complex terms as something positive: 'this apparent enemy of life, this *negative man*, – he actually belongs to the really great forces in life which *conserve and create the positive*' (*Genealogy*, Essay III, §13). Humanity suffers from itself, and the ascetic priest offers a way of making this suffering bearable. He does so by offering an explanation for suffering.

For Nietzsche, it is beyond doubt that humankind is *sick:* 'man [...] is *the* sick animal' (*Genealogy*, Essay III, §13) and is so precisely because what characterises its existence is self-experimentation. We are not beings of a predetermined nature. Unlike the tiger, who has an ecological niche that harmonises with its abilities and possibilities, humanity has lost its niche. We live in the domain of culture, this is our 'natural' realm: we are 'naturally' socially constructed creatures whose relationship with nature is problematic. The very fact that we can talk of nature as opposed to culture betrays our sense of not belonging in the world we inhabit. Humans, for Nietzsche, thus attempt to come to terms with existence by struggling with it rather than letting the conditions of life be dictated by circumstances, as the other animals do. Not least, we do so by seeking to live lives that are meaningful, and in doing so we actively seek to construct this meaning. To be human is to want to be in control, to desire to dominate our environment rather than let our environment dominate us. To this extent, humanity always lives in virtue of its desire for a *future:* 'man', Nietzsche says, is 'the still-unconquered eternal-futurist' (*Genealogy,* Essay III, §13). The price to be paid for this, however, is that we suffer from our own existence. The urge we have to grasp the world in terms of meaning is frustrated; life itself hurts. The ascetic priest thus testifies to the fact that humanity is a manifest contradiction. It is 'a courageous and rich animal', but necessarily as a consequence of this is also 'the most endangered', 'the one most seriously ill': the sickest of all sick animals (*Genealogy,* Essay III, §13). It is this propensity to suffer that gives rise to the human tendency to self-torture (and self-torture can also, for us, involve hurting others; see the second essay of the *Genealogy*). This self-torture, however, in its most spiritual form is what makes our kind carry on living. Just as the philosopher Schopenhauer's 'enemies' tempted him back towards the very existence he renounces in his philosophy so there is a propensity in humankind in general to respond in this way: 'even when he [man] *wounds* himself, this master of destruction, self-destruction, – afterwards it is the wound itself which forces him *to live*' (*Genealogy,* Essay III, §13; for Nietzsche's discussion of Schopenhauer see *Genealogy,* Essay III, §7). The ascetic priest is thus an expression of 'the healing instinct of life' (*Genealogy,* Essay III, §13). The concepts of guilt, sin, damnation, etc., serve to turn the resentment of the sufferer back on him or herself. In this way, the sufferer becomes trained to survey, discipline and overcome his or her own feelings (*Genealogy,* Essay III, §16). The problem is that the priest does not cure but merely perpetuates the disease (*Genealogy,* Essay III, §17). This is where priestly asceticism can become sinister.

The real issues concerning the meaning of the ascetic ideal revolve around the question of its power and how to confront it (*Genealogy,* Essay III, §23). Above all, what is at stake here is the question of *purposes.* The ascetic ideal 'has a *goal*' of such generality that all 'the interests of human existence appear petty and narrow when measured against it' (*Genealogy*, Essay III, §23). It is a supreme ideal in so far as it offers an interpretation of all times, races, of humanity in general which seeks to subordinate all of them to a *single purpose*. This is the secret of its power over us. It 'rejects, denies, affirms, confirms only with reference to *its* interpretation' of the world (*Genealogy*, Essay III, §23). It believes it has 'unconditional *superiority of rank* over any other power' (*Genealogy*, Essay III, §23). Science, Nietzsche adds, stands as the most recent representative of this ideal – and, indeed, would be nothing without it. Likewise, the modern 'free spirits' are not opponents of the ascetic, not least '*because they still believe in truth*' (*Genealogy*, Essay III, §24). There is only one kind of *genuine* opponent of the ascetic ideal, 'these are the comedians of this ideal' (*Genealogy*, Essay III, §27). To embody this ideal and yet be a comedian means to be *ironic,* to parody the very ideal you embody – as Nietzsche himself does. Asceticism, therefore, is not something easily dismissed by Nietzsche. One ought, in fact, to be grateful to it, for it gave humanity one essential thing: without it 'the *animal* man, had no meaning' (*Genealogy*, Essay III, §28). The meaning of the ascetic ideal can now be grasped: '*This* is what the ascetic ideal meant: something was *missing,* there was an immense *lacuna* around man, – he himself could think of no justification or explanation or affirmation, he *suffered* from the problem of what he meant' (*Genealogy*, Essay III, §28). Our propensity to suffer is part of our identity. The urge to negate this propensity (see Zarathustra's discussion of 'the last man', for a discussion of which, *see* **Overman**) is a sign of sickness and lack of vitality: 'Man, the bravest animal and the most prone to suffer, does *not* deny suffering as such: he wills it, he even seeks it out, provided he is shown a *meaning* for it, a *purpose* of suffering' (*Genealogy*, Essay III, §28). What has plagued humanity is, it follows, not suffering itself but the very meaninglessness of its suffering. The great achievement of the ascetic ideal was that it managed to provide a reason, a justification, for our suffering. 'Within it, suffering was given an interpretation' (*Genealogy*, Essay III, §28). The problem was that this interpretation actually made humanity *suffer even more:* it internalised suffering through its use of the concept of guilt and its reinterpretation of this concept in terms of sin. 'But in spite of all that – man was *saved*, he had a *meaning*, from now on he was no longer like a leaf in the breeze, the plaything of the absurd, of "non-sense"; from now on he could *will* something […] the *will itself was saved*' (*Genealogy*, Essay III, §28).

Further reading: Allison 2001; Fraser 2002; May 1999; Minson 1985; Natoli 1985; Schacht 1983.

BAD CONSCIENCE

Bad conscience, Nietzsche tells us, is a 'serious illness' generated by the fact that primitive proto-human beings ended up being 'imprisoned within the confines of society and peace' (*Genealogy*, Essay II, §16). Such beings were creatures of the passions: they were used to acting on their drives but were now obliged to curtail them. Consequently, 'the poor things were reduced to relying on thinking, inference, calculation, and the connecting of cause and effect, that is, to relying on their "consciousness", that most impoverished and error-prone organ!' (*Genealogy*, Essay II, §16). Consciousness came to the fore in the domain of the development of human culture. However, from this it did not follow that the instincts disappeared. On the contrary, they now had to find new paths to discharge themselves: 'All instincts which are not discharged outwardly *turn inwards* – this is what I call the *internalization* of man: with it there now evolves in man what will later be called his "soul"' (*Genealogy*, Essay II, §16). Thus, the instincts were turned back on the human being itself. Obliged to exist within the social straitjacket of convention and custom, 'man impatiently ripped himself apart, persecuted himself, gnawed at himself' (*Genealogy*, Essay II, §16). Being endowed with bad conscience, in other words, means feeling bad about oneself, suffering from one's own existence (guilt). That is why the person dominated by bad conscience is all too prone to self-loathing. An increasingly rich inner world was created by this event: man suffering from himself created the 'bad conscience' as a consequence of 'a forcible breach with his animal past, a simultaneous leap and fall into new situations and conditions of existence, a declaration of war against all the old instincts' (*Genealogy*, Essay II, §16). This event is '*momentous*', for it changes 'the whole character of the world [...] in an essential way' (*Genealogy*, Essay II, §16): humanity is an animal that has ceased to be as one with the rest of the animal kingdom. This is an accident (a result of the dice throw of chance), and a moment of 'promise', for it implies an as yet unfulfilled potential in humanity to become something more than merely animal.

Nietzsche notes that two assumptions are made by this theory (*Genealogy*, Essay II, §17). First, the change in circumstances that created bad conscience was not a matter of gradual evolution but 'a breach, a leap, a compulsion, a fate which nothing could ward off' (*Genealogy*, Essay II, §17). Second, the 'shaping' of the human population, which according to the account he offers in the *Genealogy* begins with the violence of transferring the human animal into society, also concludes violently with the invention of the state. The 'oldest "state"' that emerged was a tyranny, which worked on the raw material of humanity until it rendered it 'not just kneaded and compliant, but *shaped*' (*Genealogy*, Essay II, §17). Society and state, in other words, began with an act of violent oppression, not with a contract, as the classical liberal theorists (such as empiricist philosopher John Locke) argue. Primitive populations were invaded by 'some pack of blond beasts, a conqueror and master race' (*Genealogy*, Essay II, §17) and subordinated by them. These conquerors, however, are not the ones in whom bad conscience grew. Rather, they are its precondition: bad conscience 'would not be there if a huge amount of freedom had not been driven from the world, or at least driven from sight and, at the same time, made *latent* by the pressure of their hammer blows and artists' violence' (*Genealogy*, Essay II, §17). The tyranny of invasion, the coercion of populations by their conquering force marks the beginning of bad conscience. The same 'force' that motivates these 'artists of violence and organizers', that builds states, is turned back on itself to make bad conscience (*Genealogy*, Essay II, §18). It is thus a result of 'that very instinct for freedom (put into my language: the will to power)' (*Genealogy*, Essay II, §18). Human instincts, now imprisoned along with the human body in state and society, turn in on themselves and thus create an inner world, a realm of subjectivity. Man now suffers from himself. Bad conscience, it follows, is '*active*', not reactive: it creates an inner realm of meaning, imagination and beauty as a means of compensating for the inability of the drives to express themselves externally. Selflessness, self-denial, self-sacrifice: all these belong to this realm and emerge from this condition. Bad conscience is thus an expression of humanity suffering from itself as a result of being *made* to be social (*Genealogy*, Essay II, §19). It is expressed in *nausea,* and is hence a 'sickness [...] but a sickness rather like pregnancy' (*Genealogy*, Essay II, §19), for out of it comes the rich intellectual and creative potential that characterises modern humankind, exemplified by the sovereign individual and the Dionysian man.

Further reading: Allison 2001; Ansell-Pearson 1991; Butler 2000.

BECOMING

The view that reality, such as it is, is in a ceaseless state of flux. The notion of becoming as Nietzsche understands and advocates it can be traced as far back as the fifth century BC and the philosophy of Heraclitus. For Heraclitus, the universe is an eternally burning fire. It consists of four different states: fire, air, water, and earth, each of which can be transformed into the other. Fire turns into water, which turns finally into earth, and earth can turn into air, then water and finally fire: the universe is hence an endlessly returning cycle in which one state succeeds another. This is a universe with neither beginning nor end, a realm where none who dwell within it, be they gods or mortals, are able to determine its ultimate meaning or purpose. Nietzsche follows Heraclitus in so far as, for him too, 'everything has become' and does so eternally (see *Human, All Too Human*, §2). The world on Nietzsche's view, too, can only be grasped in terms of the flux of forces, as a whole that comes into states and passes through them, as a realm of ceaseless development without goal. One of the most significant ramifications of this, for Nietzsche, concerns our understanding of morality. To live in a world that is framed in terms of 'the innocence of becoming' (*Twilight of the Idols*, 'The Four Great Errors', §8) is to live free from guilt or sin. To affirm the innocence of becoming means to affirm that the world cannot be allocated a meaning that transcends it. The world is a whole but at the same time without unity. If this is the case, then we, too, are freed from all ultimate determination according to the notion of will or design when it comes to the question of our identity. No one, Nietzsche says, is the consequence of 'a special design, a will, a purpose' (*Twilight of the Idols*, 'The Four Great Errors', §8). Each of us is 'necessary, one is a piece of fate' (*Twilight of the Idols*, 'The Four Great Errors', §8), part of the whole, yet the whole cannot itself be measured, judged, or compared with anything else superior to it. No one, it follows, can be held to any ultimate account for who they are, and such an insight redeems the world, for once one has attained such a standpoint it is no longer possible to find reality lacking and to suffer from that lack. Becoming thereby challenges the moralism associated with philosophies of being. It does so not least because in so far as the world becomes not only is any unity of purpose denied it but, at the same time, the kind of grounding unity afforded to and derived from the universal conception of the subject (the 'I') is also challenged. Thus, the 'I think' of Cartesian thought or the transcendental unity of the Kantian subject, both of which are used to secure the claims of metaphysics and epistemology, are open to challenge.

See also: **self**.

Further reading: Deleuze 1983, 1987, 1990; Deleuze and Guattari 1988.

BEING

The notion of being can be traced at least as far back as the sixth century BC and an obscure, rhapsodic poem by the pre-Socratic thinker Parmenides (one of the Eleatics). For Parmenides, being denotes, first, all that which is actively engaged in existing, all that is 'be-ing', in the same sense that all those who are alive are to be included amongst the 'living'. In this sense, being means whatever exists, the totality of entities. Second, being is also that condition in virtue of which anything that exists does so at all. In this sense, the verb 'to be' is that which endows any proposition with its truth-value, e.g. 'George W. Bush *is* president', 'All Cretans *are* liars'. In turn, Parmenides holds that being is a unity; for him being has always been and always will be: it is the eternal and unchanging condition of existence. As this abiding condition, being cannot be said to be derived from anything other than itself, and certainly could not have sprung from its opposite, non-being or nothingness. If one takes this position one is a monist: reality is ultimately regarded as a single, unified and eternally stable principle. This view was to have a profound influence upon Plato (c. 428–c. 348 BC) and his Theory of Forms. Platonic metaphysics draws the distinction between appearance and reality. This distinction asserts there to be a fundamental difference between the experiential realm of the senses and the realm of the intellect or spirit. Reality, Plato argues in the *Republic,* is coterminous with the latter. The real world is not the world that is felt, seen and heard, but the world of thought. The Theory of Forms argues that all particulars have a general feature in common. Thus, if one takes three people, they can all be said to be different in terms of their appearance, character traits and the like. However, all three are human and share in common this attribute. For Plato, this means that all three are particular instances of a universal Idea of the human itself. For Plato, all the other important concepts that we have can be parcelled out in similar manner. Beauty, goodness, justice and so forth all have a Form that exists in itself and this Form is what makes any individual instance of them what it is. Whereas the realm of the senses comes into existence and passes away, i.e. is eternally subject to change, the realm of the Forms is what it is eternally. Underlying the realm of the Forms is being itself. The highest of the Forms is the Form of the Good, and it is this that endows all the others with their identity. Just as the sun illuminates the earth and so makes the realm of the visible possible so the Form of the Good is what 'illuminates' the human world, endowing it with meaning by presenting an evaluative standard whereby our actions and beliefs can be deemed either good or bad. Philosophy, in turn, has for Plato the special task of leading us toward knowledge of the good; such knowledge, if properly grasped and acted upon, will lead to virtuous deeds and individual happiness. Thus, the notion of being is conjoined within Plato's work to the concept of a universal moral code. Nietzsche has little time for this approach, advocating instead a philosophy that embraces the 'innocence of becoming'. For him, the philosophy of being is not merely pure abstraction and illusion. It is also damaging for it denigrates the only reality available to us, the world of embodiment and sensory experience, putting in its place an empty fiction to serve as the goal and purpose of enquiry and life. (See especially in this connection Nietzsche's discussions of Socrates, reason and the concepts of appearance and reality in *Twilight of the Idols*).

Further reading: Deleuze 1990; Schacht 1983.

BREEDING

When Nietzsche talks about 'breeding', as he frequently does, he is discussing those conditions which are necessary for the production of certain types of humanity. In other words, 'breeding' alludes to a formative, and therefore educational, range of practices; these practices mould humans in specific ways. 'Breeding' is the means whereby humans are shaped so as to be representative examples of certain spiritual or moral types of the species. For instance, on Nietzsche's view, to be a 'good' human being according to Christian precepts is to be a representative example of the cultivation of a certain type of person. Such a person both has beliefs and acts in ways which are characteristic of the values endorsed in the Christian system of morality. 'Breeding' is about the ideals that a culture posits as having supreme value, and which are used to ground the educational ideals of that culture. These ideals serve as the justification for forming the individuals who compose that culture. The question of breeding is most significantly dealt with by Nietzsche in the context of his discussions of morality and religion (see *Beyond Good and Evil*, §§61–2, 242, 251, 262; *Twilight of the Idols*, 'The "Improvers" of Mankind', §§2–4). It is worth noting that generally the question of breeding is not for Nietzsche to be taken in a manner akin to the cultivation and refinement of particular *races*. It is not, a matter of human biology but of the forming of human types from the multiple biological constituents that make up humanity. When he does discuss the notion of breeding in the pursuit of creating specific racial characteristics it turns out that the consequence is hardly to be lauded. The notion of 'pure blood' is the 'opposite' of something harmless (*Twilight of the Idols*, 'The "Improvers" of Mankind', §4).

A human type is a kind of person equipped with particular dominant dispositions. Such a being is 'bred' in Nietzsche's sense to the extent that the raw material of dispositions with which any social and moral system must deal are given form in one particular way or another through the valorisation of them as either worthy or unworthy. The drives, in other words, are channelled; they are rendered second nature, i.e. instinctual (*see* **drive/instinct**). By way of example, §262 of *Beyond Good and Evil* invites us to think of 'an aristocratic community', such as the ancient Greek city-state, 'as a voluntary or involuntary contrivance for the purpose of *breeding*'. Breeding, it follows, concerns the structure of the institutions and norms that bind people together in a social body. A city-state offers a specific range of conditions under which certain types of human are bred, i.e. in which they are taught to value a certain attitude toward life. What is in the first instance bred in the aristocratic Greek *polis,* Nietzsche contends, is a limited type of person. The individual is limited because the survival of the community is the ruling power of its social order. Such communities are usually founded in conditions under which they must either survive or perish and because of this 'every aristocratic morality is intolerant [...] it counts intolerance itself among the virtues under the name "justice"' (*Beyond Good and Evil*, §262). One day, though, the fearful conditions pass and life gets easier. In consequence, by degrees the old morality loses its authority; it no longer seems necessary since it has ceased to be 'a condition of existence', and therefore the limits imposed by it vanish. Consequently:

> Variation, whether as deviation (into the higher, rarer, more refined) or as degeneration and monstrosity, is suddenly on the scene in the greatest splendour and abundance, the individual dares to be individual and stand out. At these turning-points of history there appear side by side and often entangled and entwined together a glorious, manifold, jungle-like growth and up-stirring, a kind of *tropical* tempo in competition and growing, and a tremendous perishing and self-destruction, thanks to the savage egoisms

which, turning on one another and as it were exploding, wrestle together for 'sun and light' and no longer know how to draw any limitation, any restraint, any forbearance from the morality which stored up such enormous energy, which bent the bow in such a threatening manner – now it is 'spent', now it is becoming 'outlived'.

(*Beyond Good and Evil*, §262)

What Nietzsche is implying here is that it is the *discipline* of aristocratic, noble morality that will, through the constraints of its institutions, breed an animal with the potential to legislate with regard to its own existence. Such ability is the fulfilment of the right to make promises that, in *On the Genealogy of Morality,* characterises the '*sovereign individual*' (*Beyond Good and Evil*, §262). What becomes equally clear in the light of this is that life is something that must be lived in a self-justifying manner: the justification of existence is something that must be forged by humanity out of the activity of living. Only thus does humankind attain 'self-redemption' from its animalistic, non-human origins. The function of breeding, it follows, is to equip a *few* humans to live such lives; to educate them to become themselves in the activity of an independent existence of self-fulfilment.

Further reading: Kaufmann 1974.

CARTESIANISM

Although, strictly speaking, the word 'Cartesian' denotes something that is of or bears some direct relation to the philosophy of philosopher René Descartes (1596–1650), it has come to signify a metaphysical viewpoint that is of importance to issues concerning the nature of the self and questions in epistemology. Descartes sought to refute scepticism (the view that nothing can be known) by way of the 'sceptical method', which meant following a path of first doubting all his beliefs and then seeing what kind of knowledge could be arrived at from this initial position of doubt. Since the senses can deceive us, our beliefs derived from them can be doubted. In more extreme form, one can also doubt one's ability to distinguish between whether one is asleep or awake, that one has a body, or even that the propositions of mathematics and geometry are correct. This is because there is no way of telling whether one is being deceived constantly or not. Descartes envisages a 'malicious demon', who, God-like, has total power over his perceptions and calculating abilities. If one took this extreme position, it is indubitably the case that one thing remains certain: that even in doubting everything one still exists. This is most famously expressed in Descartes's phrase 'I think, therefore I am' (cogito, ergo sum). According to Descartes, if one then turns to the question of what this 'I' is it turns out that it is not the mechanical structure of the human body but, rather, 'soul' or 'mind'. This forms the basis of Descartes's dualism. For him there is physical stuff and mental stuff. These are different in kind, which means that they do not mix since they have essentially different properties. One need not follow Descartes's arguments in too much detail here, since the point to appreciate is that this account of knowledge resorts to the conscious subject (an individual entity endowed with thought) in order to provide the 'foundation' of knowledge (a powerful metaphor for knowledge that has exerted a profound influence on philosophy). On this view, the relationship between the human subject and the physical world that it experiences is accounted for in terms that situate the subject 'outside' the world. The 'I' is a kind of observer who is not implicated in the concrete conditions of their experiences.

For Nietzsche, such an approach to knowledge is deluded. For one thing, it is not clear that the immediate certainty Descartes attributes to self-consciousness characterises it (or indeed anything else) at all. This contention is yet another instance of the superstitious cleaving to the consciousness of the 'I' that characterises much philosophy, 'as though knowledge here got hold of its object pure and naked, as "thing in itself"' (Beyond Good and Evil, §16). Notions such as that of the 'thing in itself' (a phrase derived from Kantianism), 'absolute knowledge', or 'immediate certainty' are, says Nietzsche, self-contradictory delusions. Although everyday life might consist of people cleaving to such beliefs (and they may well need them in order to get around), a properly philosophical view would assert that all knowledge worthy of the name spurns absolutes and superlatives of this kind. Knowing something, for Nietzsche, involves being a finite entity with finite abilities engaged with a world of infinite becoming. What one can know must have limits, and such limits are precisely what impart meaning and concreteness to knowledge. The absurdity of unrealistic conceptions of knowledge is clear enough as soon as one reflects on the nature of the 'I think' and the supposed 'immediacy' of its identification with thought. Put in slightly different terms, the view that the words 'I' and 'will' refer to something self-sufficient, complete and autonomous is questionable. The assertion of the truth of the *cogito* involves 'rash assumptions', e.g. that the 'I' has causal abilities with regard to thoughts (that the 'I' does the thinking), that thinking 'is an activity and operation' on the part of the subject, that one already knows what thinking is. Even doubting the causal abilities of the 'I' means that the relation of immediacy between the 'I' and its purported content evaporates:

> a thought comes when it wants, not when 'I' want; so [...] it is a *falsification* of the facts to say: the subject 'I' is the condition of the predicate 'think'. It 'thinks': but that this 'it' is precisely that famous old "I" is, to put it mildly, only an assumption, an assertion, above all not an 'immediate certainty'.
>
> (*Beyond Good and Evil*, §17)

Even inserting an 'it' into the chain of events that gives rise to thought is to step on uncertain ground, following 'the habit of grammar' (*see* **language**) by appending to events a causal condition akin to the subject. The Cartesian conception of the self depends upon an untenable dualism that separates identity, thought and body by asserting that the consciousness is the self. As with the version of knowledge presented here, this view of the self is also something that Nietzsche consistently rejects.

Further reading: Cottingham 1992; Descartes 1986; Lampert 1993; Sedgwick 2001.

CHRISTIANITY

At his most polemical, Nietzsche claims that Christianity is a disaster. This does not mean that he does not to a deep degree respect the figure of Christ, who he goes so far on occasion to call the 'most noble human being' that has lived (*Human, All Too Human*, §475). What it does mean, though, is that Nietzsche despises the *Christian Church*: 'I call Christianity the *one* great curse, the *one* great intrinsic depravity, the *one* great instinct for revenge for which no expedient is sufficiently poisonous, secret, subterranean, *petty* – I call it the *one* immortal blemish of mankind' (*Antichrist*, §62). Christianity, Nietzsche is keen to show, is *ressentiment* morality writ large. The distinction he draws between Christ and Christianity is important here. The genuine figure of the evangelist was, Nietzsche holds, expunged from the moment Jesus was killed on the cross. To be truly Christian is, Nietzsche argues, to engage in a concrete practice that has distinct features that mark it off from the doctrinal and dogmatic conceptualisations that followed in the aftermath of Christ's life. The genuine Christian life as Jesus revealed it is realised in action, not by way of proclaiming adherence to a body of beliefs:

> This bringer of 'glad tidings' died as he lived, as he *taught* – *not* to 'redeem mankind' but to demonstrate how one ought to live. What he bequeathed to mankind is his *practice:* his bearing before the judges, before the guards, before the accusers and every kind of calumny and mockery – his bearing on the *Cross.*
>
> (*Antichrist,* §35)

What Christ exemplifies to the very end of his life is 'A new way of living, *not* a new belief' (*Antichrist,* §33). One cannot underestimate the importance of this view of Jesus when it comes to grasping fully Nietzsche's rejection of Christian principles. When Christ died, what happened next was in fact an *inversion* of his teachings, 'What was called "Evangel" from this moment onwards was already the opposite of what he had lived: "*bad* tidings", a *dysangel*' (*Antichrist,* §39). Christianity as it is subsequently codified is a priestly confidence trick, the responsibility for which can be laid at the door of Saint Paul. Nietzsche argues that for Christ himself, no adherence to a fixed body of beliefs (no *credo*) was ever deemed necessary: '*Not* a belief but a doing, above all a *not*-doing of many things, a different *being*' (*Antichrist,* §39) is what mattered to him. Above all, Christ refuses to judge. What becomes Christian faith, however, does just this sort of thing. It codifies and judges and thereby reduces the question of Christian being to simply 'holding something to be true, to a mere phenomenality of consciousness' (*Antichrist,* §39). In this way, Christian faith kills the Christian message before it is even allowed to spread. Nietzsche contrasts Christianity with the Buddhist religion to the advantage of the latter. Both may be what he terms nihilistic religions, both are expressions of *décadence.* However, the difference between them is startling. Whereas Christianity is the outpouring of *ressentiment,* Buddhism represents the consequence of hundreds of years of critical thought (*Antichrist,* §§20 ff). Buddhism has no interest in a struggle against 'sin' as the Christian faith does but rather seeks primarily to ameliorate suffering. It is, in this regard, unique in being a '*positivistic* religion': 'It already has – and this distinguishes it profoundly from Christianity – the self-deception of moral concepts behind it – it stands, in my language, *beyond* good and evil' (*Antichrist*, §§20 ff). More to the point, Buddhism delivers what it promises: it gives the adherent peace of mind, absence of desire, the negation of pain. Its priestly culture is one where asceticism has found a positive direction. Christian priestly asceticism, in contrast, promises much but gives nothing.

Nietzsche is, of course, never less than ambivalent when it comes to the figure of the ascetic priest. But with regard to the long-term consequences of priestly Christianity for human well-being, he states his viewpoint clearly enough. Institutionalised Christianity has consistently promulgated the morality of pity; it has praised and encouraged 'the "unegoistic", the instincts of pity, self-denial, self-sacrifice' (*On the Genealogy of Morality*, 'Preface', §§5 ff). Nietzsche rebels against these instincts. He reads the morality of pity as a rejection of 'life' made evident in a European culture that has become less and less at home with itself, sinister, and thus stands as a prelude to nihilism. The morality of pity is the symptom of a turning 'against life' which bespeaks an illness. This illness embodies specific 'instincts' such as pity and self-sacrifice taking control. The morality of pity is the sign of the predominance of these instincts, their orchestration and use by priests in the furtherance of their own power. The values endorsed by the morality of pity have been taken as given and unquestionable, but Nietzsche argues that they are not facts, therefore that they are not beyond doubt (*Genealogy*, 'Preface', §6). Morals are supposed to be of greater value in that the '"the good man"' has been held to further the advancement of humanity (the future of man). But what if the reverse were true? What if the 'good' were a sign of regression, 'a danger, an enticement, a poison, a narcotic, so that the present *lived at the expense of the future?* [...] So that precisely morality itself were to blame if man, as species, never reached his *highest potential power and splendour*. So that morality itself was the danger of dangers?' (*Genealogy*, 'Preface', §6). One can note here the use of the phrase 'symptom of regression'. The morality of the Christian Church, Nietzsche is telling us, is backward-looking; it represents an attempt to undercut the development of humankind that the second essay of the *Genealogy* charts as emanating from the era of prehistory. Our prehistoric past endowed our kind with the unique facet of futurity. The real *price* of morality is that it barters this futurity in exchange for present comfort. To live according to Christianity, the morality of pity, is to live 'in a smal-ler-minded, meaner manner' (*Genealogy*, 'Preface', §6); it thus means that the future potential of human excellence is to be *sacrificed* to priestly power. The 'real *history of morality*' (*Genealogy*, 'Preface', §7) that Nietzsche then seeks to narrate is designed to undermine our faith in the doctrinal and the priestly. Above all, it challenges the Christian view that we are our concepts and beliefs and embraces instead the standpoint that holds our deeds and practices to encapsulate us.

Further reading: Fraser 2002; Géffre et al. 1981; Jaspers 1961; Lippitt and Urpeth 2000; Love 1981.

CONSCIOUSNESS

Is it not possible, Nietzsche asks, that consciousness may be 'a more or less fantastic commentary on an unknown, perhaps unknowable, but felt text?' (*Daybreak*, §119). In other words, consciousness is not what philosophy has generally taken it to be. The Cartesian view, for example, holds thought, consciousness and the 'I' to be a unity and different in kind from corporeality (the body and the realm of feelings and instincts). Nietzsche argues that the distinction philosophers are frequently tempted to make between consciousness and instinct (*see* **drive**) is a false one and that this error underlies one of their central delusions. This is the delusion that philosophical thought is capable of untainted objectivity. Nietzsche thus seeks to collapse the distinction between the instinctual and being conscious.

> Just as the act of being born plays no part in the procedure and progress of heredity, so "being conscious" is in no decisive sense the *opposite* of the instinctive – most of a philosopher's conscious thinking is secretly directed and compelled into definite channels by his instincts. Behind all logic too and its apparent autonomy there stand evaluations, in plainer terms physiological demands for the preservation of a certain species of life.
>
> (*Beyond Good and Evil,* §3)

Consciousness is subject to the workings of the drives and to environmental and physiological pressures about which it usually remains completely unaware. Philosophical evaluations, it follows, are not autonomous, rational decisions but interpretations of these pressures, ways of dealing with them. If this is the case for the philosopher, it is no less so for everybody else. We are creatures whose consciousness (and above all self-consciousness) characterises us often in decisive ways, but not in the ways tradition has thought to be decisive.

Language is a crucial factor here. Both *Daybreak* and *On the Genealogy of Morality* take communal living to be the decisive condition governing the emergence of humanity from nature. Out of this communality, Nietzsche notes in *The Gay Science,* language springs. We are self-conscious beings precisely to the degree to which our ancestors were social creatures compelled by the conditions of their existence to enhance their communicative abilities (*Gay Science,* §354). The need to communicate generated an ever-increasing reliance on signs (language), and the continual use of such signs led to an intensification of what began as rudimentary consciousness. It is for this reason that 'the development of language and the development of consciousness [...] go hand in hand' (*Gay Science,* §354). To be conscious, in other words, is to be a being endowed with language. Consciousness, however, is not as important to existence as we have been tempted to make it. It neither denotes the ground of being, as Platonism held, nor is it a prerequisite of life. '[W]e could think, feel, will, and remember, and we could also "act" in every sense of that word, and yet none of this would have to "enter our consciousness" (as one says metaphorically). The whole of life would be possible without, as it were, seeing itself in a mirror' (*Gay Science,* §352). One should note from this that the equation of thought with consciousness is, for Nietzsche, a mistaken one. A being need not be conscious in order to think. Nor is reason defined by way of conscious thought. Our rational abilities emerged, rather, as coping mechanisms capable of dealing with the demands of life.

See also: **self**.

Further reading: Deleuze 1983; Katsafanas 2005.

DARWINISM

Darwinism is the theory of evolution by the mechanism of 'natural selection'. According to this theory, all living species have emerged as a consequence of being locked into a 'struggle for existence' over limited resources. Darwin's theory, proposed in *On the Origin of Species* (1859), argues that the rich diversity of complex life forms on the earth can be explained through random variations that occur between generations of individuals. Some variations are fortunate enough to favour the survival of a species, some are not – something that is resolved by the contingent factor of environmental conditions. Evolution, which occurs over vast spans of time, is thus driven by an unwitting mechanism rather than by teleological principles. Nietzsche clearly understood many of the issues that Darwinian thought raised, and many of his ideas have a Darwinian tinge to them. Thus, for example, the origins of consciousness are accounted for by him in terms of the human need to communicate, which itself is dictated by environmental conditions. Likewise, his notion of the economy of the preservation of the species or his analysis of the development of the aristocratic *polis* (*Beyond Good and Evil*, §262; *see* **morality**) have a clear evolutionary flavour as does the notion of genealogy. Doubtless, this may in part have owed something to Nietzsche's early interest in the writings of English political economist Walter Bagehot, whose *Physics and Politics, or Thoughts on the Application of the Principles of 'Natural Selection' and 'Inheritance' to Political Society* (1872) Nietzsche cites in the *Untimely Meditation,* 'Schopenhauer as Educator' (§8). Nietzsche was also acquainted with Herbert Spencer's theory of 'social Darwinism' (a Lamarkian perversion of Darwin, and not in reality derived from it). Bagehot was clearly a figure Nietzsche admired, Spencer not. Nietzsche's attitude to Darwin is nevertheless often ambivalent, sometimes antagonistic. Primarily, he is suspicious of the notion that life is essentially characterised by a 'struggle for existence' (*Twilight of the Idols,* 'Expeditions of an Untimely Man', §14). This notion, for Nietzsche, implies that the realm of nature is constituted by life being in a state of permanent reaction to conditions, rather than through an active, constitutive engagement with them. For Nietzsche, nature is a realm of abundance, squandering and excess. In such a context, it is the struggle for power that matters, not mere existence, for life is aggressive, 'a *power-will* acted out in all that happens' (*Genealogy,* Essay II, §12).

Further reading: Moore 2002; Moore and Brobjer 2004; Richardson 1996, 2004.

DEATH OF GOD

Along with the sentence from *Twilight of the Idols* 'What does not kill me makes me stronger' ('Maxims and Arrows', §8), the announcement of the madman in *The Gay Science* (§125) that 'God is dead' probably most encapsulates the Nietzsche of popular imagination. What the death of God may mean and what it can be construed to mean by careless readers are, however, different matters. For one thing, the proclamation does not mean that a living being called God has literally died. Rather, the death of God signifies the demise of belief in the metaphysical certainties that have hitherto served to support the values of Christianity and hence European culture. It is first alluded to in §108 of *The Gay Science:*

> *New struggles.* – After Buddha was dead, his shadow was still shown for centuries in a cave – a tremendous, gruesome shadow. God is dead; but given the way of men, there may still be caves for thousands of years in which his shadow will be shown. – And we – we still have to vanquish his shadow, too.

Belief in God is presented in terms of a 'shadow' that casts itself across the domain of our understanding and its future. In other words, it is not something that one can escape from easily. Our dispositions and desires, our habitual ways of doing things, of thinking and hence of interpreting our environment and ourselves, preclude a straightforward escape from the consequences of holding metaphysical beliefs. Just because we reach a point where God is no longer believed in does not imply that what is associated with such belief vanishes with him (see Nietzsche's later discussion on the 'moralisation' of the concept of guilt in the second essay of *On the Genealogy of Morality*). A passage from *Daybreak* makes a similar point: 'We still draw the conclusions of judgments we consider false, of teachings in which we no longer believe – our feelings make us do it' (§99). According to this view, we are creatures dominated by our dispositions and the customs that emanate from them, rather than by rationality. We prejudge and thereby assert the significance of things according to the predominance of certain feelings and habits. This is so not least in relation to the implications that these habitual ways of judging have for how we view morality:

> Wise and noble men once believed in the music of the spheres: wise and noble men still believe in the 'moral significance of existence'. But one day this music of the spheres too will no longer be audible to them! They will awaken and perceive that their ears had been dreaming.
>
> (*Daybreak,* §100)

For Nietzsche, belief in the Christian God and the affirmation of the metaphysical view that holds values to have an existence independent of the people who do the evaluating go together. One cannot have the one without first affirming the other: Christian morality and metaphysics are conjoined. They also permeate our cultural milieu and thereby shape many of our most unquestioningly held beliefs.

Where is the limit of the influence of metaphysics upon our thinking to be placed? Consider the comments below, which follow directly on from §108 of *The Gay Science:*

> Let us beware of thinking that the world is a living being. Where should it expand? On what should it feed? How could it grow and multiply? We have some notion of the nature of the organic; and we should not interpret the exceedingly derivative, late, rare, accidental, that we perceive only on the crust of the earth and make of it something essential, universal, and eternal, which is what those people do who call the universe an organism. This nauseates me. Let us even beware of calling the universe a machine: it is certainly not constructed for one purpose, and calling it a 'machine' does it far too much honor. [...] The total character of the world [...] is in all eternity chaos – in the sense not of a lack of necessity but a lack of order, arrangement, form, beauty, wisdom, and whatever other names there are for our aesthetic anthropomorphisms. [...] [H]ow could we reproach or praise the universe? Let us beware of attributing to it heartlessness and unreason or their opposites: it is neither perfect nor beautiful, nor noble, nor does it wish to become any of these things; it does not by any means strive to imitate man. None of our aesthetic and moral judgments apply to it. Nor does it have an instinct for self-preservation or any other instinct; and it does not observe any laws either. Let us beware of saying that there are laws in nature. There are only necessities: there is nobody who commands, nobody who obeys, nobody who trespasses. Once you know there are no purposes, you also know that there is no accident; for it is only beside a world of purposes that the word "accident" has meaning. Let us beware of saying that death is opposed to life. The living is merely a type of what is dead, and a very rare type. Let us beware of thinking that the world eternally creates new things. There are no eternally enduring substances [...]. But when will we be done with our caution and care? When will all these shadows of God cease to darken our minds? When will we complete our de-deification of nature? When may we begin to 'naturalize' humanity in terms of a pure, newly discovered, newly redeemed nature?
>
> (*Gay Science,* §109)

For Nietzsche, we think metaphysically in all sorts of ways, but perhaps especially in the way in which we contemplate nature. Even when we think in terms that appear to be remote from the anthropomorphism that characterises much of metaphysics we are enmeshed within it. To talk of the universe as being governed by 'laws' as natural scientists do is to think in a manner that does not escape from metaphysics. This is because the belief that impersonal laws govern the universe is an extension of the urge to comprehend nature in terms amenable to human concerns. To think thus is to dwell in the shadow of belief in God. To announce the death of God, it follows, is to proclaim that one has perceived the limit of a way of thinking that characterises our self-understanding most deeply. It means to take the first step on the path of the 'naturalisation' of humankind, i.e. of rethinking the questions of our relationship to the world and of who we are. However, to speak of a world devoid of purpose and hence also of accident, of a realm to which even crude mechanistic concepts ought really not to be applied (and where, one should add, the traditional concept of 'will' is redundant [see **will to power**]) brings with it dangers. The one who expresses the limits of metaphysics runs the risk of appearing to look somewhat eccentric. His view of the world invites the attribution of madness:

> *The madman.* – Have you not heard of the madman who lit a lantern in the bright morning hours, ran to the market place, and cried incessantly: 'I seek God! I seek God!' – As many of those who did not believe in God were standing around just then, he provoked much laughter. Has he got lost? asked one. Did he lose his way like a child? asked another. Or is he hiding? Is he afraid of us? Has he gone on a voyage? emigrated? – Thus they yelled and laughed. The madman jumped into their midst and pierced them with his eyes. 'Whither is God?' he cried; 'I will tell you. We have killed him – you and I. All of us are his murderers. But how did we do this? How could we drink up the sea? Who gave us the sponge to wipe away the entire horizon? What were we doing when we unchained the earth from this sun? Whither is it moving now? [...] Is there still any up or down? Are we not straying as through an infinite nothing? Do we not feel the breath of empty space? [...] Do we hear nothing as yet of the gravediggers who are burying God? Do we smell nothing as yet of the divine decomposition? Gods, too, decompose. God is dead. God remains dead. And we have killed him.'
>
> (*Gay Science,* §125)

As befits something that brings implications that are maddening, the death of God is proclaimed here in the public domain of the marketplace by a madman. One should not, however, conclude that the madman is Nietzsche (tempting, perhaps, in the light of his later mental breakdown). What we are presented with is, rather, a literary device. This device is designed to emphasise the point that the initial gesture marking the 'naturalisation' of humanity, which requires nothing less than the 'de-deification of nature' (*Gay Science*, §109), is profoundly unsettling. This is because such a gesture must appear to bring with it things that seem to be unnatural, i.e. implications that run counter to the deep-set inclinations that pattern our daily lives.

According to the parable of the madman, we have entered an age where belief in God has withered away. How has this happened? What is most striking is that the madman claims that it is *we* who have killed God. In simpler terms, modern science, according to Nietzsche, has begun to explain the world in a manner that no longer requires the notion of a living divinity to animate its innermost workings. God has become redundant, but the consequences of such redundancy are, for the present at least, obscure. Hence, before leaving, the madman dashes his lantern on the ground and says:

> My time is not yet. This tremendous event is still on its way, still wandering; it has not yet reached the ears of men. Lightning and thunder require time; the light of the stars requires time; deeds, though done, still require time to be seen and heard. This deed is still more distant from them than the most distant stars – and yet they have done it themselves.
>
> (*Gay Science*, §125)

Is the death of God a disaster? Not for everybody, it seems, as the opening of the fifth book of *The Gay Science* (§§343–83, which were added in 1887) tells us:

> *The meaning of our cheerfulness.* – The greatest recent event – that 'God is dead,' that the belief in the Christian God has become unbelievable – is already beginning to cast its shadow over Europe. For the few, at least, whose eyes – the *suspicion* in whose eyes is strong enough and subtle enough for this spectacle, some sun seems to have set and some ancient and profound trust has been turned into doubt; to them our old world must appear daily more like evening, more mistrustful, stranger, 'older'. But in the

main one may say: The event itself is far too great, too distant, too remote from the multitude's capacity for comprehension even for the tidings of it to be thought of as having arrived as yet. Much less may one suppose that many people know as yet what this event really means – and how much must collapse now that this faith has been undermined because it was built upon this faith, propped up by it, grown into it; for example, the whole of our European morality. This long plenitude and sequence of break-down, destruction, ruin, and cataclysm that is now impending – who could guess enough of it today to be compelled to play the teacher and advance proclaimer of this monstrous logic of terror, the prophet of a gloom and an eclipse of the sun whose like has probably never yet occurred on earth? [...] [W]e philosophers and 'free spirits' feel, when we hear the news that 'the old God is dead,' as if a new dawn shone upon us [...] At long last the horizon appears free to us again, even if it should not be bright; at long last our ships may venture out again, venture out to face any danger; all the daring of the lover of knowledge is permitted again; the sea, our sea, lies open again; perhaps there has never yet been such an 'open sea'.

(Gay Science, §343)

The death of God is thus above all best grasped as an *event*. More specifically, it is a cultural event whose implications are potentially devastating: the destruction of faith brings with it the loss of legitimacy of the values that derived their justification from that faith, and hence the justification for the hegemony of Christian Europe and its culture is challenged. This destruction of Christian values is dangerous, for it initiates nihilism, the belief that nothing is true and anything is permitted. Yet, it is also exhilarating, for with the death of such values comes the invitation to experiment, to embark upon an adventure of thought that is unbounded by the horizon of traditional morality, a consequence which will take Nietzsche into the territory of experi-mentalism. Does one simply overcome metaphysics once one has embarked upon the adventures of the mind that the death of God makes possible? To affirm such a conclusion would be too easy (see *Gay Science,* §344; *see* **knowledge**).

See also: **Zarathustra**.

Further reading: Kaufmann 1974; Lampert 1986; Lippitt and Urpeth 2000; Schacht 1983; Schrift 2000; Stegmaier 2001; Young 2006.

DÉCADENCE

Décadence, Nietzsche says, is anarchy of the instincts. It is the propensity to choose what is bad for oneself. As such, *décadence* is a
symptom of decline. For Nietzsche, the figure of Socrates sums up
the decadent type (*Twilight of the Idols,* 'The Problem of Socrates').
Socratic moralism is the product of its originator's realisation that he
himself represents a crisis of the norm that is the Ancient Greek
psyche. The drives and passions that constitute the abiding condition
of organic life are, for Nietzsche, channelled in various ways to constitute human identity. A different ordering of the drives yields different cultures and, hence, beings endowed with different arrays of
dominant instincts. Socrates appears on the scene of a Greece where
the organising of the dominant instincts has begun to disintegrate.
This is a social world which is in decline in so far as the dominant
customs that make it what it is are on the wane. It is a world already
falling under the spell of *décadence.* Socrates' reaction to this problem
is to turn to reason and dialectic. In other words, he seeks to confine
the threatening anarchy of the drives by caging them in rationality.
Thus, the claim that 'Reason = virtue = happiness means merely: one
must imitate Socrates and counter the dark desires by producing a
permanent daylight' (*Twilight,* 'The Problem of Socrates', §10). The
problem for Nietzsche is that this represents a typically decadent
response to the problem, for it turns away from the spontaneous
conditions of active existence in favour of a world of contemplative
reflection.

The meaning of *décadence* is, however, as with so many things in
Nietzsche, never clear-cut. In Nietzsche's last complete book, *Ecce
Homo,* a deeply original work (possibly Nietzsche's most original: an
at times outrageously funny text, packed with spiked comments about
others, oozing self-parody), he claims that in order to have insight
into decay and decadence one must actually *be* decadent, for one has
thereby the wherewithal to resist it (*Ecce Homo,* 'Why I Am So Wise',
§1). Being ill, it turns out, is a precondition of seeing beyond one's
own everyday world. *Daybreak* was written in an intense state of
intellectuality brought on by uninterrupted headache that lasted for
three days punctuated 'by the laborious vomiting of phlegm' (*Ecce
Homo,* 'Why I Am So Wise', §1). In better health, the insights of this
book would not have been possible. *Daybreak,* as a work of 'dialectical
clarity', reflects its author in a state of decadence, his physiological
trauma. Nietzsche then reminds us that, for him, dialectics is symptomatic of *décadence* (recalling 'The Problem of Socrates'). 'After all

this do I need to say that in questions of *décadence* I am *experienced?*' (*Ecce Homo*, 'Why I Am So Wise', §1). This, though, is only half the story, for Nietzsche is both decadent and anti-decadent.

Being both is a matter of *perspective* (*see* **perspectivism**) and deliberately invokes Nietzsche's image of himself as a wearer of masks (*Beyond Good and Evil*, §40), an embodiment of contrary views on life: one person who is himself a wealth of oppositions and stuggles. Such oppositions and internal conflicts are what make human beings rich in potential.

Thus, to take a famous example, it is not a matter for Nietzsche of being in favour of either noble morality *or* slave morality: 'there is, today, perhaps no more distinguishing feature of the *"higher nature"*, the intellectual nature, than to be divided in this sense and really and truly a battle ground for these opposites' (*Genealogy*, Essay I, §16). 'I am a *décadent*, [but] I am also its antithesis' (*Ecce Homo*, 'Why I Am So Wise', §2). *Décadence* may mean choosing what is bad for you but Nietzsche says he always 'instinctively' selected the correct means of recovery, which is why his philosophy expresses his 'will to health, to *life*' and enacts its self-overcoming.

Further reading: Schacht 1983; Scott 1998; Thiele 1990.

DIONYSUS/DIONYSIAN

Dionysus is the Ancient Greek God of Festivals. According to the young Nietzsche, Dionysian festivals 'centred in extravagant sexual licentiousness', where 'the most savage natural instincts were unleashed' (*Birth of Tragedy*, §2). The figure of Dionysus emerges as an expression of the feeling of ecstasy that accompanies the sense of loss of the individuated self (the socially constructed identity of the 'I'). In the festivals of Dionysus, such a state was brought about by, for example, the use of narcotic draughts, which gave rise to intense emotions that caused 'everything subjective' to vanish 'into complete self-forgetfulness' (*Birth of Tragedy*, §2). Dionysian intoxication, Nietzsche argues, reaffirms the relation between humanity and nature. Individuated humanity is alienated from nature (as an individuated being one is cut off both from the world of nature and also from experiencing a sense of belonging within the community of one's fellow beings), but in the Dionysian moment this alienation is overcome. Thus, 'nature which has become alienated, hostile, or subjugated, celebrates once more her reconciliation with her lost son, man' (*Birth of Tragedy*, §1). In so far as the principle of individuation is negated so, equally, are the social barriers separating person from person: the force of social convention, in other words, is overturned. In *The Birth of Tragedy*, the Dionysian is contrasted with the Apollinian. The bringing together of these two opposing principles, Nietzsche argues, underlies the greatness of Ancient Greek tragedy (epitomised by the works of Aeschylus and Sophocles). The Dionysian finds its first expression in the orgiastic poetic outbursts of Archilocus (c. 711 BC). All art, according to *The Birth of Tragedy*, can be comprehended in terms of the Dionysian–Apollinian opposition: 'every artist is an "imitator", that is to say, either an Apollinian artist in dreams, or a Dionysian artist in ecstasies, or finally – as for example in Greek tragedy – at once artist in both dreams and ecstasies' (*Birth of Tragedy*, §2).

Nietzsche abandons the Apollinian–Dionysian opposition in his so-called 'middle period' works (*Human, All Too Human, Daybreak, The Gay Science*, Books I–IV). However, the figure of Dionysus returns and gains pivotal importance in his later writings. Dionysus is a grand but ultimately 'ambiguous tempter god' whose 'last disciple and initiate' the mature Nietzsche comes to regard himself to be (*Beyond Good and Evil*, §295). This is a god conceived of not in terms of solemnity and pomp, neither monotheistic in spirit nor dogmatic and doctrinal, but a god who stands for the plural virtues of dance, laughter and experimentation. It is not, in short, a god of metaphysics or one that points to a 'beyond' outside the confines of embodied existence. The Dionysian now epitomises creativity, as is witnessed by Nietzsche's conception of a 'monological' aesthetics (*see* **art**). To be Dionysian is to affirm life, not least through the teaching of eternal recurrence. It is to overcome the inherent suffering of existence identified by pessimism, not however by negating pain but by trans-figuring it through celebration of the rich and dangerous possibilities of our animal nature (i.e. the potential for the Overman). The Dionysian is once again linked by the later Nietzsche to the concept of tragedy and its unparalleled achievement of welding expressive force and formal content (see *Twilight of the Idols*, 'What I Owe to the Ancients', §5). It is

> the will to life rejoicing in its own inexhaustibility through the *sacrifice* of its highest types [...] *Not* so as to get rid of pity and terror, not so as to purify oneself of a dangerous emotion through its vehement discharge [...] but, beyond pity and terror, *to realize in oneself* the eternal joy of becoming [...].
>
> (*Twilight of the Idols*, 'What I Owe to the Ancients', §5)

Through the affirmation of becoming, the Dionysian transfigures the transience of existence. The multifaceted personality of writer J. W. von Goethe (1749–1832), the figure Nietzsche admires most and most consistently, encapsulates this. Goethe is no mere 'German event but a European one' (*Twilight of the Idols*, 'Expeditions of an Untimely Man', §49). Goethe, for Nietzsche, was a man of strong passions and instincts who 'surrounded himself with nothing but closed horizons' as a means of fulfilling the aspiration for '*totality*' (*Twilight of the Idols*, 'Expeditions of an Untimely Man', §49). For Goethe, the passions, willing and reason are not separate spheres but are to be integrated to form a unity. He is a man who 'disciplined himself into a whole, he *created* himself' (*Twilight of the Idols*, 'Expeditions of an Untimely Man', §49). In short, we are presented here with the figure of the most rounded human being. He is both cultured and intellectual, yet able to celebrate his own embodiment, a being of self-control who is, in consequence, able to allow his passions full creative rein. In Goethe we find 'a man of tolerance, not out of weakness, but out of strength [...] a man for whom nothing is forbidden, except it be *weakness*' (*Twilight of the Idols*, 'Expeditions of an Untimely Man', §49). Such a being is the most emancipated person imaginable: an example of the sovereign individual alluded to in the *Genealogy*. This is the person who '*no longer denies* [...]But such a faith is the highest of all possible faiths: I have baptized it with the name *Dionysus*.' (*Twilight of the Idols*, 'Expeditions of an Untimely Man', §49). The Dionysian, therefore, is encapsulated by Goethe's self-fashioned personality. This is a persona that is both one of passion and discipline, of freedom achieved in virtue of constraint, of fatalism that stands amidst life with a sense of gratitude for simply having existed at all. This is what Nietzsche alludes to as 'Dionysian pessimism' (*Gay Science*, §370).

Further reading: Del Caro 1981; Kemal et al. 1998; Krell and Wood 1988; Rampley 2000; Winchester 1994; Young 1992; Yovel 1986.

DRIVE/INSTINCT

Nietzsche's understanding of these terms reflects the tendency of his philosophy to conjoin the normally separated realms of nature and culture, body and society (*see* **naturalisation of man**). As they imply, the notions of drive and instinct contain naturalistic implications akin to the conception of nature and human identity suggested by Darwinism. A drive is a brute compulsion, such as the drive to seek sustenance or the drive to reproduce one's species. However, the great majority of drives are far less tangible than these; for example, Nietzsche considers the urge to interpret the world morally as an expression of the dominance of certain socially organised ensembles of drives. Because he considers the individual as a nexus of drives or instincts, Nietzsche often approaches questions concerning one's identity (*see also* **self**) in terms of embodiment. The self is a realm of drives, a fashioning of bodily instincts. Significantly, however, when it comes to the human, animal drives and instincts are always already enmeshed within, refashioned and articulated by way of culture. Nietzsche's various accounts of the drives and instincts reflect this attitude clearly enough.

The discussion of the drives offered in *Daybreak*, §119, presents a case in point. Whatever the degree of a person's self-knowledge, Nietzsche argues, 'the totality of drives' that makes them who they are will elude their cognisance. Even the most basic of these drives can hardly be delineated, let alone easily determined: 'above all the law of their unknown nutriment remains unknown' (*Daybreak*, §119). This is because the question of what serves to satisfy a particular drive is a matter that can only be answered in terms that are contingent: there is no necessary connection between what a drive is and what might satisfy it at any given time. On the account Nietzsche develops here, we are webs of drives, beings driven by impulses of desire that seek satisfaction in the only way possible for them: by means of our daily experiences. 'Experiences' are thus akin to morsels of food thrown into a den filled with hungry animals competing for sustenance.

> To express it more clearly: suppose a drive finds itself at the point at which it desires gratification – an exercise of its strength, or discharge of its strength, or the satisfaction of an emptiness – these are all metaphors: it then regards every event of the day with a view to seeing how it can employ it for the attainment of its goal.
>
> (*Daybreak*, §119)

Note how Nietzsche is wholly aware of the metaphorical nature of his discussion. He now introduces another metaphor. The drive is a delicate plant: deny it nourishment and it will weaken, wither and finally perish. The most evident example of this (the basis of Nietzsche's metaphorics here) is that of the drive for sustenance. This drive exemplifies all others in that unless they are sustained in some manner all drives die. Without the satisfaction of this drive for food the organism as a whole ceases to be; consequently, hunger 'is not content with *dream food*' (*Daybreak*, §119). Other drives remain more intangible precisely because their means of survival (of 'sustenance') and even their demise do not have such clearly concrete aspects or possibly catastrophic consequences. Such drives can thrive on dreams. Our dreams, in other words, are compensatory nourishment for unsatisfied drives. A person may dream of taking revenge, of glorious music, of having sex: all make up for what one's drives failed to receive during the waking hours. Such dreaming, Nietzsche adds, is intimately bound to bodily sensations: dreams are 'very free, very arbitrary interpretations of the motions of the blood and intestines, of the pressure of the arms and the bedclothes, the sounds made by church bells' (*Daybreak*, §119) and the like. Awake or asleep, our drives are constantly engaged in fervent activity, and this means that being asleep and being awake are not states of existence that are different in kind. The waking world of consciousness, no less than the dream world of the unconscious, is governed by the same illogical logic. 'Experience', in other words, is an active interpretation of sensations and situations rather than a pure flow of sensory information received passively by the mind as if it were a blank sheet. Experiencing means, to some degree or other, actively inventing. Individual identity, in turn, is open to being interpreted in terms of the drives, too. Who 'I' am is an articulation of which drive happens to get satisfied most and, in consequence, ends up stronger than the rest: 'To our strongest drive, the tyrant in us, not only our reason but also our conscience submits' (*Beyond Good and Evil*, §158). Tyrannical drives lead to neurosis and self-harm (witness Nietzsche's discussion of how one ought to be lenient to criminals, who are often best understood as being victims of their drives [*Daybreak*, §202]).

Where drives are many, chaotic in their rampant activity, capable of thriving or dwindling, instincts are patterns of behaviour formed by organising the raw material of the passions. Which drives dominate in a person is a matter of the individuated body, of a person's biography and tastes. Instincts, in contrast, concern the larger realms of the social body and the species as a whole. Thus, Nietzsche talks of the instinct for the economy of the preservation of the species (*Gay Science*, §1). Likewise, there are instincts for evaluating things according to commercial considerations (*Daybreak*, §175), instinctive tastes (e.g. modernity's taste for 'sensualism'), the 'religious instinct', instincts appropriate to a 'higher' kind of human being, or the 'English instinct' (*Beyond Good and Evil*, §§14, 53, 62, 188). Understood this way, instincts are tied to culture and the social realm. Used this way, 'instinct' means acting according to dictates that have been learned but to such a degree that one does not need to ponder before an action in order to 'reflect' upon it: instinct, for the human animal, is a matter of second nature. Culturally speaking, the instincts are bound up with those norms that serve to bind a community together. Such norms fashion a community's members by imposing upon them rules of behaviour. Instincts are, in this way, *learned* patterns that serve to endow life with an order and hence meaning. One will cleave to such meaning in the face of absurd conditions: '*Instinct* – When the house burns down one forgets even one's dinner. Yes: but one retrieves it from the ashes' afterwards (*Beyond Good and Evil*, §83). Instincts can work well and thereby allow a mode of existence (a way of life, a culture) to thrive. However, they can also begin to fragment, a situation which leads to cultural collapse. Such a view is especially evident in the discussion of Socrates that Nietzsche offers in *Twilight of the Idols*. For Nietzsche, Socrates represents a rebellion against all the ancient Hellenic instincts (*Twilight of the Idols*, 'The Problem of Socrates', §4). Specifically, the anarchy of Socrates' own instincts is living evidence that the dominant instincts of his culture have begun to turn against themselves (*Twilight of the Idols*, 'The Problem of Socrates', §9). Against the instincts Socrates pits the forces of reason and consciousness. In effect, Nietzsche argues, he seeks to impose a new hierarchy of the drives on the ancient Greek world. The Socratic view that drives and instincts have nothing to do with philosophy is something that Nietzsche questions. For him, in contrast, philosophy is largely based in unconscious and instinctive activities, simply because thought itself is (see *Beyond Good and Evil*, §3).

Further reading: Bataille 1992 [1945]; Deleuze 1987; Schacht 1983; Schrift 2000.

ECONOMY OF THE PRESERVATION OF THE SPECIES

The Gay Science opens with the contention that all humans act with one ultimate aim, 'to do what is good for the preservation of the human race' (§1). At first glance, it might seem as if Nietzsche is making a claim about laudable motives linked to the survival of the human race. However, it turns out that the aim of 'doing good' does not originate in what most people might think of as 'good' motives (i.e. feeling love or concern for others). Rather, Nietzsche is discussing a deeply ingrained 'instinct' (largely unconscious) that springs from the collective nature of humankind. We are all subject to an instinctive desire to think and act with a view to mutuality. This constitutes nothing less than the human 'essence'. In less flattering terms, people are what Nietzsche elsewhere calls 'herd animals' (*Gay Science, §1*). We are collective beings, and it is this collective nature that defines us. The most important element of this collective nature is invisible, i.e. unconscious. Humans, like all life forms, are driven by the need to survive. The unconscious force of our collective nature focuses individual action on the general aim of preserving the species as a whole. We are communal beings. The communality Nietzsche has in mind here is, however, far from the kind that might be associated with collectivism. Even though people are often tempted to designate others as 'good' or 'evil' according to the likely consequences their actions have for others, Nietzsche tells us that such a subjective-instrumental attitude takes a small-scale view of human qualities. Such a standpoint is in reality inadequate. One might like to think of a world composed of 'good' and 'bad' individuals, the former kind, selfless, moral and worthy; the latter selfish, immoral and contemptible. However, this view ignores the possibility that what appear to be amongst the most harmful people might really 'be the most useful when it comes to the preservation of the species' (*Gay Science, §1*). For Nietzsche, a more intelligent assessment of those human qualities that might be deemed 'useful' or 'good' must bear in mind the larger issue of human preservation. Such an issue does not get fixated upon the narrower realm of consequences for others that characterise the actions of some possibly very unpleasant individuals. Considered thus, some individuals and feelings that one might generally view as evil because of the pain and resultant moral repugnance they give rise to might not be altogether bad. The harmful person, Nietzsche suggests, may well be a vehicle bearing violent or repulsive instincts that, it turns out, might be needed for human survival: 'Hatred, the mischievous delight in the misfortune of others, the lust to rob and dominate, and whatever else is called evil belongs to the most amazing economy of the preservation of species' (*Gay Science, §1*).

As ought to be clear from this, Nietzsche is contending that human life is (in part at least – and certainly much more than one might like to admit) maintained by conditions that are both diverse and contrary. Differing and occasionally conflicting human propensities gain their sense from the way in which they function not simply in relation to each other (between individuals and even within a single individual) but in relation to the wider question of human preservation. Taken as a whole, these conditions of preservation make up an economy of relations. Diverse human propensities (our instincts, drives and passions, the consequences of which are in some instances violent and vile) are not to be evaluated merely from the standpoint of those on the receiving end of them (the victim). One can also adopt the viewpoint of a universal standard that concerns the continuation of life. This standard is that of the general economy of human existence. Such an economy, Nietzsche notes, is both 'expensive' and 'wasteful': it is fundamentally stupid in its squandering of material resources. Nevertheless, such an economy can be proven, Nietzsche asserts, to have preserved humanity right up to the present, and it is thus not to be easily dismissed. Consideration of the general economy of human preservation means bearing in mind the potential usefulness of all human characteristics rather than just those that might have agreeable consequences for others. Thus, what might from one standpoint be dangerous, violent, threatening and unsettling might equally also be considered representative of the drives that promote human life. What is generally abhorred could therefore also be inspiring, creative and nurturing when taken in the context of its importance to the preservation of the species. The pointed question that follows this discussion is meant to prick us: are any of us today able to live in a fashion even remotely capable of damaging the species? To acknowledge such an overarching economy of human preservation would mean living in a world devoid of guilt, a world where noone would ultimately be responsible for being who he or she is. This would be so because every individual would be, in one way or another, an articulation of this economy and receive their justification thereby. They would thereby be endowed with inclinations that, whether called 'good' or 'evil' from current perspectives, would have value when viewed from the perspective of their place within the universal structure of human preservation. No one, seen from this standpoint, could be said to be 'guilty' of anything. However, as long as we dwell in a manner that refuses to acknowledge the irresponsibility that the economy of the species would bring with it we are condemned to living 'in the age of tragedy, the age of moralities and religions' (*Gay Science*, §1).

One consequence of Nietzsche's discussion of the general economy of human preservation is that human life is rendered open to being interpreted as a series of unconscious ruses, a sequence of pranks played upon an unknowing human pride by the guiding and yet invisible economy of its instincts. Thus, although the author of tragedy may foreground in his or her art the bleak aspects of life and in this way is seen as advocating something negative, he or she is in reality expressing something positive: tragic narrative gives depth and significance to existence. Such depth and significance endows life with meaning and so advances 'the faith in life' and the 'interests of the species'. People in general do not differ so much in kind as in degree from the great tragedians. All of us, whether refined or vulgar, are dominated by 'the drive for the preservation of the species' and hence this general economy. In whatever form it may be manifested (competing, designing, criticising, building, painting or sculpting art, writing literature, poetry, philosophy, trading in stocks, loving, hating, protecting, colonising, seeking vengeance), human culture is interpretable as an expression of this drive. Naturally, philosophy furnishes for Nietzsche a good illustration of this. Meditative thought at its most complex conceals a drive for preservation that may on occasion appear wondrous. Yet, beneath all remains a web of drives articulating themselves. Philosophy thus can be interpreted as a play of concepts flitting across a landscape where 'folly, [and] lack of reasons' dominate (*Gay Science*, §1).

The economy of human preservation is universal only in so far as the continuation of human life goes. Such an economy bestows significance on a life devoid of any core sense derived from objective conditions (there is no God to endow life with sense). In this way, the economy of human preservation bestows possibility upon human existence. It facilitates the cultivation of the belief that existence is worthwhile, that whoever one might be, however one's life might turn out, it will not have amounted to mere senselessness. For Nietzsche, to be human is to be subject to the need to find (if needs be, to invent) sense if we are to affirm life (see the Third Essay of *On the Genealogy of Morality*). It is in the light of this view that history is rendered open to being viewed as a passing parade of purposes and meanings. History, in this regard, is always the history of morality. Take a look back at every teacher of morality, says Nietzsche, and one will in essence find someone who has offered a reason and justification for being here. That history is really comedy is made clear by the fact that every teaching that has claimed to grasp the eternal has always, at some point, been sundered by another claiming the same authority:

> There is no denying that in the long run every one of these great teachers of a purpose was vanquished by laughter, reason, and nature: the short tragedy always gave way again and returned into the eternal comedy of existence [but] human nature has nevertheless

been changed by the ever new appearance of these teachers of the purpose of existence: It now has one additional need – the need for the ever new appearance of such teachers and teachings of a 'purpose'. Gradually, man has become a fantastic animal that has to fulfil one more condition of existence than any other animal: man has to believe, to know, from time to time why he exists; his race cannot thrive without a periodic trust in life – without faith in reason in life.

(*Gay Science*, §1)

If it were possible for humanity to laugh at itself, the sense of the tragic would vanish. Faced with abiding laughter at the prospect of the human condition the tragic genre of art would no longer be possible. However, we are beings for whom life must make sense: we crave meaning. This requirement is a constituent of our nature; it is in fact the defining demand that humanity brings to bear upon its own existence. This demand is answered, at least up to now in human history, by the teachings of morality, which create the conditions wherein we can continue to exist, reassured by the belief that the events of our lives are meaningful however much suffering we happen to endure. Nietzsche's contention that we are governed by this great economy allows for a characteristic challenge to be posed with regard to our conceptions of 'good' and 'evil'. Although it is not uncommon to see Nietzsche represented as a thinker who stands morality on its head, what he claims here is that contemporary morals need not so much to be overturned and abandoned as resituated. It is not a matter of rejecting what are now called 'good' qualities in favour of those commonly deemed 'evil' but rather of accounting for *all human propensities* in terms of their place within the general economy of our preservation. Such a strategy is, however, perhaps more shocking than the alternative just mentioned. This is because the very inclusiveness of this standpoint denies the critic the opportunity of adopting the relatively straightforward stance of attacking Nietzsche for advocating 'immoral' things. What are called 'evil' propensities, it turns out, have a positive value, but this is no less the case for those deemed 'good'.

As is so often the case with Nietzsche, it is essential to consider this last claim in the context where it is situated in order to grasp the subtlety of his position. Thus, in the wake of this discussion, Nietzsche stakes the equally provocative claim that humanity has usually been advanced not by people deemed 'moral' but by the 'strongest and most evil spirits' (*Gay Science*, §4). These are the true preservers of the human species and are likened to inflammable substances, in so far as they always rekindle passions that are lying dormant in humanity and in so doing challenge us to affirm life and thereby continue the existence of our kind. What is surprising concerns the identity of such individuals. Nietzsche can provide a list of names: these human explosives, beings that stand against morality and are thus accounted 'evil' by their contemporaries, include Socrates, Buddha and Julius Caesar. Such men preserve humankind by spurring it to reconsider existence. All, however differently, provoke a response in others by giving rise to passion and the desire for meaning (be it through argument, contemplation of spirituality, or material conquest). Significantly, the teachers of morality included in this list are harbingers of the new; they are always revolutionaries. They are beings who, viewed from the standpoint of the norms of their own times, seem *evil* (see also *Daybreak*, §18). This is because the great teachings of morality always arrive on the scene as something shocking, strange and destructive to the dominant guiding forces of convention and tradition. All great ethical teachings redefine social relationships, overturning the norms that marked hitherto unquestioningly accepted boundaries and beliefs. Hence, for Nietzsche, both the spiritual and material relations that constitute culture are open to being refashioned by new moral discourses. Read in the context of the great economy of human existence, values no longer denote timeless virtues but are now taken to be subject to the vicissitudes of history, governed by the invisible rule of the economy of human preservation.

Further reading: Sedgwick 2007b.

EMPIRICISM

An empiricist is a philosopher who stresses the priority of experience when it comes to explaining what human understanding is and how it works. In its modern form, empiricism is normally regarded as dating from John Locke (1632–1704) and his *Essay Concerning Human Understanding* (1690). In this text Locke argues that all our ideas and concepts originate in our experiences rather than being innate in the mind (as rationalist thinkers such as Descartes believed). For Locke, famously, the human mind is something akin to a blank sheet of paper or an 'empty cabinet' that is subsequently written upon or filled up by our experiences. Scottish Enlightenment philosopher David

Hume (1711–76) is also another central figure within empiricism, although his approach and terminology differ in some ways from Locke's. For Hume, our concepts are representations derived from our experiences and are akin to little pictures constructed out of them. Human understanding, in turn, is rooted in the predominance of individual habit or custom. We are social beings driven to act on our experiences according to a mechanism that works in a manner no different from that of a dog. Unlike Locke, Hume develops a more nuanced social theory to accompany his empiricist approach (indeed, one might at times be tempted to call him a 'social epistemologist'). Various attempts have been made to recuperate Hume's empiricism for later philosophical purposes. Most famously, perhaps, is the interpretation offered by Anglo-American analytic philosophers, who like to see him as a methodologist who follows the rigours of the hard sciences. However, other approaches are possible, such as the interpretation offered by Deleuze. For Deleuze, whereas the rationalist begins with concepts, such as 'unity', 'wholeness', 'the subject', and then searches for how these notions are embodied in the world of experience, the empiricist begins with the notion of fluid 'states of things' and then asks how it is possible to generate concepts out of them. Empiricism, when understood in this way, does not begin with theory but practice, the practice of concrete engagement with the world. An empiricist is not, on this view, a theoretical person but an experimental one; someone who does not think 'is' but rather always thinks 'and', i.e. a maker of connections and conceptual mechanisms rather than a formulator of abiding conceptual structures. This view is heavily influenced by Deleuze's Nietzscheanism (for example, the notion of experimentation; also that of becoming).

Nietzsche himself is without doubt indebted to aspects of empiricism. Like the empiricists, he cleaves to the notion that the realm of the body and the senses is what forms the starting point for any genuine account of what it is to be a person (to be a person is to be an embodied being). Likewise, Nietzsche no less than Hume thinks that habits are what make us the kind of animals we are. Thus, Hume is right in arguing that our habits underlie our faith in causality. However, where Hume, in spite of the social aspect of his thought, tended to stress the role of individual habit in the formation of concepts and judgements, Nietzsche argues that our habits are species habits, i.e. shared, the product of the long prehistory that makes up the story of the development and emergence of morality. It is not individual habits but species habits that are important (*Will to Power*, §550). It is not clear either that Nietzsche is an empiricist in the sense that Hume and Locke are when it comes to the nature of our concepts. Although the early unpublished essay 'On Truth and Lie in a Non-Moral Sense' tends to follow a combined empiricist approach in holding our concepts to be derived directly from sense experience by way of an act of conceptual abstraction, Nietzsche's later texts do not endorse quite the same view. Thus, in *Beyond Good and Evil* (§20), the Lockean account of the origin of our ideas is deemed 'superficial' because it does not take account of the cultural and linguistic conditions that underlie our philosophical vocabulary. In short, Nietzsche would no more accede to the notion of the immediacy of empirical experience than he does to the view that the self-consciousness of the Cartesian 'I think' has immediacy. Likewise, it is hardly possible to ignore Nietzsche's scathing comment that figures such as Locke and Hume constitute 'a debasement and devaluation of the concept "philosopher"' (*Beyond Good and Evil*, §252). What Locke and Hume lack (as examples of the typically 'English') is 'real *power* of spirituality, real depth of spiritual insight, in short – philosophy' (*Beyond Good and Evil*, §252).

Further reading: Deleuze 2001.

ENLIGHTENMENT, THE

The Enlightenment was an intellectual movement in France (also in Britain in the form of the 'Scottish Enlightenment') that arose during the eighteenth century with the writings of Diderot, Hume, Kant, Rousseau, Smith and Voltaire. Kant's maxim 'Dare to understand!' captures the underlying optimism that inspired Enlightenment thought and its faith in the redemptive powers of rationality. Such a faith was promulgated in the aftermath of the example of the sciences and, especially perhaps, Newton's achievement in the *Principia Mathematica*. Enlightenment thinkers expressed faith in reason's ability to solve social, political, intellectual and scientific problems. They also tended to be aggressively critical of what they regarded as the regressive influences of tradition and religion, countering these with an affirmation of humanism, the ideal of progress, an espousal of a politics of toleration and free thinking. That said, not all Enlightenment thinkers were unrepentant atheists like Diderot. Voltaire, for instance, passionately believed in a non-Christian deity, whilst Hume was phlegmatically agnostic about such things (even so, his criticism of belief in miracles displays a characteristic Enlightenment commitment to embracing scepticism when it comes to metaphysical beliefs). Needless to say, the term 'Enlightenment' does not denote a homogenous body of doctrine. It had its critics, even on the inside. Thus, Hume often undercuts the Enlightenment faith in reason in his *Treatise*, and Rousseau's writings are often associated with the development of counter-Enlightenment thinking. Nietzsche's thinking, while ambivalent with regard to the virtue and vices of the spirit of Enlightenment, clearly owes a significant debt to it. This is especially so with regard to the books he wrote in the late 1870s and early 1880s (*Human, All Too Human, Assorted Opinions and Maxims, The Wanderer and His Shadow, The Gay Science*, Books 1–4). *Human, All Too Human*, for instance, was originally dedicated to the memory of Voltaire and adopts a methodological scepticism which shows the influence of Enlightenment thought and the sciences. That said, Nietzsche is often regarded by some (e.g. Habermas) as a thinker of counter-Enlightenment or as one of its 'black' thinkers (see Horkheimer and Adorno 1988). This is because his mature writings especially tend to render problematic the view of reason espoused by the Enlightenment. Probably, Horkheimer and Adorno's interpretation of this must be regarded as one of the most provocative. For them the Enlightenment abandons its rationality through transforming all questions of knowledge into issues that can be addressed only in instrumental terms. Reason, in other words, is rendered no more than a mere tool at the hands of Enlightenment thought. With this, not only is the ethical dimension of rationality lost but, at the same time, the Enlightenment's unrestrained worship of reason itself becomes irrational and dogmatic. Such irrationality leaves reason prey to being the unwitting instrument of dominant social forces, one consequence of which is the disaster of German Nazism. On their view, Nietzsche (along with de Sade) is a thinker who takes the logic of Enlightenment and works it through to its self-destructive conclusion. Thus, Nietzsche's rendering of morality as an expression of interest (noble morality, slave morality), his attacks on any attempts to ground our knowledge of ethics in objective conditions and his claim that rationality is an expression of will to power all serve to question the Enlightenment ideal of rational progress.

Further reading: Berlin 1979; Conway 1997; Gay 1988; Habermas 1988.

EPISTEMOLOGY

The philosophical term for theory of knowledge. The main concerns of epistemology are the meaning of the term 'knowledge', the limits and scope of knowledge and its reliability. Philosophers have often concerned themselves with the difference between knowledge and belief or the question of the degree to which the senses or rationality determine what knowledge is. For Plato (c. 428–348 BC), rational abilities are intrinsic to human identity and reflected in the objective order of things (the famous theory of the Forms). Aspects of this approach were developed by seventeenth- and eighteenth-century rationalism. The philosophers associated with empiricism offered an alternative approach. For the empiricist, knowledge is a direct result of the human ability to have impressions via the senses. In turn, Kant responded to the empiricists by arguing that it is not possible to reduce all knowledge to being a consequence of sensory experience. For Kant, all experience is negotiated by *a priori* conditions that are independent of experience. Thus, where an empiricist like John Locke held the mind to be like an empty cabinet waiting to be furnished by experience, Kant argued that the cabinet (to continue Locke's metaphor) was structured in a manner that made it amenable to having experiences in the first place. Kant's epistemology thus argues for a rejuvenated metaphysics. Nietzsche is, in some respects, indebted to empiricism. However, he criticises Locke and Hume in various ways. He is frequently highly critical of Kant's philosophy and often scathing about Plato; but he is not always as distant from them as might first appear. In general, one clear stance does emerge from Nietzsche's writings concerning his own epistemology: he doesn't have one. Indeed, the very urge to render philosophy primarily in terms of epistemology is, for Nietzsche, suspect and counter to the spirit of genuine philosophical activity:

> Philosophy reduced to 'theory of knowledge', in fact no more than a timid epochism and doctrine of abstinence – a philosophy that never gets beyond the threshold and takes pains to *deny* itself the right to enter – that is philosophy in its last throes, an end, an agony, something inspiring pity.
>
> (*Beyond Good and Evil*, §204)

In other words, for Nietzsche, philosophising properly understood is an activity that offers more than the mere construction of 'theories' about how we know things. Ultimately, philosophy for him is better understood as a form of 'legislation': it is an activity that does not seek to tell us how reality really is but rather aims to control it through interpretation. Thus, *Beyond Good and Evil* (§§204 ff.) constructs the case for viewing philosophy as a legislative enterprise. Nietzsche regards traditional epistemology, which seeks to uncover the basic conditions of our knowledge, as little more than an uncritical extrapolation of the underlying presuppositions of metaphysics. Epistemology must be overcome, even if it turns out that metaphysics itself cannot be entirely abandoned (*see* **knowledge**). The epistemologist's desire to present a transparent account of the nature of knowledge founders upon the fact that the subject (the Cartesian 'I think') does not make an adequate foundation upon which to develop an account of knowledge. For Nietzsche, subjectivity is produced by environmental forces (the material conditions of life), practices, norms and linguistic conventions (also material conditions, but cultural ones). To be a subject, it follows, means to be bound by a context: all of us must speak from a particular perspective whenever we make a judgement. In turn, perspectivism implies that there is no 'knowledge' as such, as traditional epistemology presupposes. There are, rather, many possible 'knowledges' or standpoints from which the world may be viewed.

Further reading: Clark 1990; Grimm 1977; Wilcox 1974.

ETERNAL RECURRENCE

This notion, Nietzsche tells us, can be traced back to Ancient Greece and the fifth-century BC philosopher Heraclitus (*Ecce Homo,* 'The Birth of Tragedy', §3). Nietzsche's teaching of eternal recurrence is first announced in §341 of *The Gay Science,* where it is deemed the 'greatest weight'. How, the text asks the reader, would you respond if at some point a demon were to appear before you in a moment of lonely solitude and confront you with the news that your life will be repeated exactly as it has occurred in even the smallest of details? Would one curse at the thought of this idea or respond to the prospect with joy and affirmation? To be gripped by this thought, Nietzsche says, would be to have one's attitude toward life, to one's every deed and moment, subject to the most decisive of judgements. This is because the affirmation of the eternal recurrence of all that has been and will be would be an affirmation of existence to a degree that cannot be exceeded. To say 'yes' to eternal recurrence is to bestow upon life the greatest seal of confirmation that one can. That eternal recurrence is linked intimately to the figure of Zarathustra and his extolling of the idea of the Overman is made clear enough by considering that the following section of *The Gay Science* (§342) relates the opening of Zarathustra's journey as it is later told in *Thus*

Spoke Zarathustra. In *Zarathustra,* eternal recurrence is both announced
again and subsequently affirmed (*Zarathustra,* Part III, 'On the Vision
and the Riddle', §3; Part IV, 'The Drunken Song', §§9–12). Here,
the embracing of eternal recurrence is the joyful affirmation of
meaningfulness in a fleeting world of becoming devoid of ultimate
sense. All that is becomes and passes away; thus, every joy is condemned to extinction. Through eternal recurrence, however, all that
is transient is rendered eternal, and life is thereby celebrated.
Nietzsche toys with various conceptions of eternal recurrence. It is
sometimes discussed in his notebooks as a scientific hypothesis. In *The
Will to Power* (§1066), for example, the view is proffered that an
infinitely lasting universe composed of finite material must, sooner or
later, always return to the same pattern and hence repeat endlessly.
Such speculation might well be considered an at-best flawed thought
experiment, for it presupposes too much. However, whether one is
tempted to consider it in cosmological terms or not, the fact that
eternal recurrence is a regulative conception cannot be ignored. As
such, it serves Nietzsche well, for it allows him to present his philosophy as well suited to dealing with what he regards to be the central
challenge posed by human existence. This is the question of how to
bestow upon it a degree of sense that does not succumb to the nihilism that results from the death of God while yet, at the same time,
refusing to turn back to the kind of faith exemplified by Christianity.
In the face of this dilemma, Nietzsche affirms the possibility of preserving sense in the face of meaninglessness by conjoining the
Dionysian creative aesthetic with the thought of eternal recurrence:
'I, the last disciple of the philosopher Dionysus – I the [...] teacher of
the eternal recurrence' (*Twilight of the Idols,* 'What I Owe to the
Ancients', §5). Dionysian creativity, which gains its legitimacy
through being considered as an expression of the essence of what
lives, justifies human existence through affirmation of the joys of
creative endeavour in the face of transience.

Further reading: Hatab 1978, 2005; Klossowski 1997 [1969]; Löwith 1997
[1956]; Stambaugh 1972.

FREE SPIRIT

Human, All Too Human is subtitled 'A Book for Free Spirits'. This text
stands as a public statement of Nietzsche's abandonment of Wagner
and Wagnerian music, pessimism, nationalism and romanticism in

favour of attitudes more closely associated with the Enlightenment (the first edition of *Human, All Too Human* was dedicated to the memory of Voltaire). Enlightenment, as Kant famously characterised it, is the liberation from myth and superstition, which is replaced by rational critical thought. It is for him summed up by the motto '*Dare to think!*' Regarded in this light, Nietzsche's conception of the free spirit could be taken as being akin to the Enlightenment free thinker: a person who asks for reasons where others are content to abide with faith (*Human, All Too Human*, §225). The free spirit, however, is a rather more ambiguous figure than this straightforward view implies. Thus, if one turns to the second part of *Beyond Good and Evil*, entitled 'The Free Spirit', things become more complex. Here, the free spirit is epitomised by the notion of the 'philosopher of the future', which is a being of legislation and commanding (*see* **philosophy**). Such spirits, Nietzsche tells us, are not to be confused with those who espouse 'modern ideas' (*Beyond Good and Evil*, §44). They are certainly not democrats, liberals, or supporters of the belief in equality; nor do they have an uncritical faith in the sciences. The free spirit is, rather, linked explicitly by Nietzsche to the notion of will to power and stands in contrast to the dominance of modernity and mass culture. Such a being is necessarily opaque and courts ambiguity when it comes to the issue of liberation from the dominant norms of society: 'Is it any wonder we "free spirits" are not the most communicative of spirits? that we do not want to betray in every respect *from what* a spirit can free itself and *to what* it is then perhaps driven?' (*Beyond Good and Evil*, §40). The free spirit is hence a mysterious being, a wearer of masks rather than a promulgator of Enlightenment and supporter of scientific method. Free spirits, in other words, are prone to disguises, for this is a necessary requirement for the satisfaction of their desire to abandon faith and the craving for certainty (*Gay Science*, §357). The free spirit is, it follows, a figure that radiates as much darkness as it does light.

Further reading: Lampert 1986, 2001.

GENEALOGY

In Nietzsche, the term 'genealogy' denotes a method for the analysis of the different dominant modes of ethical discourse (morality). It is presented in *On the Genealogy of Morality*, and subsequently mentioned in *The Antichrist* (§§24, 45), *Ecce Homo* and *The Case of Wagner* (in a

footnote by Nietzsche at the very end of the text). A similar histor-
icising and naturalising approach can also be found in Part V of
Beyond Good and Evil, 'On the Natural History of Morals'. In
Genealogy, Nietzsche argues that the meaning of morality and moral
language (i.e. of the meaning attributed to words like 'good', 'evil'
and 'bad') is not to be interpreted in terms of ideas of 'usefulness' or
'altruism' – a view he attributes to 'English psychologists', amongst
others. Instead, for him ethical systems can best be understood by way
of reference to the historical conditions under which they emerged
and from which they subsequently developed. Telling the story of
this emergence is telling the story of their 'genealogy'. Ethical systems
thus emerge from socio-historical conflagrations which, it turns out,
reveals them to be immured in power struggles. Moral language, it
follows, cannot be exhaustively accounted for by way of reference to
disinterested conceptions of 'good' and 'bad', but is an expression of
interests. The use of the word 'good' can, Nietzsche argues, signify
the presence of very different social perspectives and therefore also
represents two very different (and indeed competing) modes of evaluation. These are the evaluative methods designated by the terms
'noble morality' and 'slave morality' (the one a moral system of 'good
and bad', the other of 'good and evil'). A genealogical investigation
reveals that purportedly universal values (not least the values denoted
by the ultimately triumphant slave morality discourse of 'good and
evil') have their origins in narrower specificity. Consequently, the
moralist's pretensions to transcendence are defused by a speculative
historical analysis of the origins of their ethical language. What genealogy shows is not merely that value judgements (the hidden origins
of which, it is claimed, are revealed in etymology) are expressions of
environmental conditions and the interests that are intrinsic to such
conditions. This approach also undoes what Nietzsche holds to be the
misconception that ethics is grounded in a free subject (i.e. in the concept of freely willed agency). The moral agent, Nietzsche argues, does
not exist behind their actions in some mysterious substratum. To think
this is metaphysics pure and simple. Subjects are not, in other words,
'free' to choose to do one thing or another; they are pieces of fate (to
recall a phrase from *Twilight of the Idols*). Being an agent means doing – its
nature is a concrete rather than theoretical issue. The self, in other words,
is revealed through what it does in the domain of practice (*Genealogy*,
Essay I, §13). Genealogy thereby destabilises moral discourse. It does
not, however, represent an attempt to abandon it. Thinking 'beyond
good and evil', Nietzsche says, does not mean transcending 'good and
bad'. The immoralist, in other words, is not an amoral being.

Further reading: Acampora 2006; Allison 2000; Blondel 1991; Fink 2003; Foucault 1977; Geuss 1999; Minson 1985; Schacht 1994; Siemens 2001a; Spinks 2003.

GOOD EUROPEANISM

Although *The Birth of Tragedy* presents us with a call to arms in the pursuit of a revitalised German culture, attainable by way of the music of Wagner, Nietzsche soon rejects this in favour of what he terms 'good Europeanism'. A stark contrast exists between the youthful Nietzsche and the more mature writer of *Human, All Too Human* and after. The mature Nietzsche's work bears witness to the demise of nationalistic sentiment in favour of the celebration of a unified European culture. Such unification is, for Nietzsche, the consequence of modernity, with its ever-faster exchanges of information, burgeoning commercial activity and means of travel. In the aftermath of such developments, traditional national barriers are threatened and, with them, the existence of the nation state (*Human, All Too Human,* §475). To be a good European means, for Nietzsche, to be someone who is part of this self-overcoming of European identity, which is nothing less than the self-overcoming of Christianity. One thereby embraces the notion of the free spirit (*Beyond Good and Evil,* Preface).

Further reading: Detwiler 1990; Krell and Bates 1997; Lampert 1986, 1993.

HERD

This is one of Nietzsche's favourite words for referring to many of the dominant trends in modernity. Humans are, in his view, in an essential way herd creatures. In other words, they have a general tendency, as a consequence of the psychology inherited from their origins in prehistory, to be creatures of conformity. Originally, the individual did not exist, only the community. Out of the need for communal security in primitive communities 'we' and 'you' constituted the concrete conditions upon which survival rested and were hence always afforded the greatest importance. The individual is a late and coincidental outcropping of normative structures (the web of habits, customs and traditions) that make up the human world. For this reason: 'The *you* is older than the *I;* the *you* has been pronounced holy, but not yet the *I:* so man crowds toward his neighbor' (*Zarathustra,* Part I, 'On Love of the Neighbor'; see also the discussion of the emergence of the individual as exchanger in the second essay of *On the Genealogy of Morality*). In turn, things one might usually invest with a quantum of individuality are, for Nietzsche, just as prone to be devoid of it. Consciousness, for example, about which humanity feels so much pride and which is often taken to epitomise individuality, is for Nietzsche at least as amenable to being regarded as representing herd mentality in microcosm, for it is a feature that springs from our communal nature and the development of language. Our self-interpretative abilities, which come to constitute an essential aspect of the kind of animal we are, thus emerge from a realm of shared practices and traditions: what we tend to think of as being 'individual' about ourselves is not quite as individual as we might like to think. The unique nature of the individual is, in turn, something that is fashioned rather than given. Indeed, for Nietzsche this is something that springs from the unconscious, embodied self not the consciousness of the 'I'. Whereas the 'I' is still overwhelmingly communal the self is a complex channelling and refraction of the hierarchical forces that are at work in all social orders no less than individuals. For Nietzsche, the history of humankind begins with a brute animality that is by turns shaped by primitive communality (the morality of custom) and the emergence of shared identities and the ability to make promises, which give rise to the development of self-interpretative abilities. Only then comes the sovereign individual, whose transcendence of normative compulsion and constraint pays testimony to the forming of an individuality out of what was once common and shared. The herd is, it follows, the precondition of the individual, which is an accidental but ultimately inestimably valuable consequence of communal existence. For Nietzsche, what is appalling about modern life, replete as it is with talk of equal rights, democracy, and the emergence of the nation state, is that it represents something regressive, a sliding backwards to an earlier prehistoric normative structure. Modernity is, at its worst, Christianity writ large: the diminution of individuality in favour of a revitalised collectivism. Nietzsche cannot comprehend how such a collectivism might not ultimately pose a threat to the individual but actually serve to cultivate it. Hence, his dismissal of the 'herd' mentality is often accompanied by anti-socialist sentiment:

> Socialism is the fanciful younger brother of the almost expired despotism whose heir it wants to be; its endeavours are thus in

the profoundest sense reactionary. For it desires an abundance of state power such as only despotism has ever had; indeed it out-bids all the despotisms of the past inasmuch as it expressly aspires to the annihilation of the individual.

(*Human, All Too Human,* §473)

That said, Nietzsche is no liberal, either. For he sees in market capit-alism and liberalism an evil that is no lesser in terms of its tendency to conformism and the eradication of the individual: 'Liberalism: in plain words, *reduction to the herd animal*' (*Twilight of the Idols,* 'Expeditions of an Untimely Man', §38).

HISTORICAL PHILOSOPHY

The approach to questions of knowledge (not least in the moral and aesthetic spheres) that Nietzsche develops in the text of *Human, All Too Human.* Historical philosophy embraces the notion of becoming as opposed to being, and with this seeks to produce historically informed accounts of the nature of our concepts. Its historicism is what characterises it most essentially. Historical philosophy is in part inspired by the positivism of the physical sciences and can be con-trasted with metaphysical philosophy. The approach suggested by the notion of historical philosophy is pursued in Nietzsche's late works in the form of genealogy.

See also: **knowledge.**

HISTORY

Nietzsche's most sustained discussion of the nature of history is offered in the essay 'On the Uses and Disadvantages of History for Life' (1874 – the second *Untimely Meditation*). The essay opens with a quotation from Goethe's *Poetry and Truth:* 'In any case, I hate everything that merely instructs me without augmenting or directly invigorating my activity'. This quotation serves to illustrate Nietzsche's intentions from the outset of the essay. He wishes to show 'why instruction without invigoration, why knowledge not attended by action, why history as a costly superfluity and luxury [...] must be seriously hated by us – hated because we still lack even the things we need and the super-fluous is the enemy of the necessary' (*Untimely Meditations,* Essay II,

'Forward'). At the same time, Nietzsche affirms the need for history, albeit in a different sense from the need for history that belongs to the 'idler in the garden of knowledge' (*Untimely Meditations,* Essay II, 'Forward'). There are, for him, *two* aspects to history: one is life enhancing, the other is life negating. We may live in an historical age and this can be one of our great virtues, but 'virtues can be as damaging as vices: the "historical sense" is a hypertrophied virtue' (*Untimely Meditations,* Essay II, 'Forward'). What, one may ask, is it to be an historical being? One can begin to answer this question by considering non-human animals. Non-humans live *unhistorically.* They are, for the most part, contented. The human being, in contrast, is an animal that is dogged by memory (*Untimely Meditations,* Essay II, §1). Of course, we can forget things temporarily: we can become lost in activities, in the company of others, etc, but all humans are sooner or later called back to contemplating what memory delivers them over to. One is, of course, delivered from such misery by death. However, this itself confirms the knowledge 'that being is only an uninterrupted "has-been", a thing that lives by negating, consuming and contradicting itself' (*Untimely Meditations,* Essay II, §1). Happiness, it follows, is the exclusive province of the ability to forget – which implies that happiness and history are incompatible. A being unable to forget even for a moment will never know happiness in any shape or form. It is not merely happiness that is at stake here, but also action, which requires forgetting. A life would in principle be possible without (conscious) memory. But a being unable to forget would perish through inaction. Historical thought needs, it follows, to be given limits beyond which it must not be allowed to trespass 'if it is not to become the gravedigger of the present' (*Untimely Meditations,* Essay II, §1). To do this one would need to be able to estimate the 'plastic power' of individuals, peoples and cultures. Such power is to be understood as an individual's or a culture's ability to draw into itself what is past and essentially foreign to it. Some peoples and cultures are more able to assimilate what is foreign to them than others. The greater the ability to assimilate, the greater a person's inner nature. The strongest nature would encounter no limit to the degree to which it could incorporate the past into its self-understanding. Cultural good health thus requires a degree of history and a degree of the unhistorical to be present: 'the unhistorical and the historical are necessary in equal measure for the health of an individual, of a people and of a culture' (*Untimely Meditations,* Essay II, §1). The ability to live and feel unhistorically is the fundamental ground of human life: it is akin to an atmosphere, without which life is not possible. In turn, thought, reflection, comparison and the like (i.e. the employment of past experiences for present purposes) impose limits on this unhistorical nature and only thereby does humanity attain its true being. Action presupposes the shrugging-off of history and memory: 'no painter will paint his picture, no general achieve his victory, no people attain its freedom without having first desired and striven for it in an unhistorical condition' (*Untimely Meditations,* Essay II, §1). Actions of such kinds depend upon the assertion of the absolute right of the present to be what it is; conscience is subverted. Thus, every great historical event is paradoxically born out of an 'unhistorical atmosphere' (*Untimely Meditations,* Essay II, §1), wherein its agents elevate themselves to a '*suprahistorical*' vantage point. Historical humans, in contrast, look to the past as a means of being impelled toward the future. The future presents itself as a realm of possible happiness, somewhere where past wants and miseries will be overcome. 'Suprahistorical men', on the other hand, see past and present as a unity.

> Just as the hundreds of different languages correspond to the same typically unchanging needs of man, so that he who understood these needs would be unable to learn anything new from any of these languages, so the suprahistorical thinker beholds the history of nations and of individuals from within, clairvoyantly divining the original meaning of the various hieroglyphics and gradually even coming wearily to avoid the endless stream of new signs.
>
> (*Untimely Meditations,* Essay II, §1)

History, in other words, is guided by *need*. As such, history can never be a 'pure' science, in the sense in which mathematics might be said to be. However, the extent to which life needs history 'is one of the supreme questions and concerns in regard to the health of a man, a people or a culture' (*Untimely Meditations,* Essay II, §1). This is because when history 'attains a certain degree of excess, life crumbles and degenerates, and through this degeneration history itself finally degenerates too' (*Untimely Meditations,* Essay II, §1). History, Nietzsche now argues, has relevance to humankind in three respects: as a being who (i) 'acts and strives', (ii) 'preserves and reveres' or (iii) 'suffers and seeks deliverance' (*Untimely Meditations,* Essay II, §2). The three relations outlined here correspond to three kinds of history: the monumental, the antiquarian and the critical: 'Each of the three species of history which exist belongs to a certain soil and a certain climate and only to that: in any other it grows into a devastating weed' (*Untimely Meditations,* Essay II, §2).

Monumental history pertains to those who are active and engaged in the struggle for a specific goal. Such persons stand in need of teachers and models to emulate but, finding them lacking in the present, turn to the past. History becomes a means of fortification, of gaining strength in order to pursue a chosen end. The monumental consciousness unites past struggles with their present struggle to constitute a 'chain [that] unites mankind across the millennia like a range of human mountain peaks, that the summit of such a long-ago shall be for me still living, bright and great' (*Untimely Meditations*, Essay II, §2). Thus, a faith in continued human accomplishment underlies monumental history. This notion of the historical serves the belief that it is possible to elevate humanity – that what remains of a great person's life are his or her monumental deeds. The value of this view of the past for the present lies in the implication that since greatness was possible it ought to be possible again. At the same time, monumental history does unutterable violence to the past: it eradicates the myriad differences that mark each historical period. Properly grasped, the nature of history would doubtless be found in a multiplicity of small accidents. History, in other words, involves an essential *contingency*. For Nietzsche, the monumental mode of history rules over the antiquarian and the critical modes in so far as the essence of historiography resides in its ability to inspire powerful persons, yet its dominance leads inexorably to the damaging and destruction of the past. Whole parts of the past are susceptible to being forgotten or despised because of it. This is the case whether it is used by the powerful or the resentful and powerless. *Antiquarian history* is that mode of historical understanding that 'preserves and reveres' (*Untimely Meditations*, Essay II, §3). This attitude regards the past with the gratitude due to that from which it has itself sprung into existence. The antiquarian attitude seeks to preserve that which was the case in order to hand it on to those who follow. 'The history of his city becomes for him the history of himself; he reads its walls, its towered gate, its rules and regulations, its holidays, like an illuminated diary of his youth and in all this he finds again himself' (*Untimely Meditations*, Essay II, §3). The 'I' thereby situates itself in the context of a 'we', and from the vantage point of this 'we' the individual feels his or her life to have a meaning that extends beyond the transitory: the individual becomes the embodiment of the spirit of their house, city, race or culture (examples could include any talk of the 'German soul', the 'British spirit' and the like). Antiquarian history makes people feel contented with their lot. The downside of this mode of historical understanding is its narrow field of vision: it has the potential for parochialism in the extreme. What is other than it the antiquarian attitude is incapable of understanding or sympathising with at all. Likewise, all that is associated with the past of the community is accorded equal reverence: there is a lack of discrimination and blandness. Sensibilities thereby harden. Life becomes ritualistic and empty and the living culture that the antiquarian attitude celebrates begins to wither under the weight of undiscriminating veneration. The need for *critical history* is amply demonstrated by the above. This is an attitude toward the past that seeks to break it apart, and, by dissolving its apparent unity, ultimately to condemn it. 'It is not justice which sits here in judgment; it is even less mercy which pronounces the verdict; it is life alone, that dark, driving power that insatiably thirsts for itself' (*Untimely Meditations,* Essay II, §3). Life, which needs forgetfulness to live, sometimes needs to suspend this very condition in order to continue. Critical history counters forgetfulness, 'it wants to be clear as to how unjust the existence of anything – a privilege, a caste, a dynasty, for example – is, and how greatly this thing deserves to perish' (*Untimely Meditations,* Essay II, §3). Ages that destroy the past by being critical of it are always the most dangerous, for they lack stability. Self-loathing can arise from critical history, since to understand the past in a manner that judges it and finds it wanting is also to understand elements of oneself in this light.

All cultures stand in need, Nietzsche argues, at various times, of the three modes of historical understanding that his essay outlines as means of the preservation of life. What, then, of the present? Nietzsche's view is clear enough: the present is dominated '*by the demand that history should be a science*' (*Untimely Meditations,* Essay II, §4). This demand contradicts 'the demands of life' in so far as it requires that all constraints be removed in the search for objectivity and truth. Knowledge has become a fetishised consumerist product:

> Knowledge, consumed for the greater part without hunger for it and even counter to one's needs, now no longer acts as an agent for transforming the outside world but remains concealed within a chaotic inner world which modern man describes with a curious pride as his uniquely characteristic 'subjectivity'.
>
> (*Untimely Meditations,* Essay II, §4)

Modern culture is thus an anachronism: 'it is not a real culture at all but only a kind of knowledge of culture' (*Untimely Meditations,* Essay II, §4). What then follows in the text is a swingeing attack on contemporary German nationalism. Talk of modern historical objectivity, in fact, conceals partiality: 'naïve historians call the assessments of the opinions and deeds of the past according to the everyday standards of the present moment "objectivity" [...] they call all historiography "subjective" that does not accept these popular standards as canonical' (*Untimely Meditations*, Essay II, §6).

There is, indeed, rejoicing now that 'science is beginning to dominate life': that condition may, possibly, be attained; but life thus dominated is not of much value because it is far less *living* and guarantees far less life for the future than did a former life dominated not by knowledge but by instinct and powerful illusions.

(*Untimely Meditations*, Essay II, §7)

(This is, one should recall here, the age of modernity, of mass production, and as such demands the subjugation of the individual to 'labour in the factories of the general good' (*Untimely Meditations*, Essay II, §7). The realm of knowledge, like modern society, is a sphere dominated by efficiency of production, market supply and profit). Science, when imported into history, demands that all reality be understood as historical, that it lack any essential unhistorical core. Science denies the eternal and has 'a profound antagonism toward the eternalizing powers of art and religion, for it hates forgetting, which is the death of knowledge, and seeks to abolish all limitations of horizon and launch mankind upon an infinite and unbounded sea of light whose light is knowledge of all becoming' (*Untimely Meditations*, Essay II, §10). Which, one must therefore ask, is to preponderate: science or life? The answer is life, because a knowledge that annihilates the conditions of life annihilates itself. Consequently, Nietzsche argues, science requires regulation.

Four years later, Nietzsche extols a modified view, opposing the virtues of 'historical philosophy' to an illusory and rigidifying 'metaphysical philosophy' with its eye set on the eternal (see *Human, All Too Human*, §§1–3). Historical philosophy teaches one to be less ambitious in one's pretensions about the extent of one's knowledge. It opposes the universal truths of dogmatic thought with more modest claims, whose reliability resides in their specificity. History, in fact, refutes metaphysics in a way that philosophical argument alone cannot do. Where it was once necessary to demonstrate that God does not exist, as soon as a historical account is offered of how the belief in God arises and acquires its power and value, the refutation of God by any other means becomes pointless (*Daybreak*, §95). Historical narrative, in other words, refutes in its very nature by offering an explanation that avoids the terrain of metaphysical debate. This use of history characterises the later, more polemical phase of

Nietzsche's thought. In *On the Genealogy of Morality*, for example, Nietzsche's 'thoughts on the *descent* of our moral prejudices' (Preface, §2) present the reader with a combined historical/genealogical account of the 'line of descent' of moral practices and codes. The *Genealogy* itself, Nietzsche tells us, is the inheritor of the historical mode of enquiry first hinted at in *Human, All Too Human*. In the later work, however, we are offered nothing less than the 'real *history of morality*', i.e. 'that which can be documented, what can actually be confirmed and has actually existed, in short, the whole, long, hard-to-decipher hieroglyphic script of man's moral past!' (*On the Genealogy of Morality*, Preface, §7). The moral past is an historically sedemented *text* and it requires proper interpretation. The *Genealogy* thereby asserts the relevance of history to the study of ethics in a sense that is decisive. The history in question is no mere story of predefined ethical concepts but claims to be an account of the emergence of moral practices and concepts themselves. Morality, in other words, is historically constituted. Thus, for example, the attack Nietzsche mounts on English psychologists accuses them of the traditional philosophical lack of '*historical spirit*' (*Genealogy*, Essay I, §2). They think in a manner 'that is *essentially* unhistorical' when they take the commonly accepted altruistic meaning of the word 'good' as a given. For Nietzsche, in contrast, one can only grasp the precise significance of moral language once the historical context from which it was forged has been delineated. Thus, 'the real breeding ground of the concept "good"' (*Genealogy*, Essay I, §2) is to be found not in a long forgotten act of altruism but in a historical realm dominated by class differences, struggle and issues of interest. The good originally were '"the good" themselves, mean-ing the noble, the mighty, the high-placed and the high-minded' (*Genealogy*, Essay I, §2). The concept 'good', it follows, does not arise out of altruistic 'usefulness' but rather is an expression of power. The origin of the 'good' hence lies in what Nietzsche calls noble morality. The word 'good' expresses a 'pathos of distance', a feeling of being differentiated from those inferior to you. It is in this feeling of superiority and power that 'the origin of the antithesis "good" and "bad"' (*Genealogy*, Essay I, §2) lies. From this initial positing of value, all other ethical forms emerge – not least that of slave morality, which is a reaction to the nobility's dominance by those who are their victims (see *Genealogy*, Essay I, §10). There is good reason for the victim's response: historically, the noble is always encountered as an invader and bringer of violence. Thus, Nietzsche notes, the nobles of Ancient Roman, Ancient Greek, Arabic, Germanic (i.e. Goth and Vandal), Japanese and Scandinavian (i.e. Viking) cultures all left 'the concept "barbarian"' (*Genealogy*, Essay I, §10) in their wake. Central to the account of the origins of morality offered in *Genealogy* is the historicisation of ethics. History undermines the authority of the divinity purported to underlie the origin of values. The *Genealogy*'s second essay, '"Guilt", "Bad Conscience" and Related Matters' seeks to offer an account of the origins of humankind's ethical nature in general. This nature, Nietzsche argues, springs from the concrete practices that make up human prehistory. Such practices (essentially violent and rooted in the primeval relation between creditor and debtor) endowed humanity with a 'moral memory' (*Genealogy*, Essay II, §3). On Nietzsche's account, the meaning of morality (and indeed the concept of meaning as such) is historically generated from webs of practices. It is also, Nietzsche argues, essentially linked to power.

Essay II, §12 constitutes one of the most startling sections of the *Genealogy*. Here Nietzsche offers a development of the power thesis that is at the same time woven into the theme of the historical development of law and punishment. Questions about origins and purposes, he argues, are separate issues. There is a tendency to ignore this: 'moral genealogists' (stupid as ever) tend to find a purpose in something and interpret this as its origin. Take the example of law: it is possible to see in law today the enactment of a purpose, e.g. 'revenge or deterrence' (*Genealogy*, Essay II, §12). 'But "purpose in law" is the last thing we should apply to the history of the emergence of law' (*Genealogy*, Essay II, §12). The cause of a thing's emergence and its possible practical uses are issues that are of a different order. Anything that exists is always susceptible to being 'interpreted anew, requisitioned anew, transformed and redirected to a new purpose by a power superior to it [...]' (*Genealogy*, Essay II, §12). This claim is mounted in the light of Nietzsche's contention about the immanence of power. Power is expressed through *interpretation*: 'everything that occurs in the organic world consists of *overpowering, dominating,* and in their turn, overpowering and dominating consist of re-interpretation, adjustment, in the process of which their former "meaning" and "purpose" must necessarily be obscured or completely obliterated' (*Genealogy*, Essay II, §12). The point here is to show us that 'interpretation' is not just a matter of formal hermeneutic concern (i.e. purely textual interpretation); it is an *organic and concrete activity* that is characteristic of life itself. In turn, Nietzsche argues that the interpretation of a thing *necessarily* overwrites previous senses that may be attributed to it. Moreover, it does so to the extent that such senses may become *irretrievable*. Consequently, however well one might have grasped 'the *usefulness* of any physiological organ (or legal institution, social custom, political usage, art form or religious rite) you have not yet thereby grasped how it emerged' (*Genealogy,* Essay II, §12). The current *purpose* of a thing is therefore not to be confused with 'the reason for its existence' (*Genealogy,* Essay II, §12). We are guilty of confused thinking if we believe, for instance, that 'the eye is made to see, the hand to grasp' (*Genealogy,* Essay II, §12). To hold such a view would commit one to an absurd metaphysical position, i.e. the view that seeing came *before* eyes, grasping *before* hands. All purposes are *signs.* Every purpose shows that 'the will to power has achieved mastery over something less powerful, and has impressed upon it its own idea of a use function' (*Genealogy,* Essay II, §12). Purposes, in other words, always already concern relations of *power.* Our view of history must change if we accept this argument. '[T]he whole history of a "thing", an organ, a tradition can to this extent be a continuous chain of signs, continually revealing new interpretations and adaptations, the causes of which need not be connected even amongst themselves, but rather just follow and replace one another at random' (*Genealogy,* Essay II, §12). History is an amalgamation of conflicting purposes, but this very variety and multiplicity of purposes means that history is devoid of conceptual unity, of *a* purpose. The development of organs, customs, etc., is thereby *not* to be grasped in terms of a '*progressus* towards a goal, still less is it a logical *progressus*' (*Genealogy,* Essay II, §12). It is, rather, better understood as a series of 'more or less mutually independent processes of subjugation exacted on the thing [...] The form is fluid the "meaning" even more so' (*Genealogy,* Essay II, §12). With this in mind, one can turn to the concept of punishment. Punishment can be differentiated into two aspects. On the one hand, there is the aspect of punishment that exhibits 'relative *permanence,* a traditional usage, a fixed form of action, a "drama", a certain strict sequence of procedures' (*Genealogy,* Essay II, §13). In other words, punishment has one aspect that is linked to conventions, practices, i.e. ways of doing things. On the other hand, there is a characteristic that is defined by way of its '*fluidity,* its meaning, purpose and expectation, which is linked to the carrying out of such procedures' (*Genealogy,* Essay II, §12). On the basis of 'the major point of historical method' (outlined in *Genealogy,* Essay II, §12), the practices, conventions, etc., 'will be older; predating its use as punishment' (*Genealogy,* Essay II, §13). The sense of punishing 'was only *inserted* and interpreted into the procedure' (*Genealogy,* Essay II, §12) after the fact. The procedures that characterise punishment were not, it follows, '*invented* for the purpose of punishment' (*Genealogy,* Essay II, §12). The attribution of a sense to punishing is something that comes much later: what we call 'punishment' does not pertain to a single sense but a plurality of *senses,*

> a whole synthesis of 'meanings': the history of punishment up to now in general, the history of its use for a variety of purposes, finally crystallizes in a kind of unity which is difficult to dissolve back into its elements, difficult to analyze and, this has to be stressed, is absolutely *undefinable.* (Today it is impossible to say precisely *why* people are actually punished: all concepts in which an entire process is semiotically concentrated defy definition; only something which has no history can be defined.)
>
> (*Genealogy*, Essay II, §12)

It follows that the *purpose* of punishment can never be given in absolute terms to the extent that punishment has a history. This is because history is always the history of competing purposes. It is still possible to see how the history of punishment is characterised by a range of 'elements', whose syntheses 'change valence' so that one aspect or another temporarily dominates. However, what punishment *means,* Nietzsche concludes, is always going to be an 'uncertain, belated and haphazard' matter (*Genealogy,* Essay II, §13). History, it follows, is governed by an essential, unpredictable contingency with regard to its content and direction. There is no core to history: no single narrative thread constitutes it. Likewise, one cannot think of history on this view without invoking the concept of power, since history consists of struggles between competing interests that defy resolution. Both points take us into the domain of values and morality and a point made in *Thus Spoke Zarathustra* with regard to the self's journey through history being evaluative expressions of embodiment (*Zarathustra,* Part I, 'On the Gift-Giving Virtue'). For a discussion of this, *see* **self**.

Further reading: Ansell-Pearson 1991; Foucault 1977; Hillard 2002; Janaway 1998; Kaufmann 1974; Lemm 2007; Stambaugh 1987.

'I'

See **self**.

INSTINCT

See **drive/instinct**.

JEWS

The question of Nietzsche's relationship to the Jews is undoubtedly rendered contentious by the claims made by various Nazi exegetes in the 1930s and 1940s that National Socialism was the natural home of his thought. In spite of the Nazi desire to render him in such terms, however, Nietzsche was no rabid anti-Semite (something which cannot be said of his sister Elizabeth, who subsequently became close to Hitler). In fact, according to Nietzsche, the anti-Semite is (to pick just two examples) a distorted individual (*Ecce Homo*, 'Human, All Too Human', §2) and a philistine creature of *ressentiment* (*Genealogy*, Essay II, §11; Essay III, §26). Such feelings as the hater of the Jews has are for Nietzsche both despicable and run counter to his vision of good Europeanism. Nationalism, he notes, is the underlying cause of anti-Semitic feeling in Europe, for within the context of the bordered nation state the Jews' 'energy and [the] higher intelligence' (*Human, All Too Human*, §2) garnered from their accumulated spirituality makes them successful, and success in turn provokes jealousy and hatred. Such hatred, for Nietzsche, is endemic in much of Europe and is borne witness to by the vast bulk of anti-Jewish literature that is spewed forth (*Human, All Too Human*, §475). It is, he adds, obviously the case that no culture exists that has not produced unpleasant individuals, and it is 'cruel' to require that the Jewish people ought somehow to be exceptions to this rule. It may be the case that

> the youthful stock-exchange Jew is the most repulsive invention of the entire human race. Nonetheless I should like to know how much must, in a total accounting, be forgiven a people who, not without us all being to blame, have had the most grief-laden history of any people and whom we have to thank for the noblest human being (Christ), the purest sage (Spinoza), the mightiest book and the most efficacious moral code in the world.
>
> (*Human, All Too Human*, §475)

Thus, it ought, for Nietzsche, to be impossible for the average non-Jewish European to regard Jewish people without at the same time considering the long history of cruel victimisation that has been inflicted upon them. In this regard, the Jewish culture is rendered akin to a mirror, for in it is inscribed the all too often concealed violence and bad conscience of European culture itself. Indeed, Nietzsche claims that the Jews are in fact to be thanked for preserving whatever continuity exists between the world of Ancient Greece and

Europe – another facet which might help explain anti-Semitic rancour. That the text of *Human, All Too Human* was written as a rebuttal of Nietzsche's youthful relationship with anti-Semitic musician Richard Wagner is doubtless also significant. For with this work he seeks early on to mark himself off as no longer participating in the confidence trick he considers anti-Semitic sentiment to represent. Nietzsche thus writes as one who has, to some extent, suffered from the malady he castigates. The German nationalistic tendency to xenophobic feeling was not, he tells us, something he was entirely immune to: 'May it be forgiven me that I too, during a brief sojourn in a highly infected area, did not remain wholly free of the disease [...]?' *(Beyond Good and Evil,* §251). What is problematic in contemporary culture, Nietzsche adds, is the degree to which sentiments of this kind are tolerated at all, let alone acted upon. At the same time, however, Nietzsche's language, the degree to which it is on occasion prone to immoderate turns and twists of style, might seem to be able to be turned back upon him by way of accusation of the existence of some unconscious anti-Jewish feeling. It is simple enough, for example, for a careless reader of the *Genealogy* or *The Antichrist* to find confirmation of the view that Nietzsche regards the Jews with an at times spitefully critical eye. The designation here of slave morality and the ethics of *ressentiment* as originating in Jewish hatred for the noble, for instance, can easily provoke thoughts of, at the very least, unwitting racism. That said, one can counter such a claim by noting that the *Genealogy* not only contains explicit condemnations of anti-Semitism but also that the identity of the contemporary European Jew is not being addressed here at all. Rather, what is being discussed is the ancient priesthood – a group whose direct inheritors, it turns out, are modern-day anti-Semitic Christians *(Genealogy,* Essay II, §11).

Further reading: Golomb 1997; Golomb and Wistrich 2002; Kaufmann 1974; Mandel 1998.

KANTIANISM

The approach to philosophy first developed by Immanuel Kant (1724–1804). Kant's *Critique of Pure Reason* (1781, revised 1787 – often referred to as the first *Critique*) is one of the most radical and thought-provoking texts in the history of modern philosophy. This text, along with the second and third *Critiques* (concerned with practical reason and aesthetic judgement respectively), forms a systematic articulation of the scope of our reason. Kant's central contention in the first *Critique* is that although, following the claims put forward by empiricism, experience is essential to knowledge, there nevertheless exist transcendental principles independent of experience that make it possible. One can think of this matter in the following way: for an empiricist, we have sensory experience, and this kind of experience impresses itself upon the mind in such a way as to create concepts. Our concepts, it follows, are copies of sense impressions (little pictures). One of the problems with this account is that it does not explain how it is possible for us to recognise experiences in the first place. For Kant, the answer to this issue lies in the fact that there are principles already in the mind which allow us to do just this. He calls these *a priori* principles, and they can, he argues, be arrived at independently of experience (for example, the 'pure intuitions' of space and time). The point of such principles is that they are universal, in the sense that all human beings must think according to the rules they stipulate in order to be able to think at all. In this way, for Kant, the objectivity of knowledge is secured. We can know the phenomenal world (the world as we are able to experience it, empiricist-style) because we have abilities that allow us to do so. At the same time, the world as it 'really' is (the noumenal world) must remain eternally unknown to us. The realm of the noumenon is the ground of the appearance of the phenomenal object one encounters experientially. However, all one can say about the noumenon takes the form of 'negative knowledge'. The 'thing in itself' is and must always be a blank space about which no concrete knowledge can be formulated, in spite of its being the underlying condition of the world that we can discuss and hence have knowledge of.

The main aspects of Kant's philosophy of which Nietzsche is critical are to be found in Kantian epistemology and moral theory. For one thing, he challenges the Kantian claim that one can derive the objectivity of our knowledge of the *a priori* from its necessity. The necessity of a way of thinking does not confer the kind of objectivity that Kant thinks it does. All that such necessity shows is that we are the kind of animal that needs regulative beliefs (*Will to Power*, §530). One thus needs to replace the Kantian question 'How are synthetic judgements *a priori* possible?' with the more nuanced 'Why are such judgements necessary?': 'that is to say, it is time to grasp that, for the purpose of preserving such beings as ourselves, such judgements must be *believed* to be true' (*Beyond Good and Evil*, §11). The 'thing in itself' also gets a critical mauling. Nietzsche was influenced in this respect by his reading of F. A. Lange's account of historical materialism (1866).

On Lange's reading, if one is a materialist, then the phenomenal world (i.e. that world open to our experience by way of the senses) is the only one we can comment upon meaningfully. In consequence, any metaphysical reality one cares to imagine must be, at best, pale and indeterminate. Nietzsche, in similar vein, comments in *Human, All Too Human* that although there might possibly be a metaphysical world all that can ever be said of it is that it will always be inaccessible and lacking concrete value to us: 'Even if the existence of such a world were ever so well demonstrated, it is certain that knowledge of it would be the most useless of all knowledge: more useless than knowledge of the chemical composition of water must be to the sailor in danger of shipwreck' (*Human, All Too Human*, §9). In his later thought Nietzsche takes a more sceptical view even than this. He does not merely object to the view that things in themselves could be said to exist in a meaningful sense but additionally holds that the assertion of the existence of a noumenal reality conceals a hidden moral agenda. Above all, Nietzsche believes that Kant, in cleaving to this notion, passively reproduces the moral metaphysics of Platonism. In Kantianism, Plato's dubious distinction between the world of experience and the world of concepts, between appearance and reality, is maintained. All knowledge, on Nietzsche's view, concerns concrete experience, above all the practical concerns of human beings. Our knowledge is a consequence of environmental and biological demands. What we 'know' comes down to what we need to know in order to get by. The view that we can have access to a reality beyond such needs is a fantasy. Moreover, it is a damaging fantasy, for it tempts us to believe that there is a reality beyond our lived concrete concerns. Thus, the Kantian thing in itself is a mere residue of the conceptual fetishism that has infected the philosophical tradition since the time of Socrates. It is the last remnant of the philosophical concept of being. To think in terms of the thing in itself is to think in terms that invoke another reality, a 'beyond' that is the product of a 'moral optical illusion' (*Twilight of the Idols,* '"Reason" in Philosophy', §6). In other words, the claim that there is an objective reality is in fact, on Nietzsche's view, a concealed expression of 'moral prejudice'. Kant, no less than Christian metaphysics, conceals moral principles in a realm beyond experience and in this way tucks them safely away beyond criticism. It should come as no surprise, then, that Nietzsche is highly critical of the Kantian 'Categorical Imperative', which claims that morality is capable of making objective demands upon us, irrespective of what our wants and desires might be (captured in the injunction to act only in such a way that one can will the principle underlying one's action to become a universal law). Morality, for Nietzsche, is not about universality (at least, not in this sense), for morals are always a matter of interest and hence particularity.

Further reading: Bennett 1966, 1974; Bowie 1990; Chadwick and Cazeux 1992; Kant 1964, 1970, 1976, 1983, 1987; Körner 1955; Sedgwick 2001.

KNOWLEDGE

Nietzsche is a thinker who consistently questions the validity of traditional philosophical accounts of knowledge. He is, for example, a vehement critic of the quest for 'immediate certainty', epitomised by the purported immediacy of the *cogito* ('I think') that Descartes famously invoked in order to ground his epistemology (see below). Likewise, 'metaphysics', be it in Platonic or Kantian form, is also an object of Nietzschean derision (which is not to say that he does not share some features with both thinkers). Nietzsche questions the value of such approaches when it comes to the task of properly understanding what knowledge is. He also questions the tendency that philosophers have to think that they can provide an account of reality that is free from all the travails and ambiguities of everyday life and talk:

> I take this from the street. I heard one of the common people say, 'he knew me right away.' Then I asked myself: What is it that the common people take for knowledge? What do they want when they want 'knowledge'? Nothing more than this: Something strange is to be reduced to something *familiar*. And we philosophers – have we really *meant* more than this when we have spoken of knowledge? What is familiar means what we are used to so that we no longer marvel at it, our everyday, some rule in which we are stuck, anything at all in which we feel at home.
>
> (*Gay Science,* §355)

Thus, the word 'knowledge' is generally used to render something out of the ordinary familiar and thereby negate anything unsettling about it. Talk about 'knowledge', to put it another way, can all too frequently be little more than a matter of interpreting ambiguous or unsettling experiences in a manner that renders them compatible with everyday understanding. What is striking about the attitude Nietzsche adopts here are his claims that 'familiarity' and everyday usage provide the best framework within which to understand the meaning of the word 'knowledge' and that philosophers, no less than anybody else, abide by this condition in their discussions of it. A 'philosophical' account of knowledge all too often amounts to no more than yet another attempt to make the unfamiliar familiar. The psychological desire for comfort, it follows, haunts the philosopher's attempt to construct an account of knowledge:

> To trace something unknown back to something known is alleviating, soothing, gratifying [...]. Danger, disquiet, anxiety attend the unknown – the first instinct is to eliminate these distressing states. First principle: any explanation is better than none. [...] Thus there is sought not only some kind of explanation as cause, but a *selected* and *preferred* kind of explanation, the kind by means of which the feeling of the strange, new, unexperienced is most speedily and most frequently abolished – the most *common* explanations.
>
> (*Twilight of the Idols*, 'The Four Great Errors', §5)

Nietzsche invites us to consider the possibility that philosophers, like everyone else as he sees it, are really more interested in feeling 'at home' in the world than in attaining 'knowledge' concerning it. Such a claim may be sweeping and contentious. It also exemplifies Nietzsche's generally provocative approach to philosophical questions. For Nietzsche, thinking about knowledge is not an activity in which one engages in order to formulate an abstract epistemology, Cartesian style. More important for him is challenging the reader into thinking critically about the status of his or her own beliefs. Is it, Nietzsche asks, always that important that one holds the 'right' answer to a philosophical question? Or is such an attitude destined to yield frustration and a distorted conception of the world we inhabit?

The Gay Science, §355, suggests that philosophical talk about knowledge may well end up amounting to little more than an unwitting rationalisation of the everyday beliefs and attitudes of a philosopher's time. Nevertheless, although Nietzsche often contends that 'knowledge' is something that must be understood in terms of its relation to the influences of the practices and habits of everyday life, he develops this approach in complex and challenging ways. One aspect of this complexity is evident in Nietzsche's refusal to develop a formal theory of knowledge (*see* **epistemology**). This tendency might tempt one to regard Nietzsche's writings as lacking overall coherence: he is an 'unsystematic' thinker. On occasion, Nietzsche asserts one thing and then elsewhere something else that appears contrary to that prior assertion; but this is more due to the fact that he is endlessly suspicious of the drive to systematic abstraction that is evident in philosophy than to any lack of coherence. The view that one is entitled to change one's mind about things is neither incoherent nor irrational. Nietzsche's thought develops. Also, his thinking tends to be very subtle in its nuances: one must always be careful that one comment that seems to praise something and another that seems to criticise it are really dealing with the same subject matter in the same context. Nietzsche frequently reveals a virulently critical attitude toward other philosophers, especially those who seek to develop theoretical systems (e.g. Kant or Hegel). This is related to Nietzsche's conception of intellectual honesty, which for him is essential for genuine thought and brings with it the demand that one accepts the fact that existence is not 'systematic'. Nietzsche enjoys formulating paradoxes and contradictions, not for the mere fun of it but because such things demonstrate both the conditions of thought and its limitations.

Nietzsche's conception of knowledge is above all bound up with a metaphysical contention. He holds that reality is essentially a matter of 'becoming' rather than 'being' (see *Gay Science,* §357). In other words, for Nietzsche, transformation is a fundamental feature of existence. Consider the claim made at the opening of the early, unpublished essay 'On Truth and Lie in a Non-Moral Sense'. Here Nietzsche tells the story of how some intelligent animals situated near some insignificant star invented a thing called 'knowledge'. However significant the invention of knowledge may have seemed to these animals, they were ultimately doomed: the sun that kept them alive extinguished, and, with that, they had to die. On this view, knowledge is bound to the domain from which it arose; it is a result of human existence and will vanish when we do. Notice, too, that knowledge is deemed a direct consequence of human attitudes and requirements, not something that bears an essential relation to any ultimate reality. This lack of connection with reality is most manifest in the question of the nature of consciousness and its relation to how we understand knowledge. For Nietzsche, consciousness is simply one sort of becoming amongst others: there is nothing 'fundamental' about it, even if it is rather special and to be valued. Nietzsche thereby initiates a criticism of the manner in which the nature of knowledge has been understood by questioning the significance that consciousness has in relation to existence, and hence its adequacy as a means of grasping it. He also questions the view that 'knowing' something means being *certain* about it.

Consider, in relation to both these issues, the philosophy of René Descartes (1596–1650). Descartes sought to refute the philosophical scepticism of his time by demonstrating the existence of at least one certain claim to knowledge. However much I may doubt I know anything it always remains the case that I am still thinking: the fact that I exist is necessarily true whenever I am thinking. This is most famously expressed in the phrase 'I think, therefore I am' (*cogito, ergo sum*). The 'I' in question, it turns out, is defined in terms of its consciousness. Thus, both certainty and consciousness serve to ground Descartes's epistemology. For Nietzsche, we cannot be defined as living or thinking beings solely in terms of our consciousness. He refuses to acknowledge that there are any 'facts' of consciousness suitable for the construction of a theory such as Descartes's. Thought, rather, is much more a matter of instinct (see *Beyond Good and Evil*, §3). Indeed, '"Thinking", as epistemologists conceive it, simply does not exist: it is a quite arbitrary fiction, arrived at by selecting one element from the process and eliminating all the rest, an artificial arrangement for the purpose of intelligibility' (*Will to Power*, §477). Thus, there are no mental 'facts' as epistemology traditionally conceives them. To put the matter another way, Nietzsche rejects the view that philosophy is about first principles. For him, no epistemologically certain starting point exists whereby an analysis of the nature of knowledge could be developed. This kind of approach is evident in *Human, All Too Human* (1878), which develops a contrast between 'metaphysical philosophy' and 'historical philosophy'.

According to *Human, All Too Human*, 'Almost all the problems of philosophy once again pose the same form of question as they did two thousand years ago: how can something originate in its opposite, for example rationality in irrationality, [...] logic in unlogic, [...] truth in error?' (§1). Metaphysical philosophy responds to this question by holding that rationality cannot originate in unreason, nor can logic emerge from illogic, or truth from error. For the metaphysician, such categories emanate from a 'miraculous source' lurking behind experience. Metaphysical philosophy, in short, claims access to a knowledge that cannot be demonstrated by *experience*. Such an approach claims a suprahistorical perspective: the metaphysician thinks he or she has access to a realm of timeless reality and truth. This attitude, however, is rooted in an error:

> All philosophers have the common failing of starting out from man as he is now and thinking that they can reach their goal through an analysis of him. They involuntarily think of 'man' as

an *aeterna veritas* [...] as a sure measure of things [...]. Everything that the philosopher has declared about man is, however, at bottom no more than a testimony as to the man of a *very limited period of time*. Lack of historical sense is the family failing of all philosophers [...] But everything has become: there are *no eternal facts*, just as there are no absolute truths. Consequently what is needed from now on is *historical philosophizing*, and with it the virtue of modesty.

(*Human, All Too Human*, §2)

Historical philosophy rejects the belief that contemporary humanity can be taken as the basis for making sweeping metaphysical judgements about 'reality'. On such a view, 'everything has become', which is another way of saying that the only knowledge we can have is of empirical experience, or so-called 'appearances'. Taken in this way, what metaphysical philosophy relegates to the secondary status of 'appearance' is in fact all there is. Everything, in so far as all that is can be grasped in terms of appearances, 'has become'. This is an approach that Nietzsche cleaves to throughout. Perhaps most tellingly, this approach is manifest in the account of morality he develops by way of the notion of genealogy.

If one does away with the metaphysical belief in 'eternal facts', then, Nietzsche argues in one of his last texts, one might just as well dispense with the notion even of 'appearances', too: 'The real world – we have done away with it: what world was left? the apparent one, perhaps? [...] But no! *with the real world we have also done away with the apparent one!*' (*Twilight of the Idols*, 'How the "Real World" Finally Became a Fable', §6). In so far as one understands the world in terms of becoming one also abandons the categories that lead us to conceive of it metaphysically; thus the notion of 'appearance' must be rejected for it, too, epitomises the attitude of metaphysics. Nietzsche argues, therefore, that philosophers have tended to confuse reality with unreality: they have been led by conceptual fetishism to mistake the concept for reality and, in so far as concepts appear to yield an unchanging reality, a stable world of 'being'. In consequence, philosophy has inverted the relationship between cause and effect by interpreting 'being' as the precondition of 'becoming', when the opposite is the case. This is why metaphysical philosophy is drawn by the tendency to take thinking as primary while relegating the conditions that culminated in thinking to the level of the secondary and derivative. For Nietzsche, things are, of course, the other way around: life is possible without thought, but it is not possible to think without being alive. Talk of 'knowledge' (hence also of 'truth', 'reason', or 'logic') necessitates an account that acknowledges the conditions under which such concepts have arisen. Such conditions are neither inherently rational or logical, as metaphysicians hold.

Nietzsche's is a critique that is to some degree indebted to empiricism, and especially Hume's version of it. He follows Hume in denying that any metaphysical claim asserting that being and reality are akin can be derived from experiential particulars. Equally, our rational abilities are not intrinsically 'rational' but habitual. However, where Hume's *Treatise* deals with habit in terms of habituation resulting from the individual's experience, for Nietzsche our habits are specifically that: they are *ours,* shared, derived from the nature of our species, a matter of shared customs and instincts rather than individual habituation. Likewise, where empiricists like Locke and Hume regard our concepts as being derived from experience, Nietzsche does not accept this view. Thus, Locke's account of the origin of our ideas is 'superficial' (*Beyond Good and Evil,* §20) precisely because it ignores the linguistic, cultural and historical factors that constitute the fashioning of concepts. Nietzsche rejects the empiricist view that our concepts are mere 'representations' of sensory input. Our rational abilities do not facilitate the representation of an objective reality, nor are they mere copies of our sensory impressions since the force of inherited habit necessarily distorts their significance. Another name for this inherited bundle of distortions is 'reason': '"Reason" is what causes us to falsify the evidence of the senses. If the senses show becoming, passing away, change, they do not lie' (*Twilight of the Idols,* '"Reason" in Philosophy', §2). Nietzsche thus adheres to a kind of empiricism, in so far as he avers that what the senses tell us is true if it were possible to take them on their own terms. But Nietzsche differs from the classical empiricists in that, for him, our *concepts* do not and cannot correspond to our sensory impressions, since they are always interpreted beforehand by our cultural-habitual apparatus. This is because concepts are not representations of sensory impressions (empiricism) nor are they rules (Kantianism), but *interpretations* of experience that render it amenable to us by imposing upon it the character of predictability. The ability of our concepts to yield knowledge, therefore, is limited to their practical application. What we 'know' must, in consequence, always be subject to 'the police of mistrust' (*Gay Science,* §344). Knowledge concerns what is likely, not certain. But, at the same time, knowledge is essentially *practical* in so far as it only emerges as a consequence of human needs. Nietzsche's attack on those philosophical accounts of knowledge which seek to render it in terms of timeless 'objectivity' springs from the fact that they cannot resist interpreting concepts in a manner that undercuts this instrumental value. Philosophers betray

> their lack of historical sense, their hatred of the very idea of becoming [...] All that philosophers have been handling for thousands of years is conceptual mummies; nothing real has ever left their hands alive. They kill things and stuff them, these servants of conceptual idols, when they worship – they become a mortal danger to everything when they worship.
>
> (*Twilight of the Idols*, '"Reason" in Philosophy', §1)

Metaphysical philosophy is, it turns out, the opposite of knowledge. It is fetishistic idolatry in the form of the adoration of the concept. Concepts are, for Nietzsche, intimately bound up with language: 'We set up a word at the point at which our ignorance begins, at which we can see no further, e.g., the word "I", the word "do", the word "suffer": – these are perhaps the horizon of our knowledge, but not "truths"' (*Will to Power*, §482). In other words, linguistic terms mark the limits of human knowledge rather than guaranteeing that what we know is a genuine representation of experience. Simply put, language is not concerned with questions of this type.

Given all the above, Nietzsche nevertheless considers questions about knowledge as being important. In order to grasp why this is so, one needs to recall the contention Nietzsche makes at the beginning of both *Human, All Too Human* and *Beyond Good and Evil*. This is the claim that something can arise out of its opposite. For Nietzsche, knowledge not only can but also actually does arise out of metaphysical errors of various kinds. That it is possible to trace the source of knowledge back to these errant conditions does not warrant the inference that knowledge is thereby condemned to a state of permanent error and falsehood. It is, for Nietzsche, possible for thought to attain a certain kind of 'objectivity' – although this need *not* be the same kind of objectivity that metaphysical philosophy equated with the truth of being. Consider in this connection §110 of *The Gay Science:* 'Origin of Knowledge'. Once, Nietzsche argues here, 'the intellect produced nothing but errors'. Some of these errors had positive consequences and they assisted in the preservation of human life. Because of this these errors were passed on to future generations and became 'erroneous articles of faith' (*Gay Science*, §110) about the nature of reality. These errors take us back into the problem of language, or what Nietzsche calls the 'metaphysics of language, in plain talk, the presuppositions of reason' (*Gay Science*, §110). Such presuppositions include the belief that there exist 'things', also 'equal things', that the world around us is composed of substances, discrete entities ('bodies'), that how things appear to us is how they really are, that the notion of good as it applies to human existence denotes the 'good in itself' (*Gay Science*, §110). The point about such beliefs, for Nietzsche, is not their objective truth value but the fact that they have proffered a framework within which it has been possible for human life to flourish. Metaphysical errors are, to this degree, amongst the facilitators of the survival of the species. Indeed, it is the very utility of these beliefs that made sure they became 'almost part of the basic endowment of the species' (*Gay Science*, §110). Such beliefs became an essential constituent of the way we think; they eventually came to make up the structure of habits and customs upon which human society unquestioningly relies in order to exist. In this way, errors became 'truths' or, in more accurate language, norms for regulating human behaviour and thought alike. It was only much later in the story he is relating, Nietzsche tells us, that the ability to place these assumptions in question, to doubt them, occurred. Thus emerged the question of truth: 'it was only very late that truth emerged – as the weakest form of knowledge' (*Gay Science*, §110).

Clearly, Nietzsche considers talk about 'knowledge' to mean talking about the habitual beliefs we have inherited that allowed our ancestors to survive. Whether or not such habitual ways of thinking really 'represent' reality is neither here nor there. In spite of this, it becomes possible in virtue of such errors to engage in the game of raising the question of their truth. This possibility is 'knowledge', albeit in a very weak sense because the conceptual assumptions ('metaphysical errors') upon which humans relied as a means of helping them get about the world successfully continue to predominate. It is a weak form of knowledge also because in questioning such errors one must inevitably use the language that enshrines them. Even so, the question of truth, as Nietzsche narrates it here, became a threat to the founding errors from which it emerged. How was this possible? The answer Nietzsche proffers involves telling a story about how 'truth', understood as the contradiction of incorrect beliefs, first appeared in the guise of asceticism. The Eleatics (who lived around 500 BC, and whose most famous follower was Plato) postulated truth as the opposite of the errors that make up our customarily held beliefs. The consequence of this was an 'inverted knowledge' that was as blind to the errors inherent in its own thinking since the Eleatic notion of 'truth' amounted to a further articulation of the conceptual habits upon which human society rested. The Eleatic notion of truth is little more than an inverted version of the beliefs that underlie the dominance of custom. What Nietzsche views as a more deft and honest approach only emerges when it was accepted that two opposed propositions can be equally 'applicable to life because both were compatible with the basic errors' (*Gay Science*, §110) that underpin custom. It is as a result of this that propositions of this kind came to be ordered in accordance with their usefulness: such propositions can be beneficial, harmful, or neither beneficial nor harmful. The last possibility is significant. For the space opened up by this third possibility made 'room for the expression of an intellectual play impulse' (*Gay Science*, §110). If one discusses things that seem to have no concrete consequences, one can say more or less what one likes without fear of censure. This is the impulse to engage in intellectual debate. Such an impulse, Nietzsche argues, finally became part of human life as much as the mental habits of custom were. Thus, 'the human brain became full of such judgements and convictions, and a ferment, struggle, and lust for power developed in this tangle' with the result that 'knowledge and the striving for the true found their place among other needs' (*Gay Science*, §110). The critical discussion of knowledge thereby gave rise to the need for truth becoming part of human nature. In this way, 'knowledge became a piece of life itself' (*Gay Science*, §110) and became ever more powerful until it collided with the earlier habitual errors that grounded the social domain. This is witnessed, for Nietzsche, by the conflict between the most cherished metaphysical beliefs (e.g. those of religion) and the desire for truth, which is driven to question such beliefs in order to maintain its integrity. Out of this emerges the human subject as a field of conflict upon which two seemingly incompatible drives struggle for power. The need for custom and stability (the great preserver of human social life) comes to be locked in conflict with the philosophical need to question the assumptions upon which such needs rest. To find oneself in such a situation exemplifies, for Nietzsche, the dilemma of being a philosopher:

> two lives, two powers, both in the same human being. A thinker is now that being in whom the impulse for truth and those life preserving errors clash for their first fight, after the impulse for truth has also proved to be a life-preserving power. Compared with the significance of this fight, everything else is a matter of indifference: the ultimate question about the conditions of life

has been posed here, and we confront the first attempt to answer this question by experiment. To what extent can truth endure incorporation? That is the question; that is the experiment.

(*Gay Science*, §110)

In other words, Nietzsche is asking here about the extent to which it is possible for human beings to stand apart from and criticise their beliefs, even though such beliefs constitute the necessary conditions of their existence.

It is now clear enough how Nietzsche can answer the question first posed at the beginning of *Human, All Too Human*. The 'need' for truth does spring from 'error'; but it is now a part of human life. To be human is always to be prey to the desire for truth, but wanting truth is never a matter of mere utility as customary, 'metaphysical knowledge' is. It follows that from the utility of some of those beliefs that helped preserve the species there arose the need that exceeds utility: the need to question metaphysics. Nietzsche can now pose a question: to what degree would it be possible for us to strive for truth and objectivity given that such striving may mean sacrificing the metaphysical errors upon which our lives rest? Pursuing 'truth', in this sense, involves criticising metaphysics, even as one finds oneself trapped within it: it means engaging in a form of sustained criticism of the very conditions of one's own life. The only way to embark upon this path is to refuse 'convictions' any 'rights of citizenship' in the domain of knowledge. Beliefs must always be regarded as being at best provisional and experimental in nature, never 'certain' (*Gay Science*, §344). Does this mean that metaphysics can be escaped from? The answer for Nietzsche is no. Even cleaving to the view that one must always hold one's concepts provisionally entails that 'some prior conviction [...] a faith' (*Gay Science*, §344) be in place. This faith, no less than any other, is a '*metaphysical faith*' (*Gay Science*, §344). The Platonic contention that truth is divine may turn out to be 'our most enduring lie' (*Gay Science*, §344) for the experimental view of knowledge enshrines within it a moral demand. This is the moral demand that truth be valued above all else at any price. Hence, the '"will to truth" does *not* mean "I will not allow myself to be deceived" but – there is no alternative – "I will not deceive, not even myself"; *and with that we stand on moral ground*' (*Gay Science*, §344). Because such a demand is unconditional it is also a metaphysical demand, for with it is affirmed the universality of an ethical principle with regard to thought. This principle states that those who seek knowledge ought to desire above all *not to deceive*.

As was mentioned earlier, Nietzsche regards any philosophy that aspires to being a mere 'theory of knowledge' as a timid and rather pathetic thing. If one confined oneself to the mere pursuit of 'theory of knowledge', one would be condemned to pointlessness. Philosophy, in order to be worthwhile, must be concrete, which for Nietzsche means placing it in the world of history and, ultimately, arguing for its 'legislative' significance. However, if the craving for knowledge is always articulated out of an ethical demand it follows that one remains inexorably situated within metaphysics. For Nietzsche, there is one possible answer to this kind of problem: a special kind of self-consciousness – self-reflexivity. To be self-reflexive entails that one grasp that all possible knowledge rests at some point or other upon presuppositions that cannot be demonstrated. To take such a view also requires accepting thought to be ultimately metaphysical in the sense that even as it craves 'objectivity' and timelessness it is condemned to remain bereft of them. Even so, the demand for truthfulness points to the fact that there may be an 'objectivity' worth seeking. To be truthful, after all, means to acknowledge that one may well be deceived, that the manner in which one thinks about a problem, even the problem itself, does not represent the only approach possible. How, though, would one police one's hypotheses? A possible answer is offered by what Nietzsche calls **'perspectivism'**.

Further reading: Clark 1990; Grimm 1977; Krell and Wood 1988; May 1993.

LANGUAGE

For Nietzsche, language is constitutive of the conditions of our rational habits and, hence, our consciousness. The basis for this contention lies in the collective nature of human beings. We are habitual creatures in the deepest sense, and our habits are collective habits and customs: they are *species habits*. To put the matter less flatteringly, as Nietzsche is often inclined to do, we do not think as we do because we are individuals but because we are 'herd animals'. Language and metaphysics, on Nietzsche's view, go hand in hand, for our habits (not least our conceptual habits) are as much a matter of language as anything else:

> To the extent that man has for long ages believed in the concepts and names of things as in *aeternae veritates* he has appropriated to himself that pride by which he raised himself above the animal:

he really thought that in language he possessed knowledge of the world. The sculptor of language was not so modest as to believe that he was only giving things designations, he conceived rather that with words he was expressing supreme knowledge of things [...] Happily, it is too late for the evolution of reason, which depends on this belief, to be again put back.

(*Human, All Too Human*, §11)

Language functions by referring to our experiences. It is because of this that we are subject to the irresistible temptation to believe that words refer to things and that these 'things' exist independently of our language. Nietzsche, however, is a nominalist. That is, he holds that names are *given* to objects rather than derived from some essential properties inherent within them. By way of language, we name 'things' – and the notion of a 'thing' is, after all, a kind of name. According to Nietzsche, the presupposition that the names we make up have 'real' entities that correspond to them shows that we are in fact always actively forming and interpreting rather than passively receiving our experiences. It is because of this presupposition that we are prey to the habit of taking words to represent the purportedly 'essential properties' of objects. Such a belief may be a necessary condition of language use; but such necessity does not of itself warrant the inference that the belief is objectively true. For Nietzsche, rather, the contrary is the case. Words and names do not represent things (as metaphysical philosophy would assert) but, just as our concepts do, they express something about our relationship with our environment: language is a means of coping with, and mastering, our environment. Indeed, Nietzsche even toys with the idea that the origins of language reside in class and power distinctions (*see* **noble morality**). Kant argued that the subjective conditions of experience (that is, how a thinking being called a subject is constituted, not a particular person's 'subjective' experiences) determine the nature of our concepts and hence knowledge. However, for Kantian thought they do so in a manner that confers objectivity upon knowledge because such conditions are necessary and universal *a priori* conditions and valid for all human beings. Nietzsche would agree that subjective conditions determine the manner in which we can make use of concepts and language. However, for him, such conditions cannot be held to confer objectivity upon our knowledge simply in virtue of their being shared. Nietzsche, like Kant, adheres to a version of empirical realism. Thus, he would take questions of what is to count as 'knowledge' as having always to start with experience. But on

Nietzsche's view we cannot, as Kant argues, trace the conditions of our experiences to a timeless, transcendental source (the transcendental subject). For Nietzsche, there is nothing about the sources of our thought that counts as 'transcendental' in any sense. One reason for this is that Nietzsche denies consciousness the causal properties that metaphysics has generally attributed to it and which Kant relies upon in order to endow the subject with the ability to be the source of meaning. Nietzsche's reason for taking this view is rooted in his claim that language constructs the world for us. The problem is that '*We are none of us* that which we appear to be in accordance with the states for which alone we have consciousness and words [...] we misread ourselves in this apparently most intelligible handwriting on the nature of our self' (*Daybreak*, §115). Language 'sees everywhere deed and doer' it 'believes in will as cause in general' (*Daybreak*, §115) and likewise creates the impression that the 'I' is a kind of substance. This belief in 'I-substance' is then projected 'on to all things – only thus does it *create* the concept "thing"' (*Twilight of the Idols*, '"Reason" in Philosophy', §5). Perhaps most shocking here is the claim that it is not us who make, arrange and thereby use language but that it is language that constitutes much of us. Language, on this view, is not a kind of conduit through which the expression of will and thought is passed but rather a power that 'manipulates' and determines thought. Beliefs, in turn, are best defined as linguistic properties. Such properties define what a speaker is, rather than the other way around. Reason is thereby transformed in its significance. Whereas philosophers have traditionally taken human rationality to set the standard according to which reality can be understood and evaluated, Nietzsche argues that it is linguistically constituted and thereby allies it to metaphysics. It is, in other words, language that bestows upon us the tendency to interpret experience metaphysically: metaphysical concepts (e.g. 'being' and 'God' – which for Nietzsche are concepts that have an uncanny relation to one another) are generated by grammatical conventions. The power of language amounts to no more than the weight of tradition and can be thought of as being analogous in this sense to the morality of custom. As with powerful customs, such is the steadfast and compelling nature of our belief in 'grammar' that 'with every piece of knowledge one has to stumble over dead, petrified words, and one would sooner break a leg than a word' (*Daybreak*, §47). Our collective linguistic nature thus offers a prime example of the force of habit or custom. One 'uses' language in a conventional manner (and to that extent without so much as noticing that one is doing so, i.e. 'unconsciously'). Human 'reason' resides in linguistic conventions. Thinking rationally means thinking linguistically: '*We cease to think when we refuse to do so under the constraint of language;* we barely reach the doubt that sees this limitation as a limitation. *Rational thought is interpretation according to a scheme that we cannot throw off* (*Will to Power*, §522). We are gripped in the iron vice of linguistic conventions to such an extent that our sensory experiences are interpreted for us in advance by way of them. It is, to this extent, not the world of the senses (of transient becoming) that is false, as Platonism claimed, but our interpretation of it: 'the senses [...] do not lie at all. It is what we *make* of their evidence that first introduces the lie into it, for example the lie of unity, the lie of materiality, of substance, of duration' (*Twilight of the Idols*, '"Reason" in Philosophy', §2). Nietzsche's approach here does not turn on questions about whether language refers to a non-linguistic reality (i.e. debates in philosophy of language since the time of Russell) or whether we can talk meaningfully of such a realm. Nietzsche believes that we can allude to such a realm, since the evidence of the senses is not of itself purely 'linguistic' or conceptual. Nietzsche's main point here is that language is to be understood as central to the way in which we interpret the testimony of the senses in virtue of the fact that it always offers us a world that is grasped in terms of causes. In turn, talk of causality presupposes the notion of the will. The belief that *A* is the cause of *B* is an analogue of the belief that the consciousness of willing is equivalent to the causal power of consciousness − it presupposes that thinking and willing are essentially causal. When we think of the world in causal terms, we do so by presupposing 'willing' in the sense that we assume there are such things as 'free will', freedom of choice, etc. In turn, the will is thought of as a constant, and, as such, it is allied to the concept of 'being', for thinking in terms of causes presupposes that the world, as a web of causes and effects, is structured by way of causality, and hence by willing: 'Being is everywhere thought in, *foisted on,* as cause; it is only from the conception "ego" that there follows derivatively the concept "being"' (*Twilight,* '"Reason" in Philosophy', §5). The key philosophical error has been to think that the word 'will' denotes an *ability,* but 'Today we know it is merely a word' (*Twilight,* '"Reason" in Philosophy', §5).

Language, then, seduces us into error by positing an illusory world of 'causes', 'willing', 'substances' and 'things' that is impossible to shrug off. That said, Nietzsche argues that our linguistic endowment of metaphysical errors is the precondition of our being able to conceptualise and engage with our environment in any manner whatsoever. Humanity has become the kind of being that negotiates its environment by asking questions about it (by talking in terms of knowledge and truth). However, issues concerning knowledge and truth can only be raised because, originally, erroneous metaphysical beliefs rooted in linguistic conventions were held, i.e. because the game of asking questions and answering with possible reasons was put in place long ago. Knowledge, to this extent, can arise from error, truth from untruth (see the opening sections of *Human, All Too Human* and *Beyond Good and Evil*). When Nietzsche talks about the 'errors' inculcated by language, it follows, he is not claiming that our words somehow 'fail' to refer successfully to things, i.e. that there exist 'things' in the world to which words might in principle be able to correspond but ultimately fail to do so. Words, on Nietzsche's view, cannot 'fail' to refer to things since nothing exists in this sense that they could fail to refer to in the first place. Although Nietzsche holds that there is a world that exists independently of our conscious mental activity and linguistic abilities (a world of becoming), a world of this kind is not composed of 'things' or 'substances', etc. We think in terms of such things because doing so is useful to us, i.e. because conceptualising our environment in terms of determinate characteristics allows us to negotiate it successfully. Language is hence best grasped as an expression of power. It testifies to the human ability to engage with its world instrumentally.

Further reading: Crawford 1988; Schacht 1983; Siemens 2001a.

LIFE

A concern with the notion of 'life' is a constant feature of Nietzsche's thought. Thus, relatively early in Nietzsche's career, the second of the *Untimely Meditations,* 'On the Uses and Disadvantages of History for Life', discusses the nature of history in the context of the degree to which it serves or impedes life. 'Life' here is understood to be 'that dark, driving power that insatiably thirsts for itself' (*Untimely Meditations,* Essay II, §3). Thus, 'life' denotes the array of unthinking biological processes that compel the living to exist. The mature Nietzsche, the writer of *Beyond Good and Evil, On the Genealogy of Morality, Twilight of the Idols* and *The Antichrist,* asserts the centrality of life with regard to the question of values. To be human is to be an animal (in texts such as the *Genealogy* Nietzsche is fond of using phrases like 'the animal man'); consequently, to be human is to be a form of life and, as such, to be subordinate to the fundamental conditions to which all life is subject. It is in the light of this view that

Nietzsche in turn renders values in terms of symptoms. The sort of values advocated in any instance tells you about the kind of life that advocates them, just as acne spots indicate something about the state of a person's hormonal system. In the light of this contention new questions can be posed with regard to the nature of values. When, in §3 of the preface to the *Genealogy*, for example, Nietzsche poses the question concerning the conditions under which values such as 'good and evil' arose, he does so only by way of a prelude to addressing the issue of the *value* of such judgements. His is a paradoxical task; for he seeks to enquire into nothing less than *the value of values*. One should note in this context that Nietzsche's contention is that humans *invented* value judgements. They are not God-given but derive from concrete, lived situations: values bespeak life. The contrivance of values depends upon there being conditions that are responded to by living beings. In turn, values can be recast in terms of a language of 'signs'. The question that can be asked of values is: are they 'a sign of distress, poverty and the degeneration of life […]?' (*Genealogy*, 'Preface', §3). Values are *signs*, and signs need to be interpreted, and the correct mode of interpretation is afforded by the criterion of what kind of life they reveal themselves to be signs of. In stark terms, then, life itself speaks through values. An affirmative view of existence reveals a healthy and vigorous nature. In contrast, a turning away from the world of concrete experience informs us of something exhausted and on the way out. This, for Nietzsche, is especially pertinent with regard to Christianity, for the latter is for him the incarnate rejection of the fundamental conditions of existence, and hence all life. The Christian reviles the world of becoming and change (which are the essential conditions of life) because in such a world suffering has no underlying sense to redeem it. Where Nietzsche's Dionysian view seeks (perhaps sometimes a little too desperately) to affirm the sufferings and terrors of existence, the Christian affirms a 'beyond' of peace and rest, a realm of safety vouchsafed by the power of divinity, as a refuge from such terrors.

Nietzsche deploys the notion of 'life' most polemically in one of his last works, *The Antichrist*. Here, Christianity is accused of seeking nothing less than the 'corruption' of humanity. Such a charge of corruption is not, he insists, a matter of 'moral corruption'. His use of the term is meant to be taken in a sense that is 'free of any *moralic acid*' (*Antichrist*, §6). 'Corruption', rather, means a loss of the 'instincts', the inclination to choose what is bad for oneself: as such, it signifies a departure from what is natural – namely, a departure from 'life'. A consideration of nature thus leads, in turn, into a discussion of the

concept of 'life' as Nietzsche deploys it, for, he insists, what is at stake
is nothing less than '*life itself*': 'I consider life itself [to be the] instinct
for growth, for continuance, for the accumulation of forces, for *power:*
where the will to power is lacking there is decline' (*Antichrist*, §6).
Since the supposedly 'highest' (i.e. Christian) values lack this will this
means they are '*nihilistic* values' (*Antichrist,* §6). Thus, Nietzsche's
attack on Christianity in *The Antichrist* is mounted in the name of 'life
itself', and what does not fulfil the demands laid down by life itself is
worthy of being indicted on the charge of decadence to stand trial in
the court of life. Christianity, which Nietzsche characterises as the
religion of pity, is inimical to life because pity and life do not mix.
Pity deprives us of strength when we feel it: 'Pity stands in antithesis
to the tonic emotions which enhance the energy of the feeling of
life'; through it suffering becomes contagious (*Antichrist,* §7). Above
all, pity 'thwarts the law of evolution', by preserving what is ready for
destruction. Pity, in turn, is the essence of Christianity, in so far as it
serves the Christian as a tool for conquering what is (or ought to be)
stronger, i.e. what is 'natural'. Nietzsche, in attacking Christian pity, is
hence attacking what he conceives to be inimical to life, what is 'anti-
natural'. In making this criticism, however, Nietzsche asserts for
himself the right to speak from a viewpoint which is coterminous
with that of 'life itself'. In other words, his *authority* to criticise
Christianity, to speak the truth concerning it, is gained from his
paying homage to life. In so doing he sets himself up as the mouth-
piece through which life itself 'speaks', whose love of life speaks in
the guise of a physician of culture: 'To be physician *here,* to be inex-
orable *here,* to wield the knife *here* – that pertains to us, that is *our*
kind of philanthropy, with that are *we* philosophers' (*Antichrist,* §7).
The word 'true' is thereby rendered in terms analogous in meaning to
'what is beneficial to life', what is affirmative (*Antichrist,* §9). It is on
this basis that Nietzsche can conclude *The Antichrist* with a judgement
concerning the *value* of Christian values: 'I […] pronounce my judgment.
I *condemn* Christianity, I bring against the Christian church the most terrible charge […] it has made of every value a disvalue, of every truth a lie,
of every kind of integrity a vileness of soul […] [It is] a conspiracy […]
against life itself' (*Antichrist,* §62).

To speak from the standpoint of 'life itself' as Nietzsche does here
is, however, highly problematic. This is because the word 'life' signifies the pursuit of a mode of existence: a life is, in this sense,
something which is lived. But a life which is simply lived, in whatever manner, is no justification. There is no means of deriving a rule
that justifies 'life itself' through the activity of simply living. If this

were so, then *any* form of life would be its own justification – even a life lived according to the metaphysical precepts of Christian doctrine is justifiable, in so far as the 'otherworldly' aspects of such a doctrine are merely lived characteristics of that form of life and we lack any means of arriving at an objective judgement of that form. If it is the case that we lack any such means, then Nietzsche would, once more, be committed to doing no more than offering us an account of the different modes of moral justification which have been formulated during that period of human development which goes to make up the history of morality. But if, as Nietzsche desires, we ought to make an attempt at evaluating different moral forms from the standpoint of life, then the term must take on a new significance in order for this to be possible. 'Life', in short, must become a category separate from what is lived, in so far as the Christian, too, lives his or her own life and the rules of justification contained within that life serve to justify it on its own terms. If this were to be the case, however, the word 'life' would have to have a metaphysical significance and Nietzsche's attack on metaphysics would be compromised.

Further reading: Kaufmann 1974; Schacht 1983.

MASTER MORALITY

See **noble morality**.

METAPHOR

One of the central aspects of Nietzsche's philosophical works, and one that sets him apart from many other philosophers, is that they are self-consciously rich in their use of metaphor. Often the metaphors he uses are deliberately provocative: truth is a 'woman'; philosophers are 'bees' or 'trees'; humanity is a 'herd', a 'mass of teeming worms', either a household pet or a beast of prey; the analysis of the origins of morality is a journey into a hidden and hitherto-unknown land. Often, Nietzsche's metaphors are multiple, tumbling one after the other in rapid succession and strategically naturalising. The effect of this is clearly deliberately provocative, for it simultaneously provokes and yet paradoxically deflects possible critical resistance on the part of the reader to a point he wishes to make. Thus, for example, the famous image of the 'blond beast' (*Genealogy*, Essay I, §11), an invader and barbarian opposed in type to the worm-like 'tame man', becomes a bird of prey descending on lambs (*Genealogy*, Essay I, §13). The concrete cultural violence of the one is thereby transformed into mere instinctive devouring. The use of metaphor in this overt way sets Nietzsche's thinking apart. It has often been the case that philosophy has placed great emphasis upon the literal and fact-stating functions of language, deeming metaphor to be parasitic upon this fundamental condition. By introducing metaphor in this overt way, Nietzsche's texts compromise the supposed stability that the privileging of literal language endows to meaning. In this regard, metaphor and becoming go hand in hand, and Nietzsche, as Deleuze has powerfully argued, appears as a nomadic figure traversing the margins of the philosophical tradition.

Further reading: Deleuze 1990; De Man 1979; Kofman 1993 [1972]; Nehamas 1985; Pasley 1978.

METAPHYSICAL PHILOSOPHY

This is the kind of philosophy that Nietzsche does not like very much. Metaphysical philosophy is set against historical philosophy. Where the one is historically informed, modest in its pretensions and inspired by the sciences and critical scholarship, the other is dogmatic, shows contempt for lived experience and the realm of the senses and engages in abstract (and largely empty) speculation resulting in timeless, universal claims that cannot be substantiated.

See also: **knowledge**.

METAPHYSICS

In general, metaphysics is taken to be the study of the fundamental nature of reality, as opposed to sensory experience. Traditionally, metaphysicians concern themselves with how the world 'really is', why it is here at all and the role of human beings within it. For Nietzsche, in contrast, metaphysics is best understood as *fundamental error*. Metaphysics, he says, is a kind of science: it is that science 'which deals with the fundamental errors of mankind – but as if they were fundamental truths' (*Human, All Too Human*, §18). For Nietzsche, knowledge (in so far as it means anything) is confined to the world of experience. One could, in a limited sense, call Nietzsche a 'materialist': he believes that the concrete world is all there is. This attitude underlies his anti-metaphysical stance. At the same time, Nietzsche does not accept some notions that might be associated with materialism. For example, he is no simple material atomist: he does not believe that the 'stuff' that gives rise to experience can be grasped in terms that replicate the language of metaphysics. Thus, the notion that there exist 'things' that pertain to the unity of what we call 'atoms' is mythology. There is a good reason for this: Nietzsche holds that atomism replicates a mistaken conception of the self (for example, the idea of an abiding, unchanging, eternal soul) generated out of an uncritical claim that the 'I' and its self-consciousness amounts to the entirety of what a self is (see **Cartesianism**). Nietzsche's most scathing comments about metaphysics are contained in *Twilight of the Idols*. Here, metaphysics is interpreted as the outcome of the worst conceptual idolatry. It erupts from the fundamental mistake of taking concepts to indicate an objective realm lying beyond our lived experience in the form of the reality of being. The history of philosophy is, in fact, the history of the working through of this deluded notion to its contradictory and self-destructive conclusion. The chapter 'How the "Real World" at Last Became a Myth: History of an Error' in *Twilight of the Idols* demonstrates supremely and in the most concentrated form possible the mature Nietzsche's approach. It is notable that in this chapter the conclusion, which is the demise of metaphysics, also marks a new beginning: 'incipit Zarathustra' (Zarathustra begins). Clearly, then, Nietzsche regards his own work as somehow having overcome metaphysics. Whether one is convinced of this will depend upon one's interpretation of such ideas as eternal recurrence and will to power.

Further reading: Clark 1990; Conway and Groff 1998; Grimm 1977; Haar 1996; Houlgate 1986; Poellner 1995; Welshon 2004.

MODERNITY

Nietzsche's thought is intimately bound up with the concept of modernity. His writings are deeply sensitive to the fact of their place within *cultural modernity*. A good example is furnished by the *Untimely Meditations* (1873–6). These essays demonstrate a concern with the relationship between modern society and culture. Such a world is portrayed as one in which change is rampant, a realm where hitherto cherished beliefs are being overturned. Witness Nietzsche's mentioning the accelerating decline of organised religion, the increased political hostility between European nations, the burgeoning of scientific research 'in a spirit of the blindest *laissez faire*', and the fact that the 'educated classes' are now held in thrall to 'a hugely contemptible money economy' (*Untimely Meditations,* Essay III, §4). Modern life is thus seen as embodying a threat: barbarism looms on the horizon as culture is overrun or perverted by financial interests. According to the third *Meditation,* education is distorted by being used as an instrument for the furthering of mercantile interests and the profit motive (something opposed by philosophy). The absorption of culture by mercantile interests is revealed in the modern desire to assert the existence of an intrinsic connection between the spheres of property ownership and intelligence and between wealth and culture. The supposedly *moral* nature of such connections is today taken as a given. Take the sphere of education, where investment stipulates a return in terms of the 'educated' person's suitability for the world of work. Such an attitude, however, constrains how much culture a person is allowed to absorb: culture is useful so long as it serves the interests of investment. Thus, the third *Meditation* ('Schopenhauer as educator') presents us with a view of the contemporary world as a realm where the demands of capital are swamping culture. From the above, it should be clear that the word 'culture' here has a specific and narrow meaning for Nietzsche. 'Culture' means the development of modes of thought that exceed our daily concerns. In the *Untimely Meditations,* modernity is characterised by the obsessive concern with efficiency and accumulation. It is a sphere that is driven above all by the need to oil the gears of the great money-making 'power-machine' of modern industry (*Untimely Meditations,* Essay IV, §6). This is also the age of burgeoning science. But science, too, is immured in the world of modernity, for it is no less susceptible than education to being enlisted by the demands of the social process. Science does not have the power to save culture through learning, for science, no less than education, can be rendered subordinate to the demands of a world dominated by production, exchange and the requirement for labour (see *Untimely Meditations,* Essay II, §7).

In the works that follow the *Meditations* – from *Human, All Too Human* to *Daybreak* (1878–81) – modern society is confronted and analysed just as directly in its economic and social registers. *Human, All Too Human* depicts modern society as something that is perma-nently on the move: it is characterised most essentially by change. Such change can take several forms. For one thing, the modern world is typified for Nietzsche by the emergence of the state (see *Human, All Too Human*, §101). Socialists, too, populate the modern landscape, agitating for revolutionary change and the destruction of individuality (*Human, All Too Human*, §§463, 473). Modern society is increasingly dominated by public opinion. Political debate may be omnipresent, Nietzsche notes, but such debate is neither genuine nor free, for it is determined by powerful financial interests: 'anyone possessing money and influence can transform any opinion into a public opinion' (*Human, All Too Human*, §447). The modern is thus characterised by the expansion of a public realm under the control of moneyed interests: it is the world of mass communication where rampant debate is never-ending and comes to look like petty squabbling, the realm of the fragmented interests of party and revolutionary politicians. As the public realm expands, so the inner realm of the individual contracts in its potential: 'Public opinions – private indolence' (*Human, All Too Human*, §482).

Nietzsche speaks against his times. This epitomises his conception of being 'untimely'. However, being able to speak against one's times does not mean that one has an identity that is independent of the spirit of one's age. From the text of *Human, All Too Human* onwards it is clear that Nietzsche considers us to be in an essential way historical beings (see his account of 'historical philosophy', *Human, All Too Human*, §§1 ff.). No one can will his or her way out of their own times. The urge to do so would amount to wishing oneself out of existence altogether. The historical mode of thought Nietzsche advocates characterises modern consciousness by way of an awareness of its own temporal situatedness. Its sense of temporality defines its self-consciousness. To be modern means to know that one is a prisoner of one's historically constituted essence:

> *In prison*. – My eyes, however strong or weak they may be, can see only a certain distance, and it is within the space encompassed by this distance that I live and move, the line of this horizon constitutes my immediate fate, in great things and small, from which I cannot escape. Around every being there is described a similar concentric circle, which has a mid-point and is peculiar to him. Our ears enclose us within a comparable circle, and so does our sense of touch. Now, it is by these horizons, within which each of us encloses his senses as if behind prison walls, that we *measure* the world, we say that this is near and that far, this is big and that small, this is hard and that soft: this measuring we call sensation – and it is all of it an error! According to the average quantity of experiences and excitations possible to us at any

particular point of time one measures one's life as being short or long, poor or rich, full or empty: and according to the average human life one measures that of all other creatures – all of it an error! [...] The habits of our senses have woven into us lies and deception of sensation: these again are the basis of all our judgements and 'knowledge' – there is absolutely no escape, no backway or bypath into the *real world!*

(*Daybreak,* §117)

The passage implies that our senses are confined within the boundaries of a horizon beyond which it would be impossible to understand or perceive anything at all. Our world is always already interpreted *before* we even get to the point of grasping it as something to be perceived. A 'perceived' world is thus a world that has already been evaluated before one is aware of it as mere sensation. There is, in this regard, no pure empirical sensation (as the philosophers of empiricism believed) since every 'sensation' represents an evaluation. More specifically, every sensory event is an expression of habit and custom.

Nietzsche is fascinated by the contemporary developments he charts and sees them in himself no less than in his social environment. In this, he too remains stubbornly and self-consciously modern, no less a representative of the spirit of his own age than his contemporaries. Even as one rages against one's time one is obliged to cleave to it. As moderns we may have become increasingly aware of being locked into our own times, but we also understand that there is nowhere else to go. The prohibition on time travel that is imposed upon us as temporal beings is as nothing compared to the psychological inability we would have when it came to dealing with the reality of a past era. All honest study of the past gives rise to the conclusion: 'Anything rather than back to that!' (*Assorted Opinions and Maxims,* §382). Transported back to another age a modern would find the 'spirit of that age' to be unbearably oppressive, bearing down 'with the weight of a hundred atmospheres' (*Assorted Opinions and Maxims,* §382). Our own time may be a prison, but all others would poison us. Every person from every age would find every other *impossible* to endure. Yet, at the same time, everyone experiences his or her own era as something that can be borne. There is a simple reason for this: the spirit of a person's age 'does not only lie *upon* him but is also *within* him. The spirit of the age offers resistance to itself, bears up against itself' (*Assorted Opinions and Maxims,* §382). We are beings who must dwell within the confines of our own times. Yet, even though it is impossible to stand 'outside' one's own age, it is possible to stand against it *from within it*. One can voice the contradictions and tensions of one's age – or, to put it in moral language, it is always possible to be the *bad conscience* of one's times.

This last point provides the key to grasping Nietzsche's relationship with modernity. However much Nietzsche detests cultural modernity he is also fascinated by it. Witness his discussions of the extent to which the power of the forces unleashed by capital can permeate the sphere of language (*Human, All Too Human*, §267). The demands of trade will ensure that 'at some distant future there will be a new language for all – first as a commercial language, then as the language of intellectual intercourse in general – just as surely as there will one day be air travel' (*Human, All Too Human*, §267). What is striking here is the harmony asserted to exist between the realms of technology and commerce (strikingly, the technical know-how needed for air travel is envisaged as inevitable) and linguistic change. Language answers to the demands of trade no less than technology answers to them. Language, commerce and identity are all subject to continual transformation. To be a modern, Nietzsche tells us, means to live in and acknowledge this state of permanent cultural unrest (*Human, All Too Human*, §285). Rapid and powerful economic activity typifies modernity and is expressed in every other level of experience. Nietzsche sees a world about him that is characterised by 'Trade and industry, the post and the book-trade [the] rapid changing of home and scene, the nomadic life now lived by all who do not own land' (*Human, All Too Human*, §475). Such social transformations have cultural and political implications. For one thing, burgeoning trade will bring about the 'abolition of nations' in Europe. One should, Nietzsche tells us, follow this trend set by economics and become 'a *good European* and [...] work for the amalgamation of nations' (*Human, All Too Human*, §475). Thus, a world dominated by economic production can offer the possibility of political change for the better (a unified Europe, for example); it can lead to technological advance; it can transform language in a manner that may lead to greater intellectual rigour. But it can also foster material greed and in doing so create superficiality and mediocrity.

Equally strikingly, modernity is for Nietzsche the realm in which social relationships are increasingly determined by impersonal relationships with technology. Modernity is the age of the machine: '*Premises of the machine age*. – The press, the machine, the railway, the telegraph are premises whose thousand-year conclusion no one has yet dared to draw' (*The Wanderer and His Shadow*, §278). The machine's inherent impersonality 'deprives the piece of work of its pride, of the individual *goodness* and *faultiness* that adheres to all work not done by a machine' (*The Wanderer and His Shadow*, §288). To dwell in modernity, in other words, is to dwell in the realm of mass production. With mass production comes loss of individuality: 'we now seem to live in the midst of nothing but an anonymous and impersonal slavery' (*The Wanderer and His Shadow*, §288). Increasing technological hegemony creates social conformity and has telling political consequences, for it teaches the 'mutual co-operation of hordes of men in operations where each man has to do only one thing' and in so doing proffers the 'model for the party apparatus and the conduct of warfare' (*The Wanderer and His Shadow*, §218). Modernity in this way threatens genuine contemplative thought. Nietzsche describes a world shaped by the power of mass production wherein contemplation and labour alike have not merely been transformed but corrupted. In such a society,

> work and industry – formerly adherents of the great goddess health – sometimes seem to rage like an epidemic. Because time for thinking and quietness in thinking are lacking, one no longer ponders deviant views: one contents oneself with hating them. With the tremendous acceleration of life mind and eye have become accustomed to seeing or judging partially or inaccurately, and everyone is like the traveller who gets to know a land and its people from a railway.
>
> (*Human, All Too Human*, §282)

Such sentiments express 'the collapse of space' characteristic of modernity (see Harvey 1989, p. 273). The landscape Nietzsche paints is scarred by railway tracks. It is a world in which ease of access to different and increasingly distant places belies the lack of concrete knowledge that the modern individual has. The modern traveller merely passes through the landscape, skating across the surface of a world that, as a consequence of the effect that this mode of interaction has on one's experience and hence one's intellect, is ever more superficial. The life of the modern traveller typifies the modern: it is not a life lived through an experiencing of concrete conditions, but a life that is increasingly that of the spectator. In modernity, it is implied, one does not encounter much at all beyond one's lazy self-image. To be a spectator is thus to be an enemy of genuine critical self-reflection. The traveller and voyager hero of Greek myth has in modern life become a passenger: a passive, distant and disconnected onlooker perusing a landscape that remains safely held at arm's length.

In a society ever less inclined to genuine contemplation, the 'free spirit' (a phrase that for Nietzsche signifies all that is praiseworthy in a person able to engage in critical reflection upon their own times and values – the subtitle of *Human, All Too Human* is *A Book for Free Spirits*) is rendered a suspect figure. What the free spirit resists is the tendency of society to transform the individual into something analogous to a piece of production-line technology, a mere piece of equipment and adjunct to the social demand for ever-increasing productivity. This notion of an emancipated thought inspires Nietzsche's mature philosophy. Thus, *Beyond Good and Evil* (1885) enacts a multifaceted attack on modern life. Philosophy, the arts and sciences, politics, nationalism, psychology and morality are all subject to criticism as expressions of modern life. For example, Nietzsche criticises modern physics and its obsession with the notion that nature must be law-like (*Beyond Good and Evil*, §22). The notion of nature's conformity to law is diagnosed as an expression of modern cultural norms: it is an example of 'the democratic instincts of the modern soul', of 'modern ideology' (*Beyond Good and Evil*, §22). As with the earlier texts already discussed, modern life is presented as embodying a 'noisy, time-consuming, proud and stupidly proud industriousness' (*Beyond Good and Evil*, §58) which has permeated even the world of academia; it is permeated by false 'free spirits' who are mere 'scribbling slaves of the democratic taste and its "modern ideas"' (*Beyond Good and Evil*, §44). Such a social realm breeds conditions ripe for the general loss of religious belief (*see* **death of God**) and a stiflingly uncritical attitude toward values: 'one manifestly *knows* in Europe what Socrates thought he did not know [...] one "knows" today what is good and evil' (*Beyond Good and Evil*, §202). Modernity, in other words, is for Nietzsche the realm of mediocrity par excellence. On the other hand, its inherent instability offers at least some hope for him of new possibilities. Such possibilities are expressed most powerfully in his notion of philosophers of the future.

Further reading: Habermas 1988; Harvey 1989; Lampert 1993; Rampley 2000; Sedgwick 2007b.

MORALITY

Nietzsche is a consistent critic of morality, at least in its Christian guise. For him, morality can be denied in two ways. First, one can hold that the 'moral' justifications people offer in support of their actions are merely ruses. Morality understood in this sense is deception pure and simple (not least self-deception). Second, there are those who believe that people do indeed act according to moral precepts but that the judgements upon which these precepts rest are illusions. This is the view Nietzsche endorses, at least in his so-called 'middle period' writings: 'I deny morality as I deny alchemy, that is, I deny their premises: but I do *not* deny that there have been alchemists who believed in their premises and acted in accordance with them' (*Daybreak*, §103). At the same time, Nietzsche is never averse to seeing in morality a useful tool for control and deception – an important aspect of his criticism of Socratic thought is that it uses morality in this way (see *Twilight of the Idols*, 'The Problem of Socrates'). At its worst, morality is open to the charge of being a fantastic delusion, for it has given rise to such illusions as the belief that there is a moral order according to which all guilt will be atoned for, all rights wronged and all righteousness rewarded. We are prone to being the victims of our own moral beliefs no less than generations were once the victims of superstitions: 'It is not *things* but opinions *about things that have absolutely no existence* which have so deranged mankind' (*Daybreak*, §563).

The tendency to undermine the pre-eminence of morality is an early trait in Nietzsche's philosophical development. It is evident as early as *The Birth of Tragedy*, which holds that art rather than morality is the genuine metaphysical activity of humankind. With the demise of Nietzsche's adherence to metaphysics, however, ethics becomes irredeemable illusion. That said, just because such beliefs are delusions it does not follow that one ought always to dispense entirely with them – or that one can (*Beyond Good and Evil*, §4). However, what is required, Nietzsche argues, is that we view morality as a profound problem. This is the basis of his main complaint about other philosophers: they have all too willingly taken morality as a given, as an already decided thing, thereby submerging the fact that it is the most troublesome of phenomena. Nietzsche would like to move beyond morality, by which he means beyond the view that moral beliefs correspond to things in the world that exist independently of us, and especially beyond the view that Christian morality is the one true morality. This, at one level, involves a dispute about origins. Whereas the Christian tradition would have us accept its concept of ethics as something that derives from divine sanction, Nietzsche would have us do some history and holds that this will provide the key for a refutation of the contention that the divine itself is the origin of moral beliefs. History, he notes in *Daybreak*, §95, refutes in a manner that no other form of argument about the concept of divinity can. As soon as one has suggested the manner in which beliefs in the divine can come about and come to be important one has pulled the rug from under them. Historical refutation is, in this regard, 'definitive', for it plays by other rules than those employed when engaging in more traditional kinds of argument about the existence or non-existence of God. In turn, with the demise of Christian metaphysics (i.e. the death of God) comes the end of the hegemony of Christian morality, for the surety of the one rests upon faith in the other.

The kind of historical refutation mentioned above is what underlies the views that Nietzsche develops initially in *Daybreak,* characterised particularly by the notion of the morality of custom. This view is then developed in texts such as *The Gay Science, Beyond Good and Evil* and, especially, *On the Genealogy of Morality.* In the opening sections of *The Gay Science,* the teachings of morality become expressions of the great economy of the preservation of the species. They are nature's way of seducing humankind into continuing to abide in a world that is ultimately devoid of sense. This view pays testimony to Nietzsche's contention that the need for morality evidences something constitutive of human nature and our need to endow suffering with sense. More shockingly, perhaps, in *Daybreak* Nietzsche puts forward the following argument:

> [M]orality is nothing other (therefore *no more!*) than obedience to customs, of whatever kind they may be; customs, however, are the *traditional* way of behaving and evaluating. In things in which no tradition commands there is no morality; and the less life is determined by tradition, the smaller the circle of morality. The free human being is immoral because in all things he is *determined* to depend upon himself and not upon a tradition: in all the original conditions of mankind, 'evil' signifies the same as 'individual', 'free', 'capricious', 'unusual', 'unforseen', 'incalculable'.
>
> (*Daybreak,* §9)

Morals, in other words, are simply ways of doing things which are stipulated by specific cultural milieux. Morality is, it follows, nothing more than the observance of practices within a tradition, and the manner in which those practices are arranged in relation to one another is what identifies any particular moral tradition. Thus, to be a moral being is first and foremost to be a creature of convention. One should be clear about what Nietzsche is saying here. He is not arguing that being obedient to conventions is a necessary condition of morality and the thoughts and deeds that flow from it, but that obedience of this kind is just what these things come down to, and nothing else. One follows stipulations of morality, therefore, to the extent that one is passive, conservative. If one places this contention in the context of Nietzsche's conceptions of historical philosophy and the role that prehistory must play in our understanding of the development of human psychology it becomes clear how this view represents an attempt to undermine traditional attitudes. As §2 of *Human, All Too Human* tells us, the nature of contemporary humanity is an issue that ought only to be addressed by considering the prehistoric conditions that gave rise to it. Historical philosophy thus begins with the contention that we have become who we are and that how we became such has left its stamp upon us. The contention that morality is simply the *observance* of customs and nothing else is an example of the practice of historical philosophy, for it stakes the claim that people today are the living legacy of the assumptions made by their prehistoric forebears, that the unconscious adherence to norms is what gave rise to us and still in large part characterises us.

Morality may be an illusion if it is understood as referring to an objective 'moral world order', but when properly understood by way of history, Nietzsche contends, its consequences are not illusory but concrete. The claim that morality was, in the first place, simply obedience to customs and no more is fruitful. For it is this contention that underlies the analysis of the emergence of the 'human animal' that Nietzsche offers in the second essay of the *Genealogy*. Convention, it is argued here, was forced upon our primitive ancestors. They had no choice, since life for them became possible only in virtue of living together in communities. Communal life brings with it specific demands. For one thing, it requires moderation of behaviour, especially the curtailment of those drives that are damaging to social cohesion and hence communal survival. As realms of mere custom and habit, the original proto-human communities that the second essay of the *Genealogy* envisages are devoid of self-conscious individuals. Nietzsche, in other words, is no liberal contractarian. He does not think of humans as being fully formed beings that just happen to be walking around in a 'state of nature' and then agree to form a civil social order, as Locke did in his second *Treatise of Government* (1681). To be human means, on the contrary, to have become so – to have been made by forces internal to the social domain in which the individual member of the community was obliged to live long before self-consciousness and the other traits that we tend to associate with personhood developed. Customs, in other words, were what fashioned the first human beings, and they did so violently – by inflicting pain upon wrongdoers who threatened the survival of the communal body. Thus, what became 'morality' was at first no more than the unconscious means to an end. In turn, the entire psychology of the human being, Nietzsche holds, flows from the punishments our ancestors inflicted upon themselves and each other in order to preserve social harmony. In simpler terms, the individual became a self-interpreting animal (and hence conscious) only in so far as it was first obliged by the tyranny of convention to engage in the social world. Morality, when understood as mere convention and custom, is thus revealed as the essential precondition of human culture.

The link between suffering and morality that the *Genealogy* identifies is essential, in Nietzsche's view, for understanding the subsequent developments that gave rise to modern humankind. The inflicting of suffering on the law-breaker produced what finally became the sense of guilt underlying what Nietzsche baptises the 'bad conscience' (*Genealogy,* Essay II). A link was thereby forged early on in human development between suffering and wrongdoing. This, for Nietzsche, explains our underlying tendency to interpret our own suffering in (sometimes absurdly) moral terms, for pain has become associated with the feeling of guilt. It is this feeling which Christianity uses to its advantage. Whereas in primitive cultures guilt was ameliorated by (on occasion dreadful) acts of sacrifice, with Christianity guilt becomes impossible to pay off because of the concept of original sin. For the Christian, we are born in debt, and this cannot be repaid: since God has sacrificed himself for our sins we are faced with an eternal indebtedness on an infinite scale. Moreover, such sinful guilt is associated by Christian tradition with the body and the drives. The consequence of this is the tendency amongst the pious to revile the world. Hence, Nietzsche's criticism of Christian faith is that it turns against the world as it really is (a world of becoming, of embodiment, of phenomena not being) in favour of a fantasy 'beyond' in which peace is assured by divine providence. One can turn to the preceding first essay of *On the Genealogy of Morality* in order to clarify Nietzsche's views on this. Here, morality is discussed not in the form of the morality of custom that is dealt with in the second essay but as a domain of overt valuation. The first essay identifies two contending camps: 'noble morality' and 'slave morality'. Each expresses a different, and ultimately incompatible, base of interests. The existence of the two reveals that struggle is intrinsic in the history of the ancient world and the moral worldview that emerged triumphant from it (which happens to be slave morality). Noble morality expresses the standpoint of ancient aristocratic classes, affirming the noble perspective as one of dominion and power. As a dominant social group, the nobility affirms itself first as 'good' and only subsequently characterises those of a lower station as 'bad'. This Nietzsche terms the 'good–bad' ethical discourse of evaluation. Such a method of valuation, Nietzsche claims, lies at the origin of all evaluative discourses, since the right of giving names and thereby defining and evaluating must be understood as being initially a privilege of those with power. The contrasting discourse of slave morality arises when the interests of those who encounter and evaluate the world from the perspective of the victim are voiced. Unlike the noble's identity, which is an expression of social domination, the slave's identity emerges out of their status as the noble's hapless victim. Helpless in the face of such dominance and thus unable to extract retribution from their oppressor, the slave takes the only form of revenge possible: he/she labels the oppressor as 'evil' and condemns them to eternal damnation at the hands of a slave-loving God. This negative evaluative deed, says Nietzsche, is the precondition of the slave's subsequent affirmation of his or her own identity as 'good'. In this way, slave morality expresses a 'good–evil' discourse of evaluation. It should be clear from this that what starts out for Nietzsche as mere custom and habit inexorably turns into something more complex. The forces of history create a world torn by conflict, overrun by envy and, with the victory of slave morality in European culture, devoid of genuine futurity. Morality, in other words, has become more complex than the original state of mere adherence to customs would seem to imply. This is because the self-interpretative abilities the morality of custom gave rise to are not ultimately passive but become in their own turn constitutive of human nature. Through morality we have become self-fashioning beings. The highest potential that can arise from this is to be found in the vision of the Overman and in the notion of the Dionysian man, beings who go beyond the dominance of the social norms that made them possible and who are, in consequence, 'supra-moral'.

Understood thus, morality is open to being viewed instrumentally. One of the most revealing examples of this is the discussion Nietzsche offers of the aristocratic *polis* in *Beyond Good and Evil,* §262 (*see* **breeding**). Here, morality is regarded as no more than a means to the creation of a certain type of human being. Morals, in other words, are systems of normative fashioning. The point of such fashioning, for Nietzsche, is not to be found in morality itself but in the kind of human beings that arise as a consequence of the dominance (maintained through customs and webs of beliefs) of one evaluative system. At its best, what is given rise to is the sovereign individual. At its worst, we are presented with a humanity that has lost all its potential for individuality. This is a humankind so subsumed within the realm of the mass culture of modernity that the potential for individuality that Nietzsche identifies hidden in the tyranny of custom is lost. A humanity such as this is Christian mass conformity writ large. Faced with this, Nietzsche comes to urge a revaluation of values.

Further reading: Ansell-Pearson 1991; Berkowitz 1995; Bernstein 1987; Conway and Groff 1998; Danto 2005 [1965]; Eagleton 2009; Hunt 1991; Lampert 2001; MacIntyre 1981; May 1999; Schacht 2001; Solomon 2003.

MORALITY OF CUSTOM

The era of the morality of custom is the era of prehistory. This prehistoric realm is, for Nietzsche, decisive when it comes to determining '*the character of mankind*' (*Daybreak*, §18). All social orders originate in prehistory and the propensity humans developed during that era to make and observe customs. Indeed, if one could go far enough back into the prehistoric past one would discover nothing but customs: 'Originally [...] everything was custom' (*Daybreak*, §9). Customs are thus the precondition of human existence. From the outset, humans were essentially social beings, and human society first existed in so far as customs were observed and arranged in the form of traditions. Traditions fix customs by relating them to one another, acting as a glue that binds all primitive social orders together. In their most ancient manifestation these conditions made up what Nietzsche terms 'the morality of custom'. In fact, Nietzsche holds two kinds of morality of custom to exist. On the one hand, there is the sort that demands the most frequent performance of customary observances. Frequency of observance implies a formal mode of consciousness, one dominated by the letter of customary prescriptions (law) and which sees all situations, however minor, as subject to these prescriptions. On the other hand, the other kind of morality of custom insists on the most demanding performance of customary requirements. Such an attitude demands that the law be observed and acted upon even in arduous cases. What is essential about each of the two kinds of morality of custom is that both demand sacrifice: 'The most moral man is he who *sacrifices* the most to custom: what, however, are the greatest sacrifices?' (*Daybreak*, §9). The answer to this question takes us into the heart of the most primitive conditions underlying morality. Whatever a morality stipulates as being of the greatest significance inevitably involves abstinence. The thing that is sacrificed (whether one considers the observance that requires frequent obedience or that which demands greatest obedience when such obedience is arduous) is what characterises and distinguishes one culture from another. Cultures are differentiated in so far as every culture is a realm of the effects of different normative demands. Such demands are established by environmental and historical conditions. Take, for example, a community that is in constant danger. In such a community, says Nietzsche, the morality that will have come to dominate will be that which is most demanding. The ethical-customary realm is, in other words, a refraction of environmental conditions. In communities of this kind, the extent of the power of tradition is exhibited by the presence of one central pleasure: cruelty. The sanctioning and high estimation of cruelty within the community reflects the conditions of its life. A hard life is endowed with meaning when it is interpreted as having the approval of the gods. Pleasure in cruelty hence becomes a virtue since it reflects the conditions that the gods are seen to have imposed upon the community. Here lie the roots of religious asceticism. In communities of this kind,

> the concept of the 'most moral man' of the community came to include the virtue of the most frequent suffering, of privation, of the hard life of cruel chastisement – *not* [...] as a means of discipline, of self-control, of satisfying the desire for individual happiness – but as a virtue which will put the community on good odour with the evil gods and which steams up to them like a perpetual propitiatory sacrifice on the altar.
>
> (*Daybreak*, §18)

Whether demanding frequent obedience or obedience to the most demanding norms, the central contention is made that all culture flows (quite literally, in some cases) from the sacrifices made to the demands of custom. There is, Nietzsche contends, no civilisation that has not sprung from this primeval combination of customs and sacrifices. Hence, all culture is an articulation of the morality of custom. That is why 'the mighty proposition with which civilisation begins: [is] any custom is better than no custom' (*Daybreak*, §16). Consequently, where there is no tradition founded upon custom and sacrifice there can be no culture. The central question of modernity is framed within the bounds of this contention. For even though modern society is the domain that bears witness to the demise of the power of custom, social order today no less than in the past still hangs by the thread of primitive ancestral rites.

See also: **morality**.

Further reading: Ansell-Pearson 1991; Sedgwick 2007b.

NATURALISATION OF MAN

Christian morality, for Nietzsche, possibly pays the most decisive testimony to the fact that the human animal is prone to exist in a state of disharmony with regard to its drives. Morality, generally speaking, is a perversion: it exemplifies 'anti-nature' in so far as it seeks to decimate the passions (*Twilight of the Idols,* 'Morality as Anti-Nature', §1). The problem is that 'to attack the passions at their roots means to attack life at its roots: the practice of the Church is *hostile to life*' (*Twilight of the Idols,* 'Morality as Anti-Nature', §1). Moralities in the form that Nietzsche applauds are expressions of a commandment of life. They are exemplary codes that serve not only to preserve life but also bring about its enhancement in the form of higher culture. Most moralities, however, have been anti-natural: they have valorised the concept of a better world lurking behind the concrete realm of experience and in this way have regarded existence as an inferior copy, or practice run, for a higher reality. To say, as Socrates did (*Twilight,* 'The Problem of Socrates', §1), that life is no good, that there is a better place than here for the spirit, denigrates existence. Such judgements, Nietzsche comments, can be turned back on the judge: to judge life harshly is to invite the harsh assessment that one is an expression of decline (*Twilight,* 'Morality as Anti-Nature', §5). Anti-natural morality must, Nietzsche argues, be overcome by way of a return to nature. This return signals the 'naturalisation of man', but one needs to be careful with regard to what this means. Returning to nature does not mean 'going back' to some innocent past but indicates a form of *ascent* (*Twilight,* 'Expeditions of an Untimely Man', §48). This involves the affirmation of the embodied self in all its hierarchical multiplicity. The prime example of Nietzsche's enactment of naturalisation is to be found in the second essay of *On the Genealogy of Morality.* Here he seeks to show how the rich terrain of the human soul can be accounted for in terms of the fashioning and policing of the body by the normative force of custom, moral imperatives and the imposition of power relations. Such practices yield a humanity that is no longer part of the realm of nature but can at the same time be accounted for in naturalistic, non-metaphysical terms. Concrete practices that fashion the human subject as an exchanger of increasingly sophisticated propensities give rise to a being that is no longer determined by way of them (exemplified by the sovereign individual). The naturalisation of humanity, then, seeks to integrate it back into the realm of nature in so far as it affirms without shame that this is where we, too, originated. This does not, however, mean that persons are capable of being accounted for in simplistic behaviourist terms. Rather, for Nietzsche, our passions must be acknowledged positively when it comes to the question of our identity.

Further reading: Conway 1995; Schacht 1983.

NIHILISM

A nihilist, at his or her most uncompromising, would be a person for whom every holding something true 'is necessarily false because there simply is *no true world*' (*Will to Power*, §15). In essence, the nihilist is a disappointed absolutist. The prime reason for this resides in Christian morality and metaphysics: the absolutism instilled by Christian belief served to fuel nihilism, and the decline of the authority of the Christian moral worldview in the modern era ignites it. It follows that nihilism is, for Nietzsche, indelibly associated with the death of God, that is, with the loss of faith in the divine that ensues once the Christian God has ceased to have explanatory value due to the achievements of modern science. Above all, for Nietzsche, the consequences of the death of God place a question mark over Christian morality, and it is the terrain illuminated by this question that he seeks to explore. No one, he notes in *The Gay Science,* has ever really considered 'the value of that most famous of all medicines which is called morality; and the first step would be – for once to *question* it' (§345). Such a question is posed in the context of 'the realization that the way of this world is anything but divine' (*Gay Science,* §346). Our interpretation of the world is revealed as something that has been long mired in falsity: we have taken our needs and projected them onto the 'world'. It was assumed that values had the characteristic of objectivity, that their existence formed an objective framework for understanding reality. But now it becomes clear 'that the world is *not* worth what we thought it was' (*Gay Science,* §346). The view that took human values to have objective properties that could be found in reality needs to be challenged. Nietzsche's point is that there is rather more at stake with this challenge than the status of a few metaphysical precepts. The stakes concern European self-understanding. The belief, enshrined in the faith in metaphysical values, that humanity is the measure of things must be overturned, and this has disturbing implications:

> We laugh as soon as we encounter the juxtaposition of 'man *and* world', separated by the sublime presumption of the little word 'and'. But look, when we laugh like that, have we not simply carried the contempt for man one step further. And thus also pessimism, the contempt for that existence which is knowable by *us?* Have we not exposed ourselves to the suspicion of an opposition – an opposition between the world in which we were at home up to now with our reverences that perhaps made it possible for us to *endure* life, and another world *that consists of us* – an inexorable, fundamental, and deepest suspicion about ourselves that is more and more gaining worse and worse control over us Europeans and that could easily confront coming generations with the terrifying Either/Or: 'Either abolish your reverences or – yourselves!' The latter would be nihilism; but would not the former also be nihilism? – This is *our* question mark.
>
> (*Gay Science*, §346)

Intellectual honesty demands that we no longer cleave to the values associated with the Christian faith. Nihilism is thereby posited as the most dangerous of possibilities arising from the loss of faith in Christian metaphysics. A notebook entry from around the same time as the above passage from *The Gay Science* was written serves to clarify the point:

> Nihilism stands at the door: whence comes this uncanniest of all guests? [...] [I]t is in one particular interpretation, the Christian-moral one, that nihilism is rooted. The end of Christianity – at the hands of its own morality (which cannot be replaced), which turns against the Christian God (the sense of truthfulness developed highly by Christianity, is nauseated by the falseness and mendaciousness of all Christian interpretations of the world and of history; rebound from 'God is truth' to the fanatical faith 'All is false').
>
> (*Will to Power*, §1)

Nihilism is therefore generated immanently by Christian values. Christianity has, over the centuries, fostered a sense of truthfulness (manifest most clearly in the scholarly disciplines, i.e. the physical sciences and philosophical and historical enquiry), and this sense of truthfulness has ultimately turned on the very metaphysical precepts from which it arose. Nietzsche's notebooks suggest two possible views of nihilism. Nihilism can be an expression of strength or an expression of weakness: it can be 'active' or 'passive' (*Will to Power*, §22). Nihilism is active when values are destroyed because they are seen as wanting with regard to an overpowering creative need. A creative person's own overriding goals drive them to question their faith in morality. Nihilism is passive when faith in values has been lost but the desire for the absolutes that characterised such faith remains in place. The pessimism of Schopenhauer is a case in point. The nihilist, a disappointed idealist, turns on the world and finds it wanting. For the nihilist, the inevitable conclusion is that things ought not to be as they are, but how things ought to be represents an unattainable fantasy. Nietzsche addresses the question of European nihilism more fully in the third essay of *On the Genealogy of Morality*, where he seeks to outline the nature of 'priestly' values and the meaning of the ascetic's contempt for embodiment. Nietzsche's conclusion is that the very conditions that nurtured nihilism have, at the same time, been the means whereby the 'animal man' was able to survive in the first place.

Further reading: Gillespie 1996; Jones et al. 1989; Havas 1995; Reginster 2006; Schutte 1984.

NOBLE MORALITY

Noble morality (or 'master morality' as Nietzsche sometimes refers to it) is one of the two basic types of ethical evaluation (*Beyond Good and Evil*, §260). It is the code that characterises the noble classes of the ancient world and also the realm in which the birth of values as such occurred (*Genealogy*, Essay I, §§2 ff.). Nobles are the dominant class in ancient social groupings, beings generally of action rather than con-templation. The noble's dominance of the social world is expressed in their evaluative language. This feeling of power is, for Nietzsche, possibly 'the origin of language itself', since naming is an expression of power over someone or something, a taking possession of some-thing by identifying it with a name (*Genealogy*, Essay II, §2). For the noble, the word 'good' springs from an attitude of self-affirmation. Their initial value judgement is, in other words, a projection and voicing of their identity. What the noble deems 'good' is really nothing more than what the noble esteems about him- or herself. 'Good' means noble and all that is associated with being so. In contrast, 'bad' for the noble denotes what is ignoble, socially inferior, lowly, common and plebeian. Noble moral language is thus characterised by the opposition 'good/bad'. However, the moral code antithetical to noble morality, namely, slave morality, also originates in the sphere of noble concerns. The noble class is not like a smooth space of harmonious norms but is a differentiated realm replete with the potential for conflict. Noble classes consist of warriors and priests. Imagine, says Nietzsche, a dispute over the spoils of war where the priests lose out due to their lack of physical power relative to their warrior comrades. The priest is likely to seek revenge for being dispossessed by turning for support to the slaves, who are relatively easy to manipulate when it comes to the stirring up of hatred for their noble masters (*Genealogy,* Essay I, §17). Slave morality is hence infiltrated by noble interests from the outset of the history of morality that Nietzsche narrates in the *Genealogy,* albeit in distorted form. Although dominant at the outset of Nietzsche's tale of the origins of 'good and bad' and 'good and evil' talk, he contends that the dominance of either noble or slave morality does not generally characterise the history of morality. Most societies are arenas of compromise, of 'mixed' moralities (*Beyond Good and Evil,* §260). The essential point about Nietzsche's claim here, though, is that morality can always be traced back to the interests that are played out within social hierarchies. Moral talk, in other words, is always an expression of interest.

Further reading: Allison 2001; Ansell-Pearson 1991; Kaufmann 1974; May 1999; Owen and Ridley 2000; Ridley 1998; Schacht 1994.

OVERMAN

Section 108 of *Daybreak* provides a clue to understanding the notion of the Overman:

> Only if mankind possessed a universally recognized *goal* would it be possible to propose 'thus and thus is the *right* course of action': for the present there exists no such goal. It is thus irrational and trivial to impose the demands of morality upon mankind. – To *recommend* a goal to mankind is something quite different: the goal is then thought of as something that *lies in our own discretion;*

supposing the recommendation appealed to mankind, it could in pursuit of it also *impose* upon itself a moral law, likewise at its own discretion.

In other words, in so far as human existence lacks any demonstrable all-embracing purpose, no universal moral injunctions can be justifiably imposed upon it. However, commending humanity to endorse a vision of the future is rather different. In so far as such a vision appeals to it humankind can choose to endorse that future and take upon itself as its own. The notion of the Overman may be thought of in this way. It is not something that is to be imposed on humanity by some superior power but an idea that, in the text of *Thus Spoke Zarathustra,* we are invited to consider imposing upon ourselves.

At the age of forty, Zarathustra, who has been living in mountainous solitude for a decade, embarks on a journey. He has a gift to give humankind. Overloaded with what he has managed to glean in his solitude, Zarathustra wishes to share the vision of the Overman. Such a vision, Zarathustra tells another solitary he happens to meet on his way down from the mountains, is an expression of his love for humanity (*Zarathustra,* Part I, 'Prologue', §2). Having arrived at the bottom of his mountain, Zarathustra is inclined to engage with pretty much anyone. His teaching is thereby announced in the marketplace of the nearest town: '*I teach you the overman.* Man is something that shall be overcome. What have you done to overcome him? All beings so far have created something beyond themselves; and do you want to be the ebb of this great flood and even go back to the beasts rather than overcome man?' (*Zarathustra,* Part I, 'Prologue', §3). Immediately, we are presented with a speech that invokes the vision of a humanity whose nature is such that it is capable of passing beyond itself. We must rethink, Zarathustra says, what it means to be human and come to see it as something that is more potential than actuality. Zarathustra's love of humanity, in other words, is a love of its ability to transcend its own nature:

> Man is a rope tied between beast and overman – a rope over an abyss [...] What is great in man is that he is a bridge and not an end: what can be loved in man is that he is an *overture* and a *going under.* I love those who do not know how to live, except by going under, for they are those who cross over [...] I love those [...] who sacrifice themselves for the earth, that the earth may some day become the overman's. I love him who lives to know,

and who wants to know so that the overman may live some day. And thus he wants to go under. I love him who works and invents to build a house for the overman and to prepare earth, animal, and plant for him [...] I love him who justifies future and redeems past generations: for he wants to perish of the present.

(*Zarathustra*, Part I, 'Prologue', §4)

Zarathustra's love for humankind is summed up in the dual images of rope and bridge. It is when a person is considered as a willing *means of crossing over from him or herself* that they become worthy of the love he has. Such a person sacrifices themselves: they will their own down-going and with it the down-going of humanity. The being for which the sacrificial exchange is made is one who is radically different from what we, as a whole, might be considered to be. In turn, Zarathustra envisions a fashioning of the earth into a dwelling place suitable for the Overman. The world is to be prepared so that it will be replete with the cultivated resources of nature that this being of supra-human futurity will need.

The Overman is, of course, a kind of metaphor for human potential. He is a representation of the most gloriously selfish creator-spirit, allied to what Nietzsche elsewhere refers to as the 'Dionysian' man. The Overman exemplifies the self-possession, autonomy and uniqueness of the sovereign individual in a modernity dominated by the impersonal forces of mass production and consumption. The Overman is, in short, a being of unprecedented freedom, not least because he has stepped beyond morality and the realm of universal injunctions:

He [...] has discovered himself who says, 'This is *my* good and evil'; with that he has reduced to silence the mole and dwarf who say, 'Good for all, evil for all' [...] 'This is *my* way; where is yours?' – thus I answered those who asked me 'the way'. For *the* way – that does not exist.

(*Zarathustra*, Part III, 'On the Spirit of Gravity', §2)

In order to attain the Overman, humanity must be passed through. In other words, human nature is not of itself an end and a goal but a means to some higher and yet to be determined end (*Zarathustra*, Part III, 'On Old and New Tablets', §4). In this way, the collective suffering that defines human existence is open to being redeemed. The fragments of our existence need to be forged into a new unity: all that is 'fragment and riddle and dreadful accident' in humankind needs to be reassembled into something that enables humanity to realise its future potential (*Zarathustra,* Part III, 'On Old and New Tablets', §3). In this way, the future lies in wait as something that may be justified and redeemed by way of the Overman: 'To redeem what is past in man and to re-create all "it was" until the will says, "Thus I willed it! Thus shall I will it" – this I called redemption and this alone I taught them to call redemption' (*Zarathustra,* Part III, 'On Old and New Tablets', §3). The Overman is hence redemptive, but in such a way that no 'after-worldly' illusions are needed in order for his redemptive potential to be communicated. In many ways, the vision of the 'last man' that Zarathustra also offers us provides a good way of understanding the vision of the Overman by way of the stark contrast it presents. Where visions of the Overman provoke sublime thoughts of autonomy, individuality and creativity, the last man's self-obsessed sterility is intended to provoke revulsion. Such a creature exemplifies the lack of what the Overman offers in abundance: futurity. The last man is a being beyond even self-contempt. All that matters to him is the pro-spect of comfortable living. This notion defines a rotten happiness: '"We have invented happiness," say the last men and they blink [...] One still works, for work is a form of entertainment. But one is careful lest the entertainment be too harrowing. One no longer becomes poor or rich: both require too much exertion' (*Zarathustra,* Part I, 'Prologue', §5). The last man exemplifies the tendencies of modern mass culture, with its dominant desire to ease the travails of existence. The world of the last man is one of minimal pain, small effort and little sins. It is dominated by trite mass entertainment and self-indulgence. The nightmare vision that the last man encapsulates reveals a pathway that leads nowhere. It turns out that most of us would prefer this, or so Nietzsche seems to believe. For when given this vision of the future as mass-conformity Zarathustra's audience laughs and applauds. For them the last man is preferable to the Overman. Consequently, individual disciples must be sought to receive his teaching (*Zarathustra, Part* I, 'Prologue', §9). These, how-ever, are abandoned by the time we get to Part II of *Thus Spoke Zarathustra,* for they are told that they need to find their own paths rather than imitate his. What is commended, then, in the shape of the Overman is no universal goal for humankind but a teaching of experimental creativity. The Overman thereby abides as, above all, a figure of tantalising potentiality, a being that would form the crown of human achievement in so far as humankind would thereby show itself capable of creating something more worthy than itself. However, such a vision, to repeat the point, cannot be imposed. For to do this would be to mimic the dishonesty Nietzsche associates with all exponents of universal morality.

Further reading: Eagleton 2009; Kaufmann 1974; Lampert 1986; Schacht 1983; Thiele 1990.

PERSPECTIVISM

It is a necessary condition of any knowledge claim that it must be made from some standpoint somewhere. 'Insofar as the word "knowledge" has any meaning, the world is knowable; but it is *interpretable* otherwise, it has no meaning behind it, but countless meanings.- "Perspectivism"' (*Will to Power*, §481). For Nietzsche, the will to truth requires perspectivism. This is because perspectivism retains the valuable desire for objectivity in knowledge while at the same time making room for reconsidering the nature of objectivity in terms of questions of interest. No single viewpoint will serve this purpose, since metaphysical philosophy has shown the questionable nature of any such enterprise. For Nietzsche, there is no such thing as 'disinterested knowledge'. All knowledge is an expression of an instrumental relation between the knower and his or her environment. Metaphysical philosophy seeks to provide a universal and unified picture of reality, claiming a vantage point outside the realm of historical experience. Nietzsche, in contrast, argues that all knowledge is bound to the particularity of one perspective or another: 'I should think that today we are far from the ridiculous immodesty that would be involved in decreeing from our corner that perspectives are permitted only from this corner' (*Gay Science*, §374). For Nietzsche, any perspective that claims to be timeless and universal condemns itself, for the world is such that it can always be understood differently. The notion that 'objectivity' means arriving at a single view of the whole, as the metaphysician understands it, should be derided and unceremoniously rejected. Nietzsche argues that the spirit of the notion of objectivity can only be maintained if one seeks to multiply the number of viewpoints to which one has access. Only in this way will something like reliable knowledge be possible:

> From now on, my philosophical colleagues, let us be more wary of the dangerous old conceptual fairy-tale which has set up a 'pure, will-less, painless, timeless, subject of knowledge', let us be wary of the tentacles of such contradictory concepts as 'pure reason', 'absolute spirituality', 'knowledge as such': – here we are

asked to think an eye that cannot be thought at all, an eye turned in no direction at all, an eye where the active and interpretative powers are to be suppressed, absent, but through which seeing still becomes a seeing-something, so it is an absurdity and a non-concept of eye that is demanded. There is *only* a perspective seeing, *only* a perspective 'knowing'; the *more* affects we allow to speak about a thing, the *more* eyes, various eyes we are able to use for the same thing, the more complete will be our 'concept' of the thing, our 'objectivity'.

(*Genealogy,* Essay III, §12)

In shorter terms: better knowledge means having a varied and rich understanding generated from the maximum possible number of perspectives. For Nietzsche, all thought is, to some degree or another, enmeshed within the habitual traps that custom has handed down to us in the form of metaphysics. To think differently would be naive. Metaphysics can nevertheless be turned against itself; truth can emerge out of error in the guise of the demand for the true (the will to truth); a kind of 'objectivity' can arise from criticism of the naive version of this concept. Such will to truth is, however, certainly not of the disinterested kind associated with the notion of value neutrality. In short, one cannot simply switch off the fundamental condition of one's engagement with the world, which is that one is immersed in it in a manner that is essentially interested. The metaphysician conceives of truth and objectivity in terms that 'eliminate the will completely and turn off all the emotions without exception' (*Genealogy,* Essay III, §12). It thereby runs counter to the conditions that make life possible. Perspectivism, in contrast, represents Nietzsche's attempt to do justice to the conditions of life within the realm of knowledge, which means understanding it in the light of the notion of the will (*see* **will to power**). The will to truth is, in fact, a kind of drive: it represents a sublimated expression of an urge to dominate. One should note, however, that an inherent tension exists between will to power and perspectivism: will to power always suggests the dominance of one kind of perspective over all others.

Further reading: Cox 1999; Hales and Welshon 2000; Poellner 1995.

PESSIMISM

The philosophy of pessimism is most commonly associated with the German philosopher Arthur Schopenhauer (1788–1860). In his most famous work, *The World and Will and Representation* (1818; revised edition 1844), Schopenhauer argued that our experience of the world is, Kantian style, determined by the constitution of the subject. In this sense, the world is representation, i.e. the world is that realm of objects that are capable of being represented by the thinking subject to itself in the form of concepts. The thinking subject is an individuated being endowed with bodily existence. However, the body is offered up to the subject in two ways. On the one hand, it is a representation (the 'I' can think of its body as an object like other objects). On the other hand, the body is that entity which is immediately captured by the notion of 'will'. Thus, an individual acts and in doing so experiences those actions as immediate expressions of his or her own will. When understood in this sense, acts are neither strictly bodily (i.e. physical/material) nor intellectual (mental) in significance. The physical and the intellectual are, rather, two aspects of a greater unity. To will is to be embodied. To be an embodied subject is to will. Conscious thought, for example, is no less concrete ('real') than an unthinking ('unconscious') physical reaction. The body of the individual is a phenomenon of will. This will can be characterised, above all, as 'the will to life'. It is against this background that Schopenhauer, much influenced by Indian philosophy, develops his pessimistic outlook. The life of the individual is the life of the will. We are driven by the will to live. Yet, every subject is destined to frustration of the desires that arise as a consequence of being so driven. The world is revealed to us as an object of desire, since we are concrete beings with appetites and needs (the need for food, the drive to procreate) that demand satisfaction. However, it is in the very nature of these cravings that their satisfaction is, at best, temporary. Thus, the satisfaction of hunger or sexual desire does not extinguish them permanently; these desires soon come back. Another way of looking at this is to say that it is intrinsic to the nature of human desire that it is doomed to miserable failure. We strive and labour for the satisfaction of various wants, but this means we suffer. To want something, on this view, is to suffer – why else would one seek a satisfaction if not to overcome the suffering caused by what one desires? Suffering is thus an innate condition of human existence. Faced with inevitable suffering, the prospect of death loses its sting. We may all be driven by the will to live but Schopenhauer's solution to the ills of existence is to advocate the renunciation of this will. Given that we are all manifestations of the will to live such renunciation is achieved only by renouncing the self. Self-renunciation is epitomised by the doctrine that the best thing for any person would be not to exist at all. In concrete terms, however, this is taken by Schopenhauer to mean that one should daily strive to deny one's desires. In short, a Buddhist attitude is advocated as a means of coping with the pain of living: asceticism. In ascetic denial one overcomes the self, and hence one's will to live, and thereby attains the purest form of knowledge possible. The true ascetic stands above his or her cravings (especially sexual ones) and in this way discovers a path that avoids the worst excesses of anxiety and suffering engendered by the fact of simply being here. The ascetic no longer lives for himself but rather lives for others (the paths of saintliness, altruism). Pessimism holds that the best thing for all of us would be not to have been born in the first place. This is because for the pessimist the world as it is may justifiably be said to be as bad as it can possibly be. Reality is so appalling that it is impossible to imagine how things could get worse.

Nietzsche's early work, *The Birth of Tragedy*, owes a great debt to pessimism. The interpretation of tragedy it offers develops the central life-negating tenet of Schopenhauer's thought, arguing that the insight into the terrors of life that pessimism contains forms an articulation of the fundamental Dionysian urge from which the highest achievements of classical Greek culture sprang. From the time of *Human, All Too Human*, however, Nietzsche deserts his early adherence to what he comes increasingly to see as a form of Romanticism (as he also does the Wagnerism associated with it in *The Birth of Tragedy*). He retains a deep gratitude and respect for Schopenhauer's thought, not least in so far as it represents a serious attempt to pose the question of the meaning of individual existence and the validity of religious ideals in a genuine manner that addresses the problem from a European perspective (see *Gay Science,* §357). Yet, Nietzsche also comes to regard Schopenhauer's pessimism as another means of valorising dangerously destructive Christian ideals. Indeed, Schopenhauer even outdoes Christianity by being in this respect even more Christian than it is (*Daybreak,* §132). By the time of *On the Genealogy of Morality*, pessimism is a 'tired' view of life, one symptomatic of 'nausea' when it comes to the reality of embodied existence (*Genealogy*, Essay II, §7). Schopenhauer himself is now a means to the end of diagnosing the meaning of asceticism. Thus, one can ask the question: what if a 'genuine *philosopher*' like Schopenhauer 'pays homage to the ascetic ideal' (*Genealogy*, Essay III, §5)? A discussion of the latter's aesthetics (*Genealogy*, Essay III, §6) reveals the answer. Schopenhauer followed Kant, who 'like all philosophers, just considered art and beauty from the position of the "spectator"' (*Genealogy*, Essay III, §6), rather than thinking the problem from within the perspective of the artist. As a result, Kant 'introduced the "spectator" himself into the concept "beautiful"' (*Genealogy*, Essay III, §6). Kant's maxim is that beauty is what gives pleasure without interest. That aestheticians under the sway of Kant can claim that 'under the charm of beauty *even* naked female statues can be looked at "without interest"' (*Genealogy*, Essay III, §6) entitles us, Nietzsche says, to indulge in laughter. Schopenhauer, like Kant, wants to think of aesthetic reflection as counteracting '*sexual* interestedness' (*Genealogy*, Essay III, §6). He thinks of it as an escape from the will, i.e. from the domain of the body. But is it not possible, Nietzsche then asks, that Schopenhauer misunderstood himself, that he was no Kantian, that 'beauty pleased him, too, out of "interest", in fact, out of the strongest, most personal interest possible: that of the tortured person to escape from torture?' (*Genealogy*, Essay III, §6). Schopenhauer, the great pessimist and hater of women, a man 'who actually treated sexuality as a personal enemy [...] *needed* enemies to stay cheerful' (*Genealogy*, Essay III, §7). Schopenhauer's enemies (most famously, Hegel – whom he hated with a vengeance) thus actually kept him going. It was his enemies who 'kept seducing him back into existence': the anger he felt toward them gave him 'his solace', 'his *happiness*' (*Genealogy*, Essay III, §7). In other words, Schopenhauer's hatreds countered his pessimism; his asceticism was a ruse of the cunning of reason whereby he was seduced into remaining in existence.

Whereas for the early Nietzsche the Dionysian, the tragic and Schopenhauerian pessimism go hand in hand, for the mature thinker tragic art is Dionysian but, because of this, deeply anti-pessimistic (see *Twilight of the Idols*, '"Reason" in Philosophy', §6). Tragedy does not confirm the logic of such pessimism but rather overcomes it in an act of affirmation that celebrates the terrors of existence by greeting them as offering the opportunity for fashioning a creative and hence fulfilling life in the face of meaninglessness. Where pessimism sees life's suffering as offering no consolation and, because of this, draining it of all meaning, Nietzsche's later Dionysian view holds that life itself must be the only thing worth affirming at all. That said, around the same time (in Book V of *The Gay Science*), Nietzsche explores the possibility of another kind of pessimism. Whereas Schopenhauer's pessimistic philosophy of the will can be characterised as '*romantic pessimism*', which is 'the last *great* event in the fate of our culture' (*Gay Science*, §370), there remains the possibility that another kind of pessimism could exist. Carelessly put, one could call this a *classical* pessimism – but the word 'classical' does not appeal to Nietzsche, in so far as it has come to be too vague in meaning. This future pessimism can, however, be given a more accurate name: '*Dionysian* pessimism'.

Further reading: Janaway 1998; Simmel 1991.

PHILOSOPHY

As far as Nietzsche is concerned, if there is one feature of philosophy that generally stands out it is that philosophy is not what it usually takes itself to be. This view is plain enough even in his first book, *The Birth of Tragedy*. Philosophy here is presented as the opposite of the Greek tragic psyche, exemplified by the antagonism between the gods Apollo and Dionysus. Where tragedy is the epitome of Greek cultural achievement, philosophy (specifically in its Socratic form) emerges as the destroyer of all that is to be affirmed in the pessimism of the ancient world. Philosophy in the form that Socratic thought and Platonism present it seeks to render reality in terms of narrow rationalistic principles. The victory of this approach signals both the emergence of metaphysics and the demise of ancient Greek culture. In its rejection of this view, *The Birth of Tragedy* reveals itself as a work of anti-philosophy: it enacts the wholesale rejection of metaphysics in favour of a sensibility that favours the aesthetic over the rational. Nietzsche's anti-philosophical stance does not last long. Only a few years later, in the *Untimely Meditations,* philosophy is opposed positively to contemporary social trends, not least the burgeoning marketplace culture of mass consumption and capitalism. For Nietzsche, a philosophy that 'wears rags' (*Daybreak,* §206) is far superior to the greed fostered by the contemporary commercial world of modernity. *Human, All Too Human* initiates Nietzsche's turn to embracing science with its developing of the idea of 'historical philosophy' (*see* **knowledge**), an approach that enacts a specifically anti-metaphysical rejection of dogmatic philosophical attitudes in favour of an embracing of becoming, history and development. Here, a more modest conception of knowledge than that of the metaphysician's is affirmed: modest truths matter, not grand ones. Clearly Nietzsche is not opposed to philosophy but rather to a specific form of it – namely, the metaphysics epitomised by Platonism and Christianity. It is this form of thought, however, which Nietzsche holds to have dominated throughout the history of the West. And, in this guise at least, philosophy is prone to being beset by error and illusion. For instance, it takes contingent concepts and categories (consciousness, logic, cause and effect, being) and elevates them without warrant to the authoritative status of holding the key to grasping the fundamental nature of reality. Later texts, such as *Twilight of the Idols,* pursue this view in polemical guise, portraying philosophy as beset by phantasms, as a conceptual fetishism bent on elevating the least concrete of notions to the level of measure of objective reality. Such is the degree of the metaphysical addiction of philosophers, says Nietzsche, that they are only happy when reality is drained of its inherently changing properties and frozen into a timeless form ('being'). Philosophy of this kind is likened by Nietzsche to conceptual mummification (*Twilight of the Idols,* '"Reason" in Philosophy', §1). Such philosophy is also clumsy and inept – witness the image of the philosopher as poor seducer of truth in the Preface to *Beyond Good and Evil.* Consider also the subsequent claim in that text that all that every great philosophy has really been is an unconscious memoir, an unwitting confession on the part of the author of their dominant drives and prejudices (*Beyond Good and Evil,* §6). Philosophers may be lovers of knowledge but they are also always prey to being as unaware of their own constitution, motives and genuine aims as everyone else generally is (see *On the Genealogy of Morality,* Preface, §1). Nevertheless, philosophy remains for Nietzsche something that is pregnant with possibility and futurity. So, it is certainly to be esteemed (see Essay III of the *Genealogy*) as a form of resistance to the power of dominant norms and as the inspirer of critical thought. The philosopher may look like a creature of asceticism, but, it turns out, this was merely a means to an altogether more ambitious end. Philosophy, in this regard, is capable of exemplifying human potential. The 'philosophers of the future' extolled in §42 of *Beyond Good and Evil* encapsulate this positive vision. Such beings represent a new kind of philosopher, which Nietzsche ventures to baptise with the name 'attempters'. Such a characterisation implies many things. Primarily, it presupposes that the future thinkers can be characterised by virtue of having some kind of *task:* an attempt toward something can be made only in the light of some kind of purpose that already justifies it. This desire for justification through purpose is, Nietzsche comments in *Twilight of the Idols,* something that frames the bounds of his 'happiness'. Such happiness is achieved by way of a formula: one proceeds via affirmation and negation to create a sense of direction culminating in a destination that signals the end of a journey (see *Twilight of the Idols,* 'Maxims and Arrows', §44). Philosophers of the future, being attempters, are also differentiated from other kinds. They are, above all, *new* philosophers (*Beyond Good and Evil,* §44). Philosophers of the future are defined by their relation to what has gone before them. Thus, the realms of history and prehistory that for Nietzsche made us the kind of beings we are speak through them no less than they do through the rest of humankind. The philosopher of the future stands upon the achievements of his or her forebears but at the same time stands apart from them because of their experimental daring.

The philosopher of the future will be passionate, a risk-taker, a celebrator of the intellect, capable also of suffering in great measure. Above all, they will be capable of affirming their own existence, they will, in short, be Dionysian beings. Philosophers of the future thus stand implacably against the strongest tendencies of their own times. New philosophers will not be 'scribbling slaves of the democratic taste and its "modern ideas"' (*Beyond Good and Evil*, §44), i.e. false free spirits. The modern 'free-thinker' considers suffering to be an objection to something. He or she desires the eradication of pain from life. This attitude is, for Nietzsche, quintessentially modern. The future philosopher will do no such thing. In so far as suffering and danger have always been what has made humanity develop into something more admirable than it was hitherto it is not to be dismissed as an outrage to life but affirmed as constitutive of its wonder. We need to be forced like plants are when light is denied them in order to develop. In other words, culture and the highest possible cultural achievements spring from provocation: humans need to be challenged into engaging with their environment with a view to mastering it in order to become more than they are. Less disconcertingly, one might say that what makes us human is the fact that we are not mere playthings of nature. We may always stand as potential victims of the ravages of nature, but in so far as we have always faced nature armed with concepts and rituals and thus with the hope of somehow subjugating or pacifying it we stand in a relation to it that no other animal does. The philosopher of the future exemplifies this. He faces life by welcoming all that it might throw at him, thereby epitomising what is admirable in humankind.

The philosopher of the future is akin to what Nietzsche elsewhere in *Beyond Good and Evil* refers to as *the* 'real philosopher'. This is the genuine article and can be contrasted with the 'philosophical worker'. Real philosophers are not dissimilar from such beings. Like the scholarly philosopher, the genuine philosophers need to possess the discipline imparted by a demanding education. Like Platonic philosopher kings, they need to climb each rung of the ladder of knowledge. However, the real philosopher passes beyond mere competence. The task of such a person demands nothing less than 'that he *create* values' (*Beyond Good and Evil*, §211). The examples Nietzsche proffers of such of 'philosophical labourers' are, perhaps, surprising given how deservedly famous they are: Kant and Hegel. Such figures, he says, have the formative task of fixing in place and expressing in formulae that are easy to assimilate a great stock of facts about values. They thereby prepare the ground for the real philosopher in the same way that workers on a building site establish a building's foundations, erect its walls, put on its roof and divide it up into spaces (rooms). Like the builder, the philosopher labourer creates a space in which life can be pursued, but they do not do so for themselves. Human life is much more than compartmentalising things. The tasks that can be pursued in existence do not find their destination in the vision of a well-established and neatly categorised world. The philosophical labourer's task, it follows, is limited. The philosopher of the future, who must be counted as the prime example of the species of '*genuine philosophers*', is different. Their task is not one of service. Their lives are gloriously selfish. They are commanders and lawmakers: 'they say, "*thus* it *shall* be!"' (*Beyond Good and Evil*, §211). In other words, their words are *decrees:* they are beings capable of establishing the 'Where to?' and 'What for?' of humankind. With a 'creative hand', such beings extend their grasp out toward the future,

> and all that is and has been becomes a means for them, an instrument, a hammer. Their 'knowing' is *creating,* their creating is a legislation, their will to truth is – *will to power* [...] Are there such philosophers today? Have there been such philosophers? *Must* there not be such philosophers?
>
> (*Beyond Good and Evil*, §211)

Real philosophers remain figures of the future. As such, they epitomise Nietzsche's conception of humanity as an animal that is defined by its futurity.

Further reading: Deleuze 1983; Deleuze and Guattari 1994; Heller 1988; Kaufmann 1974; Magnus et al. 1993; Schacht 1983.

PLATONISM/SOCRATISM

Plato (c. 428–c. 348 BC) was a pupil of Socrates (469/70–399 BC). Socrates himself never wrote anything (at least, nothing by him has survived if he ever did) but the strength of his personality appears to have left an indelible effect on the young Plato. Socrates is the key protagonist of all the Platonic dialogues except one. In the early texts especially, the reader is usually presented with a 'confused' Socrates asking other characters for assistance in his quest for knowledge of beauty, truth, courage, virtue, etc. The more the others offer by way of their beliefs, the more Socrates asks for greater precision and clarification. The consequence of this is that Socrates' interlocutors finally end up contradicting themselves and in this way are rendered victims of 'dialectic' (a game of question and answer designed to reveal the weaknesses in an argument or belief). The so-called middle-period dialogues reveal a Socrates of more systematic inclination. This is a figure who is now more interested in the issue of whether there is a 'real world' that exists independently of the world of the senses. Such a view is propounded in the famous 'Theory of Forms' in Plato's *Republic*. According to this theory, all particulars that have common features do so because they are each of them instances of a universal. Thus, if one identifies three people it is the case for Plato that each of them shares the common feature of personhood. Each individual is an example of a universal that exists independently of them. Accordingly, on the Platonic view, one can make the same point with regard to goodness, beauty, justice and the like. Thus, any instance of something that is 'just' is an example of the 'just in itself', of something that is beautiful of the 'beautiful in itself', etc. Such knowledge as one can have of the 'just in itself', etc., is attainable not in the world of sensory experience (which is a realm sundered by eternal becoming and subject to passing away and decay) but in the realm of Ideas. Reality, in other words, is not to be found in the world of the senses (as empiricism contends) but in the realm of pure intellectuality – a realm that is independent of the body and all that characterises it. The highest expression of this is the 'good in itself', which is what provides all the other forms with their form-like characteristics (what one might call the 'formness' of the forms). The concept of an objective reality thus yields a commitment to the existence of an objective morality: Socratic dialectic asserts an essential connection to exist between our knowledge of how things are, our rational abilities and how we ought to behave. To be rational, according to Socrates, means to know the nature of reality and to act accordingly. Nietzsche's dislike of this view is readily apparent from many of his writings. Socrates, with his obsessive schematism (*Birth of Tragedy*, §14) cannot accept the view that the world pertains to an essential multiplicity. For Nietzsche, Platonism and Socratism are conceptual fetishism (see *Twilight of the Idols*, 'The Problem of Socrates'). The Socratic worship of reason betrays the demise of the governing norms that allowed Ancient Greek culture to thrive.

Further reading: Dannhauser 1974; Kaufmann 1974; Small 1987; Tejera 1987.

POLITICS

The most recent Nietzsche scholarship can be said to be distinct from earlier scholarly work by virtue of the interest shown by a significant number of important critics in the politics of his thought. Nietzsche's name was associated at the times of both world wars with forces of German military domination. Doubtless, it was this association that led many writers to downplay the question of Nietzsche's relationship and relevance to political thought. There, however, remains what Dombowsky (2002) has referred to as a 'hardly defensible' tendency 'to read Nietzsche as apolitical'. In the Anglo-American context, this apolitical strand of Nietzsche interpretation can be traced at least as far back as Walter Kaufmann's claim that Nietzsche is a 'basically "*antipolitical*"' thinker (1974, p. 412). Doubtless, Kaufmann's proximity to the aftermath of the Second World War and the misappropriation of Nietzsche by Nazi exegetes provided considerable motivation to take such a sanitising stance (Kaufmann's view of Nietzsche has been explored with insight and understanding by Pickus 2003). That this view is by no means out of fashion is evidenced by the recent interpretation of Nietzsche offered by Leiter (2002). According to Leiter, Nietzsche 'has no political philosophy, in the conventional sense of a theory of the state and its legitimacy [...] He is more accurately read [...] as a kind of *esoteric moralist,* i.e., someone who has views about human flourishing, views he wants to communicate to a select few' (2002, p. 296). Nietzsche's emphasis upon a transformation of the individual, Leiter claims, renders questionable the legitimacy of associating any notion of political change with him. There are immediate objections to this kind of approach. It is unconvincing, for example, to hold that just because someone does not have an explicitly articulated *theory* of politics this necessarily means they do not have a politics and what they say or write has no political import. (In fact, such a view is contradicted by the second essay of *On the Genealogy of Morality,* which provides an account of the origins of both the State and civil society – see Essay II, §17). At the same time, it is possible to see in this kind of reaction to overtly political interpretations a pointer to a significant problem that can beset attempts to figure Nietzsche within a political agenda. Foremost among these attempts is a tendency to harmonise Nietzsche's thought with radical democratic political attitudes and contemporary political concerns (see Connolly 1988; Hatab 1995; Warren 1988; Schrift 2000). According to Dombowsky, such readings 'never proceed without notable exclusions, and thus, their arguments are seriously compromised' (2002, pp. 278–9). Prodemocratic interpretations of Nietzsche are, for example, forced to sideline his lack of sympathy for egalitarianism, or his affirmation of the necessity of domination and exploitation. Likewise, readings intent on recuperating Nietzsche for a democratic political agenda find themselves forced to ignore the fact that his espousal of agonistics can be harmonised well enough with fascist ideologies. One could doubtless express similar reservations about other interpretations that seek to recuperate a Nietzsche fit for positive political use (see the eco-friendly reading of Nietzsche suggested by Lampert 1993, p. 279). Do such things as Nietzsche's overtly anti-democratic stance or his agonism block the possibility of recuperation for democratic purposes? According to Acampora (2003), although, as Hatab (1995) claims, it may be possible to situate Nietzsche's radicalism at the outermost edge of a democratic society, the question remains open as to how it might be possible to reconcile Nietzsche's emphasis on unbridled contest with the practical demands incumbent on any kind of democratic polity. From this, it seems that Nietzsche might be best read as a thinker who unsettles our unquestioned political habits rather than as someone who offers us easy solutions to political troubles. Conway (1997) sees Nietzsche in this light. On his view, the questions Nietzsche poses defy positive resolution in such a way as to leave us facing the stark, possibly despotic political consequences of his 'immoralism'. Nietzsche, Conway tells us, 'dares to raise a calamitous, and previously unapproachable, question of political legislation: *what ought humanity to become?*' (1997, p. 3). This is nothing less than the 'founding question of politics' – the question of political legitimacy itself. Once asked 'this question cannot be returned to oblivion, and it must change us forever' because if we take the question with the seriousness it deserves the effect of this leaves us enmeshed within 'a potentially crippling dalliance with Nietzsche's "immoralism"' since '*nothing Nietzsche says* definitively rules out the illiberal political regimes with which his name has been linked' (p. 4). Taken this way, the political ramifications of Nietzsche's work cast a questioning shadow over the terrain of political theory rather than bolstering it. Such a point finds resonance in Jürgen Habermas's contention, following Horkheimer and Adorno's *Dialectic of Enlightenment,* that Nietzsche is to be counted as one of '[t]he "black" writers of the bourgeoisie' (Habermas 1988, p. 106) in so far as he seeks to unmask the rationality of bourgeois liberalism in such a way as to question the very basis of democratic societies.

Clearly, there is little consensus concerning the manner in which we are to assess or even approach the relationship between Nietzsche and politics. Kaufmann-like attempts to ignore this issue are surely misguided. This is so not least because Nietzsche himself seems to be in little doubt concerning his own political significance: 'Only after me will there be *grand politics* on earth' (*Ecce Homo,* 'Why I Am a Destiny', §1). Thus, one can neither entirely separate Nietzsche's name from politics, nor fit him conveniently within a political agenda. One possible approach is to explore both the contemporary political background to Nietzsche's thought and his response to this in both his books and other writings. Dombowsky and Cameron have provided an essential resource in this regard (Dombowsky and Cameron 2008). Another approach is to explore the economic language present in Nietzsche's writings, a project which would at least provide the means whereby the question of the nature of Nietzsche's entanglement with the political might be addressed (see Sedgwick 2005 for an analysis of *On the Genealogy of Morality* in these terms).

Further reading: Acampora 2003; Ansell-Pearson 1991; Bergmann 1987; Dombowsky 2002; Dombowsky and Cameron 2008; Golomb and Wistrich 2002; Sedgwick 2005, 2007b; Siemens 2001b; Strong 1975.

POSTMODERNISM/DECONSTRUCTION

Postmodernism is a cultural movement often linked to the philosophy of Nietzsche and Martin Heidegger (1889–1976) and what is often perceived as their abandonment of the project of Enlightenment. David Harvey's *The Condition of Postmodernity* offers one of the most astute accounts of the postmodern. For Harvey it needs to be accounted for in socio-economic terms, specifically in relation to the decentralisation and diversification that has occurred in the marketplace (the earlier Fordist model of production concentrated in a single factory being replaced by production that coordinates diverse resources as a consequence of the search for greater flexibility of production and higher profits). Thus, the different parts of a product are made in many places and then taken to another location where they are assembled. On Harvey's account, postmodernism is in fact an extension of the social processes that Marx identified in his analysis of the nature of capitalist society. Postmodernism (at least in its philosophical guise) may well, on such a view, be considered as little more than an extended apology for capitalism. Harvey's view is well argued and convincing. Nevertheless, the word 'postmodern' has been used in so many ways that it has come to be drained of all concrete meaning. 'Postmodern architecture' is not the same as 'postmodern literature', or 'postmodern philosophy'. At best, in aesthetic terms, the postmodern might be captured by the words 'playful' and 'experimental'.

A number of important writers and thinkers have been associated with the postmodern, all of whom show clear evidence of the influence of Nietzsche: for example, Jacques Derrida, Michel Foucault and Luce Irigaray. Nevertheless, the account of post-modernity offered by Jean-François Lyotard in the short essay 'Answering the Question: What Is Postmodernism?' does not betray an inevitably Nietzschean strain of thinking. In fact, an earlier dialogue (*Just Gaming*) reveals Lyotard as someone distinctly uncomfortable with a Nietzschean politics of will to power. Lyotard's is also an overtly Kantian view – something that Nietzsche would hardly have applauded with unrestrained enthusiasm. Parallels can be made, however, between Lyotard's notion of postmodernity as bringing the replacement of 'grand narratives' in favour of 'little narratives' and aspects of Nietzsche's view of knowledge. Matters are made more complex by the fact that the later Lyotard abandoned his earlier conception of post-modernism, seeking instead to express his position in terms of 'rewriting' the project of modernity (see Lyotard 1991).

Italian philosopher Gianni Vattimo has offered a more explicitly Nietzschean account of the postmodern (see his essay 'Nihilism and the Postmodern in Philosophy' in *The End of Modernity*, Vattimo 1988). For Vattimo, Nietzsche's *Human, All Too Human* marks the initiation of a postmodern outlook. Vattimo holds this work to define modernity in terms of the activity of constant replacement (the substitution of the old – of 'custom' and 'tradition' – in favour of the new). Nietzsche then refuses to offer an escape route from modernity articulated in this form. Rather, he attempts instead to radicalise modernity by seeking to turn its own most powerful tendencies against itself. The consequence of this is the rendering of the concept of truth in terms of historical contingency rather than as exemplifying metaphysical reality (*see* **historical philosophy**). Truth is thereby rendered a matter of metaphor in so far as language becomes no more for Nietzsche than an instrument that allows us to cope with the world rather than the means of objectively describing it. One consequence of this is that with the vanishing of truth comes the death of God. For Vattimo, the path from this leads to nihilism, but this is only a prelude to the birth of postmodernity. Of course, as with so many views of Nietzsche, this account ignores many aspects of Nietzsche's thought that do not accord with its premises. Thus, Nietzsche's desire to overcome *décadence* or his conception of eternal recurrence do not sit well with Vattimo's view.

A movement associated with the postmodern is deconstruction. Although a diverse field of practice is now covered by this word, it derives principally from the writings of Derrida and De Man. Both respond to Nietzsche's problematisation of truth and his use of metaphor. For De Man, the figural language present in Nietzsche's texts produces tensions that cannot be dissolved by way of recourse to conventional methodological tools. The effect of such language is to make the text undo its own logic of argumentation. In short, texts such as Nietzsche's are self-deconstructing. Thus, when Nietzsche questions the status of logic or truth he must do so in a manner that at the same time uses the very things he questions. For de Man this does not imply that Nietzsche's thinking is simply contradictory. Rather, it is challenging the limits of our conceptual abilities in the most rigorous of ways. For Derrida, the element of metaphor in Nietzsche also undoes the logic of his own claims. Thus, when he discusses women and truth in such terms, he can be read as destabilising the nature of such concepts and thereby radically throwing them into question. Derridean deconstruction, however, is no Nietzscheanism. It is far more Kantian in spirit in so far as it seeks to preserve a transcendental element in performing a critique of the domain of metaphysics. In some respects, the Kantian connection allies Derrida's work with Lyotard's. However, the two thinkers might be fruitfully contrasted in terms of how they approach Kant's oeuvre: where Derrida seeks to extend the transcendentalism of the first *Critique* (*The Critique of Pure Reason*), Lyotard concentrates on the logic of the sublime as developed in the third (i.e. *The Critique of Judgement*).

Further reading: Allison 1985, 2001; Behler 1991; De Man 1979; Diethe 2003; Giddens 1990; Habermas 1988; Hartman 1979; Harvey 1989; Hassan 1987; Jenks 1991; Koelb 1990; Lyotard 1988, 1989, 1991; Norris 1986, 1987, 1988; Rorty 1978, 1991; Sadler 1995; Schrift 1990; Vattimo 1988, 2002.

PREHISTORY

The term 'prehistory' refers to 'the tremendous eras of "morality of custom" which precede "world history"' (*Daybreak*, §18). This period consists of 'the *actual and decisive eras of history which determined the character of mankind*' (*Daybreak*, §18). For Nietzsche, it is in the era of prehistory that the essential aspects of human nature are determined. To put the matter another way, all of our most characteristic features have been fixed firmly in place long before our kind was ever tempted to dwell upon its own metaphysical, psychological or material constitution. The prehistoric world that Nietzsche paints is the reflected image of our own. It is an alien world, in so far as in it customary valuations of today are reversed. It is in this sense an inverted reflection of the present. Thus, in human prehistory, Nietzsche says, violent atrocity, deception, vengefulness, and denial of rationality were all counted virtues. Well-being, a hunger for knowledge, pity and the desire for peace were considered as dangerous; being pitied for something and engaging in work were regarded as matter of disgrace. More than this even, the epoch of prehistory was where the realm of human existence as a domain of meaningfulness was fixed. The degree to which we are today capable of endowing life with sense is something that we owe to this primeval epoch. Prehistoric times are also characterised by Nietzsche as the ones in which the concept of the fixed and unchanging was celebrated for the first time as being of the highest value. Change, in contrast, was taken to be something immoral (i.e. uncustomary) and, as such, was regarded as being 'pregnant with disaster' (*Daybreak*, §18). The term 'prehistory' hence refers to the formative period of human identity, the era in which an unknowing prehistoric humanity laid down the conditions of its future possible development through unconsciously fashioning its own defining characteristics. Prehistory points forward to us, but does so with no predetermined necessity. It is the epoch in which the conditions whereby humanity today draws up its decisive conclusions about the world were fabricated. Our prehistoric forebears were creatures of custom, and it is this which determines in a decisive sense the kinds of beings we are today: 'Do you think all this has altered and that mankind must therefore have changed its character?' If you do then think again! (*Daybreak*, §18). Becoming, Nietzsche holds, exerts an unbreakable grip on human development, and it is because of this that humankind is better comprehended as the articulation of a long-term and complex development. One consequence of this is that although we are today beings of modernity, the modern conceals within it unrelentingly primeval elements. The prehistoric era hence marks the emergence of a specifically human psychology characterised by the development of reason and conceptual thought, language, feelings of bad conscience and guilt. Prehistory is the realm of pure animality, made manifest in modern life in the fantasy that characterises outlandish dreams or loss of sanity (*Daybreak*, §312). Such 'primal experiences' are repressed by culture. For Nietzsche, if one wishes to discover what kind of being 'the animal man' is one must turn to prehistory for clarification. The 'real problem *of* humankind' is, it follows, a prehistoric rather than merely contemporary problem (*Genealogy*, Essay II, §1). In the

Genealogy, an exploration of this prehistory shows how humanity ends up being the kind of animal endowed with the ability to make promises – an ability that distinguishes us from all other animals.

See also: **morality of custom**.

Further reading: Sedgwick 2005.

PROMISE

Promising, according to the account Nietzsche gives in the second essay of *On the Genealogy of Morality,* is the precondition of a properly human existence. Our ability to promise endows us (well, a few of us) with the potential for genuine autonomy (exemplified by the sovereign individual, see *Genealogy,* Essay II, §2). The *Genealogy* offers an account of how this ability came about in the era of prehistory. Our prehistoric ancestors were creatures driven by their passions. They were also driven, for reasons of survival, into a mode of existence that involved ever-closer social cooperation. The well-being of the primitive social body hence ultimately took precedence over that of the individual, with the consequence that the individual's behaviour had to be mastered, its spontaneous passions kept in check, in order to ensure the safety and future of the community. The creation of the means of securing social stability, for Nietzsche, marks the beginning of the era of the morality of custom. Consider what happens in a situation of this kind. Forms of behaviour dangerous to the social body are discouraged by extreme punishments. The notion that one ought not to do something is, in other words, quite literally beaten and burned into the individual, who is thereby forced to associate certain actions with pain and as a result understand that they are not to be tolerated. The use of such a cruel mnemonics is, Nietzsche argues, essential to the emergence of the human animal. For, by way of such devices our ancestors learned not only to promise but also, in consequence of this requirement, became self-interpreting beings. The reason for this resides in the preconditions that must be in place in order for a promise to be made. Promises don't simply happen – if they did, the animal world would be replete with mice, cats and dogs making promises all over the place. Promises presuppose that the one who makes the promise can do so meaningfully. A promiser must have certain attributes that render them capable both of making the promise and fulfilling it. They must, for example, be able to understand the difference between past, present and future; to have made a promise presupposes that one grasps the difference between past commitments, present states and future possible situations and acts accordingly. The brute force of social conformity inculcates such abilities by regularising the individual, by forming each person in the community in terms of a common identity. To be a promiser, in other words, means being like one's fellow promisers; it means being predictable: only if we are all alike in the sense that it can be predicted that each of us will (generally) adhere to the commitments entailed by communal living can the community survive. Initially, such predictability is articulated solely in terms of the individual's relation to the community as a whole, and it is here that self-understanding originates. The individual becomes an 'I' only in virtue of his or her relation to the community. In the primitive community, the 'I' is from the first a debtor: I exist only in virtue of the community and, in consequence, I owe it my life. The community, in consequence, is a creditor and, should the communal contract (the rules that make social life possible) be broken, can call in the debt on any individual by demanding their punishment or death. This is why, as Zarathustra tells us, the 'you' is much older than the 'I' (see **self**). The long-term consequence of such discipline, Nietzsche argues, is the creation of the autonomous individual. A person endowed with autonomy of this kind is subject to the power of their own word and will. Equally, such a person has already sloughed off the tyrannical conditions that gave rise to their abilities. Where being 'moral' means adhering to the norm, being free means acting according to one's own values. Morality is, in this sense, a mere means to an end, rather than an end in itself.

PSYCHOLOGY

Nietzsche holds it to be inexorably the case that our most ambitious flights of fancy in the realm of metaphysical and moral thought are destined to fall back to earth with a bump. Such human aspirations are 'all too human'. The philosopher's search for truth reveals itself to be something rooted in contingency, as turning on 'some popular superstition or other [...] perhaps some play on words, a grammatical seduction, or an audacious generalization' that springs from the realm of the personal (*Beyond Good and Evil,* Preface). Meditation concerning the human, all too human has another name: it is called 'psychological observation' (*Human, All Too Human*, §35). Psychological reflection is a helpful means of coping with the traumas of life. With it one can 'pluck useful maxims from the thorniest and most disagreeable stretches of one's own life and thereby feel a little better: that was believed, that was known – in former centuries' (*Human, All Too Human*, §35). Psychological enquiry, it follows, is nothing new. Why, Nietzsche asks, are there no longer figures such as La Rochefoucauld (the seventeenth-century aphorist) ready to offer us psychological insight? In short, we need psychology. However useful it is in daily life, moreover, *science* cannot do without it (*Human, All Too Human*, §38). That said, psychology up to now has been too limited; it has been fettered by the force of 'moral prejudices' (*Beyond Good and Evil*, §23). What is needed, Nietzsche argues, is a 'genuine psychology' capable of resisting our most deeply held beliefs, a psychology that asks uncomfortable questions and welcomes uncomfortable answers. It may be the case that what are generally regarded as dreadful things (e.g. rancour, greed, lust for power) may be essential to the economy of human existence as a means to its enhancement. To engage in enquiring into such things is a daring adventure, for Nietzsche. Witness the manner in which he envisages an exploration of the terrain of the '*real history*' of morality in the Preface to *On the Genealogy of Morality*. Psychology is an essential tool, then, and it needs once more to 'be recognized as the queen of the sciences' (*Beyond Good and Evil*, §23). This may be a slight aimed at Kant, who regarded metaphysics as rightly occupying such a royal position (see the introduction to his *Critique of Pure Reason*). Psychology *not* metaphysics, Nietzsche argues, is 'the road to the fundamental problems' (*Beyond Good and Evil*, §23). This pursuit takes Nietzsche on a journey through the morality of custom (i.e. the normative regulation that fashioned the psychology of the human animal in the era of prehistory). In turn, the journey leads to his analysis of noble and slave morality in the *Genealogy*, and finally to the account offered of the 'psychology of the Redeemer' (*Antichrist*, §29) in *The Antichrist*. One should note, however, that as his thought matures Nietzsche understands the term 'psychology' in increasingly complex ways. As is clear from *Beyond Good and Evil*, §23, psychology is never for him a matter of telling interesting stories about 'the mind', i.e. of grasping the nature of intellect in a manner that ignores its essential embodiment. Psychology is always a matter of the body, of the moulding of the self through social practices and of the relationship between the realm of the social and the drives. In other words, psychology is a matter of physiology, too. *Twilight of the Idols* proffers psychological accounts of how beliefs are cleaved to in virtue of the dominance of habits (see 'The Four Great Errors', §5: 'The banker thinks at once of "business", the Christian of "sin", the girl of her love'). But it also renders values in terms of the more bodily language of 'symptoms': 'Morality is merely a sign-language, merely symptomatology' ('The "Improvers" of Mankind', §1; see also 'The Four Great Errors', §1).

Further reading: Kaufmann 1974; Golomb 1989; Parkes 1991, 1994.

REASON

Nietzsche's treatment of the concept of reason might provoke his readers to level charges of ambiguity and inconsistency against him. There are times when Nietzsche talks of reason as being amongst the most valuable of human achievements: 'Nothing has been purchased more dearly than that little bit of human reason and feeling of freedom that now constitutes our pride' (*Daybreak,* §18). Likewise, 'reason, knowledge, [and] enquiry' are on occasion opposed by him to deluded metaphysical belief (*Antichrist,* §23). Reason, when considered thus, appears to be allied with the sciences (although Nietzsche's attitude toward science and scholarship is complex and hard to reduce to one viewpoint). Reason can also be the 'great reason' that Nietzsche affirms with regard to embodied existence – a view put forward in *Thus Spoke Zarathustra* (*Zarathustra,* Part I, 'On the Afterworldly'; for a further discussion of this, *see* **self**). On the other hand, reason, as it has traditionally been understood, is the domain of the worst of human errors and illusions. Above all, the errors in question are linked to language. Language seduces. To a decisive degree, language constitutes our habits of thought in such a way as to make us their uncritical devotees. Within language, 'the fundamental errors of reason [are] petrified' (*Genealogy,* Essay I, §13). These frozen errors include such things as the belief that agency (as it is understood in relation to a conscious thinking subject) is the necessary precondition of all action, that substances, things, unities, stable identities, causes, being are words that denote a reality that exists independently of our mental habits and concrete concerns. Rationality, it follows, is an achievement about which we can feel some pride; but we are also prey to becoming its unwitting dupes. Our pride is misplaced as soon as we construe the significance of our rational abilities in the wrong manner. Reason is a means of coping; it is a 'tool' (*Beyond Good and*

Evil, §191) and, like every instrument, ought not to be confused with the domain to which its instrumental nature allows it to be related for practical aims. It is, it follows, one thing to claim for reason a specific (even positive) value as a tool but quite another to claim that this tool has value 'in itself'. The problem with philosophy, for the most part, is that it has all too often been led to construe reality to be determined according to rational prerequisites (e.g. the demands of logic). At its worst, this has resulted in the promulgation of philosophies of being. Philosophies of this kind conceal a conceptual fetishism which regards all that challenges the purported fixity of the concept as unworthy of serious consideration (*Twilight of the Idols*, '"Reason" in Philosophy', §5). This tendency underlies all philosophies that, like Plato's, denigrate 'appearance' and the empirical realm of the senses in favour of the unchanging 'reality' of the concept. One of Nietzsche's central complaints here is that the domain of reason and concept is, on this mistaken conception, simplistically opposed to that of the body and passion. For Platonism, the intellect and the senses do not mix since they are different in kind, the former derivative of the latter. The roots of this tendency are to be found in Plato's great teacher, Socrates. The Socratic account of rationality, which holds the passions to be chaotic and degenerate and reason the most perfect and refined of modes of existence, places reason at loggerheads with instinct (*Twilight*, 'The Problem of Socrates', §10). According to Nietzsche, Socrates does so because the instincts of his times (i.e. the norms that made up the unquestioned habitual terrain of everyday life in Socrates' contemporary world) are on the decline. Reason was forced upon Socrates:

> If one needs to make a tyrant of *reason*, as Socrates did, then there must exist no little danger of something else playing the tyrant. Rationality was at the time divined as a *saviour*; neither Socrates nor his 'invalids' were free to be rational or not, it was *de rigeur*, it was their last expedient.
>
> (*Twilight*, 'The Problem of Socrates', §10)

In other words, reason as the philosophical tradition since Plato has understood it does not really find its ground in the objectivity of 'higher' knowledge but rather emerges from a cultural crisis. Socrates and his Greeks 'had only one choice: either perish or – be *absurdly rational*' (*Twilight*, 'The Problem of Socrates', §10). Reason, it follows, has come traditionally to be opposed to passion and instinct not on any universal grounds but for contingent reasons to do with expediency.

Platonic dialectic, which asserts that a rational individual will, in virtue of their reason, necessarily act morally and attain happiness, seeks to counter the 'dark desires' of its time by bathing them in a purportedly eternal light of reason (*Twilight*, 'The Problem of Socrates', §10). Nietzsche's criticism of this conception of rationality, it should be noted here, also concerns the connection that it asserts to exist between reason and morality. Nietzsche's aim is to overturn moral presuppositions that uncritically conjoin reason, value, truth and human fulfilment (happiness) – a project related to his conception of what philosophy is really able to achieve (i.e. that it is a creative rather than merely descriptive enterprise). To claim a necessary connection between reason and morality, as Plato does, is to assert not merely that morality has an objective, rational basis but that morality is opposed to passion and desire. Nietzsche's contempt for this view resides in his belief that passion and reason are by no means diametrically opposed. On the contrary, passion and reason are closely connected, for the latter rests upon the former:

> Passion is degraded (1) as if it were only in unseemly cases, and not necessarily and always, the motive force; (2) in as much as it has for its object something of no great value, amusement – The misunderstanding of passion and reason, as if the latter were an independent entity and not rather a system of relations between various passions and desires; as if every passion did not possess its quantum of reason.
>
> (*Will to Power*, §387)

Thus, it is pure delusion to think of passions or drives as 'mere inclinations' lacking all purposive rationality. All passions have their reasons (their functional value), and it is this conception that finds its full articulation in the notion of the 'great reason' of the self already mentioned. 'Feeling', it follows, is not by definition the opposite of reasoning, for all reasoning is always an ordering of the passions and their relative modes of rationality with regard to one another; and this is where its value as a 'tool' resides. Nietzsche, it follows, does not ask us to abandon reason but, rather, to rethink the question of what it is. In this regard, one is taken from the discussion presented in a late text such as *Twilight of the Idols* back ten years to the concluding page of what is often held to be Nietzsche's first mature work, *Human, All Too Human*. Here, the reader is told that this book's aim is to bring reason to 'reason', i.e. to make us aware of the need to have a conception of rationality that is realistic and sensible.

Further reading: Haar 1996; Poellner 1995; Schacht 1983.

REVALUATION OF VALUES

Nietzsche tells us that he is a thinker prepared to offer what are, to anyone uncritically immersed in modernity, unpalatable truths (*Beyond Good and Evil*, §202). This means, amongst other things, beginning by asserting brutally enough that humans are animals, not in any metaphorical sense but literally. The metaphorical possibilities, however, can be rather too tempting: people of 'modern ideas', Nietzsche continues, are not merely animals but 'herd animals', creatures who crave a state of eternal moral certitude and an accompanying feeling of belonging at the cost of experimental daring. Nietzsche's hopes lie elsewhere, in a vision of '*new philosophers*' who dare to overturn, 'revalue and reverse "eternal values"' (*Beyond Good and Evil*, §203). To teach a revaluation of values means to attend to the question of the future of humankind by embracing the task of overcoming Christianity, with its ideal of pious, selfless virtue. The revaluation demands 'a critique of moral values, *the value of these values should itself, for once, be examined*' (*On the Genealogy of Morality*, Preface, §6). To embark upon such a project involves asking about the history of morality, to engage in the attempt to elucidate the conditions under which values were formed, developed and altered. The project of revaluation is thereby one that seeks to render morality itself questionable.

The practice of revaluation, it turns out, is not entirely new, according to Nietzsche. It originates in the historical precedent set by the Jews of the ancient world. The Jews, the authors of the Old Testament and source of the Christian tradition, were the first revaluers of values (*Genealogy*, Essay I, §7; *Beyond Good and Evil*, §46). The Jews, as the originators of slave morality, represent a revaluation that stands as a rebellion against the dominance of noble values in ancient society. Such a revaluation is an act of spiritual revenge aimed at the originators of moral discourse. Christianity, for Nietzsche, stands as the inheritor of this revaluation: its values are the values of *ressentiment* writ large and dressed up in the garb of transcendence (*Genealogy*, Essay I, §8). Christian values represent 'the revaluation of all Aryan values, the victory of Chandala values, the evangel preached to the poor and lowly, the collective rebellion of everything downtrodden, wretched, ill-constituted' (*Twilight of the Idols*, 'The "Improvers" of Mankind', §4). It is against this Judaeo-Christian revaluation that Nietzsche's own is targeted. The revaluation Nietzsche toys with towards the end of his mentally active life may be something which he is tempted to regard as being exclusively within the sphere of his achievement (*Ecce Homo*, 'Why I Am So Wise', §1). We are told in

§27 of the third essay of the *Genealogy* that he is at work on just such a project that will be entitled *The Will to Power: Attempt at a Revaluation of All Values*. It is also considered as having been to some extent brought to fruition the following year by the text of *The Antichrist* (*Antichrist*, §62). Yet the revaluation remains a notion that is elusive. Probably it is best summarised by the conclusion of the first essay of the *Genealogy*, which makes the following demand: '*All* sciences must, from now on, prepare the way for the future work of the philosopher: this work being understood to mean that the philosopher has to solve the *problem of values* and that he has to decide on the *hierarchy of values*' (*Genealogy*, Essay I, §17). The means of doing so, we are told in the preface to this text, is offered by the criterion of life. Ultimately, the notion of valuing values suggests something paradoxical. It is an injunction to tread a path of enquiry that will be fraught with contradiction and uncertainty. However, this perhaps is exactly what Nietzsche wants us to do.

Further reading: Kaufmann 1974; Schacht 1983.

SCIENCE

For the mature Nietzsche, science at its best is 'gay science' (*'gaya scienza'*). One needs to bear in mind here that the word 'science' (*'Wissenschaft'*) does not for him, as in contemporary English parlance, denote only the 'hard' physical sciences. Science, as Nietzsche understands and promotes it, is better grasped as 'scholarship' and 'critical enquiry'. 'Gay science' exemplifies this: it is joyous science, a practice of enquiry that is diverse, self-critical, engaged and engaging, undogmatic and open-ended, methodologically experimental. At its most beneficial, science is about method. It yields methodological insight. At its worst, it can take such insights and hypostatise them in a manner akin to that of metaphysics. Thus, when the physicist is tempted to speak of 'nature's conformity to law', Nietzsche judges accordingly (*Beyond Good and Evil*, §22). A view of this kind bears testimony to hidden interests (not least, the democratic soul of modernity). To speak of a 'law of nature' is to go too far, for it presupposes a nature little different from that presupposed by ancient Stoic philosophy (*Beyond Good and Evil*, §9). Understood aright, 'physics too is only an interpretation and arrangement of the world (according to our own requirements, if I may say so!) and not an *explanation* of the world' (*Beyond Good and Evil*, §14). Although it can be liberating with regard to some of our cruder prejudices, science does not escape entirely from them. Indeed, the presupposition that science simply overcomes metaphysics by explaining reality in causal-mechanistic terms (as the physics of Nietzsche's times does) merely reinvents the same old anthropological delusions of the past. At its best, science is subtle description. Scientific concepts, in other words, do no more than describe better what earlier discursive practices sought to describe (sometimes rather badly).

Whatever its virtues (and there are many, as Nietzsche's conception of historical philosophy shows), there is one thing science is not and can never be. Science is not philosophy. Put simply, it is a matter of dogged descriptive discipline versus creative freedom and power. Philosophy properly understood is about invention – most specifically, it concerns itself with the creation of values: '*Actual philosophers* [...] *are commanders and law-givers:* it is they who determine the Wherefore and Whither of mankind' (*Beyond Good and Evil*, §211). Such beings exemplify human futurity. They make use of the achievements that the sciences and the work of 'philosophical labourers' bequeath to them for truly creative purposes. Science, in contrast, can never provide such leadership. This is so not least, Nietzsche argues, because science remains in thrall to the ascetic ideal. It is, in fact, this ideal's most subtle and powerful development for it encourages genuine self-reflexivity. Science is, it follows, a necessary starting point for embarking on the adventure of philosophical enquiry, but it is not, for Nietzsche, to be mistaken for its purpose or as being something able to supply philosophy with a purpose. Another way of putting this would be to say that Nietzsche is a fan of science, but he is not its uncritical emulator.

Further reading: Babich 1994; Babich and Cohen 1999; Moore and Brobjer 2004.

SELF

According to Nietzsche, philosophers have always had a tendency to consider the self to be equivalent in meaning to the word 'I'. In other words, they have tended to take the notion of consciousness as offering an exhaustive account of human nature. Nietzsche disagrees with this profoundly. For him, the 'I' is not the self but a development of it. We are intellectual/spiritual beings who are endowed with creative potential, and this must be acknowledged and explored.

However, our spiritual nature has never been adequately treated by the approach adopted by philosophers such as Plato or Descartes (*see* **Platonism/Socratism, Cartesianism**) and their assertion of the absolute purity of the intellect or mind over and above the body. For Nietzsche, the self and the intellect are best grasped in terms of the body and drives. One of the most revealing discussions he offers is in *Thus Spoke Zarathustra*. According to Zarathustra, human existence may be characterised in the most spiritual of terms. Yet, even so, the spirit cannot be discussed without invoking the body at the same time. The spirit or intellect can go through transformations (*Thus Spoke Zarathustra*, Part I, 'Of the Three Metamorphoses') but from this any belief in the spirit being different in kind from the body cannot be inferred. Thus, Zarathustra also attacks those who proclaim belief in an afterlife (*Zarathustra*, Part I, 'On the Afterworldly'). Believers in afterworlds regard the world of the senses as an illusion, says Zarathustra. For them, living always involves the presence of a witness in the shape of a God who looks on as the ultimate beholder and judge of the universe he has made. The believer's reality is dialogical rather than monological (*see* **art**) because for them solitude is an impossibility. We are inclined to believe in afterworlds for concrete reasons, for they are an expression of 'suffering and incapacity' (*Zarathustra*, Part I, 'On the Afterworldly'). Afterworlds gain their power from the fact that suffering *in this life* is compensated for by thoughts of an imaginary future cleansed of pain. What this in reality signifies, according to Zarathustra, is that the body has wearied of itself. Metaphysics is testimony to exhaustion and the power of the body: 'a poor ignorant weariness [...] created all gods and afterworlds [...] it was the body that despaired of the body [...] it was the body that despaired of the earth and heard the belly of being speak to it' (*Zarathustra*, Part I, 'On the Afterworldly'). The sufferer's bodily exhaustion forces them to look for metaphysical comfort to counter what they cannot otherwise endure any more. In contrast, it is 'the healthy body' that 'speaks of the meaning of the earth', says Zarathustra (*Zarathustra*, Part I, 'On the Afterworldly').

Afterworlds originate in us but are themselves 'inhuman' and bespeak sterility. Importantly, the desire for metaphysical consolation does not emanate from a realm of disembodied spirituality. Rather, it has its origins in the body. And these origins point to something essential about the nature of the human spirit or intellect. The 'I' is the source of the *articulation* of metaphysical comfort; in other words, the 'I' utters the words that comfort and pacify us when we suffer.

However, the linguistically codified speaker who says 'I' is not, according to Nietzsche, the motivating force and wellspring of belief. The 'I' enunciates. However, what speaks through the 'I' is something other and greater, an entity that embraces consciousness but is yet greater than it. This entity is the body:

> Indeed, this ego and the ego's contradiction and confusion still speak most honestly of its being – this creating, willing, valuing ego, which is the measure and value of things [...] speaks of the body and still wants the body, even when it poetizes and raves and flutters with broken wings.
>
> (*Zarathustra*, Part I, 'On the Afterworldly')

Thus, when the 'I' speaks, it is obliged to acknowledge its embodiment. To be a person with otherworldly yearnings is to be someone who wishes to deny the reality of their own embodiment. Ironically, of course, even as such a person denies this reality they are driven to assert it simply in order to speak. Otherworldly 'realities' delude us about the self. They are fanciful projections instituted within the subterranean realm of bodily demands, wish-fulfilments that rely upon the insurmountable priority of the body whose reality they seek to deny.

Occasionally, Nietzsche speculates about the adequacy of even the notion of the body, but in the end the body is the thing we must believe in most:

> in all ages there has been more faith in the body [...] It has never occurred to anyone to regard his stomach as a strange or, say, a divine stomach: but to conceive his ideas as 'inspired', his evaluations as 'implanted by God' [...] – for this tendency and taste in men there are witnesses from all ages of mankind [...] For the present, belief in the body is always stronger than belief in the spirit; and whoever desires to undermine it, also undermines at the same time most thoroughly belief in the authority of the spirit!
>
> (*Will to Power*, §659)

The body reveals itself as a complex totality. It is an ordered hierarchy (*Zarathustra*, Part I, 'On the Despisers of the Body'). Thus, even though it may be the case that we are tempted to consider the 'mind' or consciousness as the highest expression human complexity and abstract ability, for Nietzsche the body exceeds our greatest imaginings of complexity. The body is 'a great reason, a plurality with one sense, a war and peace, a herd and a shepherd' (*Zarathustra*, Part I, 'On the Despisers of the Body'). In this regard, the body combines socially and hierarchically distinct roles: it is both ruler and ruled. In contrast to this, the diminutive rationality of the conscious mind is a mere 'instrument', a tool subject to the whims of this superior reason.

The self, it follows, is not defined by way of the concept of consciousness. It is not the 'I' of the Cartesian *cogito*, nor the transcendental 'I think' of Kantianism. The self is no mere collection of mental attributes susceptible to being encountered, counted and classified by an introspective self-consciousness but is, rather, a multiplicity. It is an assemblage of heterogeneous elements for which the word 'body' must stand as a rather attenuated and insufficient summary. This claim, however, does not mean that one can take Nietzsche to be yet another exponent of empiricism. On his view, the body can no more be reduced to a collection of sensory impressions than to the mode of abstract self-consciousness called 'mind' or 'intellect'. An empiricist thinks of the self as no more than a passive receptor of bodily sense impressions. Nietzsche, however, considers the relationship between *cogito,* body and self in other terms:

> 'I', you say, and are proud of the word. But greater is that in which you do not wish to have faith – your body and its great reason: that does not say 'I', but does 'I'. What the sense feels, what the spirit knows, never has its end in itself [...] Instruments and toys are sense and spirit: behind them still lies the self. The self also seeks with the eyes of the senses; it also listens with the ears of the spirit. Always the self listens and seeks: it compares, overpowers, conquers, destroys. It controls, and it is in control of the ego too. Behind your thoughts and feelings [...] there stands a mighty ruler, an unknown sage – whose name is self. In your body he dwells; he is your body. There is more reason in your body than in your best wisdom [...] Your self laughs at your ego and its bold leaps. 'What are these leaps and flights of thought to me?' it says to itself. 'A detour to my end. I am the leading string of the ego and the prompter of its concepts'.
>
> (*Zarathustra,* 'On the Despisers of the Body')

The self is a 'body'. Without its embodiment the self could not exist. Yet, the self is no mere 'thing' in the sense that an entity like a pen or a rock that is just discovered as something handy and waiting to be picked up unthinkingly is a mere thing-at-hand. Because the self is an entity it is necessarily embodied, but bodies can be of different kinds. Some are like pens and stones, in so far as events happen to them in such a way that they are always going to be victims of accident or will: the stone just lies where it happens to have rolled to; the pen rests on the table or in the gutter where it has been forgotten or lost having been used without a thought. The self, in contrast, is an entity in a different sense, for it is a *doer*. The essence of the self is activity. As such, it never merely exists but is in such a way that its engagements characterise it in an essential manner. The self's activity is, in fact, characterised by power relationships. As is clear from the above quotation, Nietzsche envisages the thinking, conscious 'I' as an abstraction and tool of the self's greater reason. Thus, the self hovers over the 'I' like an arch-surveyor and commander. The watching and listening nature of the self indicates its superiority, for it is that which always commands. Without the self and the power relations it embodies there could be no 'I', since reason for the existence of the 'I' resides in its allotted task of satisfying the self's demands. Thus, the self provides aims and makes reasons, using the senses and the mind as instruments in order to satisfy its commandments.

The self is thus a ruler and the 'I' its slave. Like all rulers, the self determines what the 'I' endures or enjoys. Yet, this determination is done in such a manner that it remains largely invisible to consciousness. As far as the conscious 'I' is concerned, the self is not an object of everyday awareness. The characterisation offered here of the self as simultaneously unknown and wise succinctly expresses its power over the 'I', for it is a 'mighty ruler' whose resplendent power is enhanced by its invisibility in the same manner as the God of the Old Testament has power of such divinity he can neither be looked upon nor represented. This invisibility at the same time denotes a structure akin to the façade of a building. Just as a building's façade hides its structure, so the 'I', if considered only at face value, conceals the hierarchical relations that constitute the self. In this sense, the 'I' is like the members of a community who fail to realise the degree to which they are subject to the rule of a superior force when they follow that community's conventions. We may aspire to transcendence by way of conscious thought, by the 'I's' flights of fancy, but the notion of such thought as freedom is an illusion. The 'I' can no more be liberated from the environment necessary to its existence than the body can stop breathing and continue to exist.

Clearly, the relationship between intellect and self as Nietzsche envisages it is always to be grasped in terms of a political and social structure. It is a social order in microcosm. The 'I' is a kind of subjected citizen, a subject of the crown, who experiences, thinks and decides only in so far as these activities in reality spring from its unperceived ruler. Thus, when told by the body to feel pain, the 'I' feels pain and wonders how this pain can be stopped, 'and that is why it is *made* to think' (*Zarathustra,* Part I, 'On the Despisers of the Body'). Joy likewise betrays the same relationship. Five features emerge from Zarathustra's discussion of the self:

1. The self is embodied and unthinkable without embodiment.
2. It is always superior to consciousness.
3. It is characterised in terms of relations of power (indeed, will to power).
4. The self is a kind of unity.
5. The self is encapsulated by notions of activity and creativity.

The self, in short, is a complex totality or, speaking like Kant, one might deem it a synthetic unity (*Zarathustra,* Part I, 'On the Despisers of the Body'). However, the apparent spontaneity of conscious thought, which Kant, as a thinker of Enlightenment, takes to be indicative of the subject's freedom, is by this account rendered pure illusion. Freedom, in turn, is not secured by liberating the hapless 'I' from its despotic ruler's grasp. 'Freedom' thought of thus is a delusion that has the opposite consequence of being liberating. In so far as philosophy has been tempted to think of consciousness as independent and superior to the embodied self it has imprisoned itself in metaphysical illusions as despotic and intellectually damaging as any tyranny can be. The 'I', rather, is miraculous precisely because it springs from this complex set of relationships and what makes personhood valuable is something that can only be truly grasped in the aftermath of this insight. What matters for Nietzsche is the realisation that the 'I' has a history. Thus, the 'I' emerges from the activities of a body shaped (often violently) by normative procedures (see Essay II of *On the Genealogy of Morality*) and is governed by the socially regimented logic of commanding (i.e. by the relations of power) that endows it with a will.

Further reading: Butler 2000; Thiele 1991; Schacht 1983.

SELF-OVERCOMING

'All great things bring about their own demise through an act of self-sublimation: that is the law of life, the law of *necessary* "self-overcoming" in the essence of life – the lawgiver is himself always exposed to the cry *"patere legem, quam ipse tulisti"* [submit to the law you yourself have made]' (*Genealogy*, Essay III, §27). Self-overcoming is hence a notion that denotes both limits and the means to their dissolution. It is, for Nietzsche, the rule that all acts of legislation, fashioning, forming by way of codes and norms produce outcomes that exceed the conditions that gave rise to them. The creation of a law, for example, always brings with it the potential that it will be applied to those who originated it. All things, in short, can be turned back upon themselves. The consequence of such a turning back is no mere formal negation but a simultaneous annulling and uplifting, a sublimation, whereby the origin itself is both retained and yet transformed into something new. A good example of this is provided by Nietzsche's discussion of the poet and writer J. W. von Goethe (*Twilight of the Idols*, 'Expeditions of an Untimely Man', §49). Goethe is a self-overcoming of the spirit of the eighteenth century: he stands both as a product of his era and yet negates it by transcending its mechanistic and rationalistic limitations. Such transcendence, however, is not achieved by way of an act of destructive barbarism but through *reinterpretation*. As the embodied reinterpretation of his times, Goethe both epitomises them and yet steps beyond them, simultaneously making manifest the potential hidden with his era even as he represents its passing. An equally telling example of self-overcoming is offered by Christianity. Christianity cultivates the 'will to truth', but in so doing creates a demand for truthfulness that turns back with a critical eye on the Christian faith and finds it wanting.

Further reading: Kaufmann 1974; Pollard 1988.

SLAVE MORALITY

Slave morality is the mode of ethical evaluation whose ancient origins lie in the psychology of those subjugated and hence moulded by others more powerful (i.e. nobles) (see *Genealogy*, Essay I, §§1 ff.). Whereas noble morality begins with an act of self-affirmation, the slave's initial positing of value starts with an act of negation. The noble class is that of the oppressor. The noble is a being of domination and bringer of suffering, who is deemed by the victims of his or her actions to be 'evil'. This reaction to noble oppression is the slave's initial evaluative gesture. Only after this, as a kind of afterthought and after-effect of this initial reactive judgement, does the slave come to affirm him- or herself as 'good'. For Nietzsche, the history of ethics is characterised by the ensuing struggle between noble and slave moralities, the outcome of which (in Europe, at least) is the victory of slave morality in the form of Christianity. What is judged to be the 'good' of ethics is thereby rooted in the hatred that the slave feels towards the victimising noble. The slave is a being of *ressentiment*. This psychological state forms the basis for the slave's positing of value. Nietzsche argues that the roots of *ressentiment* morality are to be found in the history of the Jews. In 'Jewish hatred' for the Roman oppressor lie the seeds of Christian faith and morality. One must note in this context, however, that although much of the most vehement rhetoric of the *Genealogy* and *The Antichrist* could be taken to mean that Nietzsche detests slave morality and all that is associated with it, favouring instead a resurgence of noble morality, this is not the case. It may be possible to see history as a war between these contending methods of evaluation (*Genealogy*, Essay I, §16) but, in spite of his revulsion when it comes to aspects of Christian morality, Nietzsche does not in fact argue at any point that one evaluative attitude is 'superior'. The noble's view of the world may indeed be 'healthier', but without *ressentiment* morality and a key figure associated with it (i.e. the ascetic priest) there would have been no humanity worth speaking of (*Genealogy*, Essay I, §7). Nobles may be life-affirming and well-constituted (to use some of Nietzsche's favoured rhetoric), but they are ultimately pretty stupid. The powerless, in contrast, have the benefit of intellect – or rather they have been obliged to develop their intellect by circumstances. Were it not for the intellect of those who lack power being introduced into and becoming part of human nature, Nietzsche argues, the history of humanity would not be worth anything much at all. Slave morality may stem from rancorous origins (rather than from the sentiment of love commonly associated with it) but it is not to be condemned for this reason. Nor, for that matter, is Christianity criticised by Nietzsche on account of its origins. What is worthy of criticism in Christian morals is a matter that concerns the futurity of humanity, its potential for perfection. The origins of something, Nietzsche tells us in *Genealogy*, Essay II, §13, do not serve to explain its significance. The point of Nietzsche's exposure of what he holds to be the rancorous origins of Christian morality is not so much to explain its significance as to disabuse us of any fondly held beliefs we might cleave to concerning the purity of Christian love. The divine origins that Christianity asserts to underlie its values are denied it: historical explanation is a more powerful refutation than any other form of argument (*Daybreak*, §95). Nietzsche's main objection to Christianity rests upon his contention that its norms fashion a humanity that is far from his ideal of the Overman.

Further reading: Allison 2001; Ansell-Pearson 1991; Kaufmann 1974; Owen and Ridley 2000; Schacht 1983, 1994.

SOVEREIGN INDIVIDUAL

The being that Nietzsche presents in *On the Genealogy of Morality* (Essay II, §§2–3) as the outcome and justification of the contingent and violent prehistorical events that gave rise to humanity. The sovereign individual is the outcome of the development under the tyranny of the morality of custom that gave rise to a humanity that could make promises and keep to its word. This ability, when broken off from the habitual and traditional conditions that characterise its origins, reveals a human being capable for the first time of genuine autonomy. The sovereign individual is 'supra-ethical', a creature whose endowment with '*the right to make a promise*' has led it to feel itself to be the 'completion' of humanity 'in general' and therefore its justification (*Genealogy*, Essay II, §2). Above all, the sovereign individual is a free being: it is a 'master of the *free* will' (*Genealogy*, Essay II, §2) that gives honour or feels contempt for others according to whether they, too, can stand by their word. The sovereign individual's identity is, it follows, rooted in self-mastery, i.e. his (for it is almost certainly male) autonomy with respect to circumstances, nature and all other living beings that lack the durability and reliability of an autonomous will. This is a self who now stands outside the conventional constraints of society and morality, but is at the same time aware of the privilege of '*responsibility*' that he has for himself. The sovereign individual is free in the sense that he has 'freedom and power over himself and his destiny' to such an extent that this feeling of freedom 'has penetrated him to the depths and become an instinct, his dominant instinct' (*Genealogy*, Essay II, §2). We are thereby presented with a being of passion but one whose passions are dominated by one instinct in particular: the sovereign individual's '*conscience*'. In the sovereign individual, conscience is encountered 'in its highest, almost disconcerting form' (*Genealogy*, Essay II, §3), but the original violent conditions and characteristics that constitute its precondition are now transformed in the autonomous right to self-affirmation. Resorting to a metaphor, Nietzsche notes that although now 'ripe', the notion of conscience in this form is 'also a *late* fruit' (*Genealogy,* Essay II, §3). Before, it would have 'hung bitter and sour on the tree! And for even longer there was nothing to see of this fruit, – nobody would have had the right to promise it would be there, although it is certain that everything about the tree was ready and growing towards it!' (*Genealogy,* Essay II, §3). The language Nietzsche uses thereby implies an uncanny purposive quality concealed in the unconscious conditions that drove human development.

STATE, THE

Nietzsche is a well-known denouncer of the state. In *Human, All Too Human,* he even goes so far as to envisage its inevitable demise at the hands of the forces of modernity. The modern era is characterised by a loss of Christian faith, and the state depends upon such faith in order to survive: 'The belief in a divine order in the realm of politics, in a sacred mystery of the existence of the state, is of religious origin: if religion disappears the state will unavoidably lose its ancient Isis veil and cease to excite reverence' (*Human, All Too Human,* §472). More specifically, the democratic nature of the modern state epitomises its decline. The state, Nietzsche adds, is just one mode of social organisation amongst others that have preceded it (the clan, the family) and lost their power. The waning of the state is, it follows, perfectly thinkable – indeed, a likelihood. Yet, he then adds, such dissolution of the state could be a risky experiment if it is forced. Indeed, one should not work actively towards such dissolution, since it has unforeseeable consequences. 'Let us therefore put our trust in "the prudence and self-interest of men" to preserve the existence of the state for some time yet and to repulse the destructive elements of the precipitate and over-zealous' (*Human, All Too Human,* §472). Thus, Nietzsche looks here to be taking, in the last resort, a liberal stance. The state is a necessary evil. The following section of *Human, All Too Human* reinforces the point, in so far as it questions what Nietzsche sees as the socialist's desire to extend the power of the state beyond reasonable limits. By the time of *Thus Spoke Zarathustra,* liberal prudence has given way to a deep suspicion of state power. For Zarathustra, the State is 'the coldest of all cold monsters' (*Thus Spoke Zarathustra,* 'On the New Idol'). It epitomises the deception that Nietzsche sees at work in mass culture: 'this lie crawls out of its mouth: "I, the state, am the people"' (*Thus Spoke Zarathustra,* 'On the New Idol'). Peoples, Zarathustra retorts, are the consequence of legislative creators who mould normative regimes (for example, Moses in the Old Testament). Even so, it would be wrong to conclude from this that Nietzsche is opposed to all state power. What he objects to in the modern state is its very modernity, i.e. its formalistic, egalitarian, democratic tendencies and thus its standing as representative of the drive to mass conformity. The state, it turns out, is also something that, in its ancient manifestation, gave rise to modern human beings. In *On the Genealogy of Morality,* the reader is offered the view that creators of states are brutal, repressive sovereigns who spur on in their victims the tendency to intellectuality. It is such beings who bring about the 'internalization of man' and thereby the emergence of the genuinely human soul (Essay II, §16). The state, as it is presented here, begins as a tyranny (no liberal contractarianism here! Nietzsche notes of his account) that then undergoes a self-sublimation which gives rise to justice and the rule of law. Justice, Nietzsche adds, is hence the opposite of revenge. In typical Nietzschean style, out of the most brutal conditions restraint is born.

Further reading: Ansell-Pearson 1991; Conway 1997; Kaufmann 1974; Thiele 1991; Warren 1988.

TRUTH

There is no straightforward way to summarise Nietzsche's views about truth. As with many notions, his ideas on truth develop throughout his philosophical career. Nietzsche's early discussion of the concept of truth, 'On Truth and Lie in a Nonmoral Sense' (1873), argues (in a manner akin to British empiricism) that concepts arise as abstractions of individual experiences. Thus, all concepts arise from 'the equation of unequal things' ('On Truth and Lie', §1). This equation gives rise to the belief that there is a world in nature that corresponds to our concepts rather than the particulars from which the concepts were derived. This, however, is an illusion, for 'We obtain the concept, as we do the form, by overlooking what is individual and actual; whereas nature is acquainted with no forms and no concepts [...] but only with an X which remains inaccessible and undefinable for us' in a manner akin to the Kantian 'thing-in-itself' ('On Truth and Lie', §1). There is no way of knowing what the essence of things is; consequently, all we can say about truth is that it is

A movable host of metaphors, metonymies, and anthropomorphisms: in short, a sum of human relations which have been poetically and rhetorically intensified, transferred, and embellished, and which, after long usage, seem to a people to be fixed, canonical, and binding. Truths are illusions which we have forgotten are illusions; they are metaphors that have become worn out and have been drained of sensuous force, coins that have lost their embossing and are now considered as metal and no longer as coins.

('On Truth and Lie', §1)

The concept of truth, in other words, is essentially linked to the context of its production. Truths are expressions of human interest and involvement. As such, the concept of truth does not pertain to the kind of objectivity that dogmatic metaphysics assumes. This approach is further developed in the opening sections of *Human, All Too Human* (1878), where the view is propounded that the notion of absolute, metaphysical truth is best replaced by a more modest conception derived from the examples of scholarship and science (*see* **knowledge**).

For the mature Nietzsche, the problem of truth is enshrined in the manner in which the concept has been handled, or more precisely *mis*handled, by the philosophical tradition:

> Supposing truth to be a woman – what? is the suspicion not well founded that all philosophers, when they have been dogmatists, have had little understanding of women? that the gruesome earnestness, the clumsy importunity with which they have hitherto been in the habit of approaching truth have been inept and improper means for winning a wench? Certainly she has not let herself be won.
>
> (*Beyond Good and Evil*, Preface)

Thus, Nietzsche begins *Beyond Good and Evil* with a provocative array of assertions concerning truth that openly operate by way of *metaphor*. Truth is provocatively presented in the guise of the metaphor of femininity. What is noteworthy here is the manner in which what look like questions actually operate as statements. Thus, 'is the suspicion not well founded that all philosophers, when they have been dogmatists, have had little understanding of women?' *means* 'dogmatists are dreadful bunglers who have not a chance in hell of grasping (i.e. understanding) truth'. Dogmatists are, to continue Nietzsche's metaphor, poor seducers. Significantly, this metaphor suggests that something linked essentially to the body (i.e. to desires, passions, drives and the like) is relevant (perhaps even essential) to our under-standing of what might have hitherto been considered to be the most abstract of domains (i.e. concepts and thought). The preface to *Beyond Good and Evil* thereby presents itself from the outset as an attack on a certain kind of thinking about truth: the kind of thought that the opening section of *Human, All Too Human* refers to as 'metaphysical' or 'dogmatic philosophy' (§1). But what does 'dogmatism' mean here? Amongst other things dogmatism involves the urge to system-atise, the desire to create 'sublime and unconditional [...] edifices' (*Beyond Good and Evil*, Preface). This desire has, Nietzsche adds, gained its justification from the realm of 'popular superstition [...] (such as the soul superstition which, as the subject-ego superstition, has not yet ceased to do mischief even today), perhaps some play on words, a grammatical seduction, or an audacious generalization on the basis of very narrow, very personal, very human, all too human facts' (*Beyond Good and Evil*, Preface). It should not evade our attention that Nietzsche himself, in resorting to a powerful metaphor to initiate a discussion of truth (making possibly an 'audacious generalization' or two of his own) is not immune from the seduction of such strategies. On the contrary, he is actively and self-consciously deploying just this kind of thing in order to present his own case against such practices. What might this mean? Perhaps, Nietzsche suggests, dogmatism was just a necessary prelude to something else:

> It seems that, in order to inscribe themselves in the hearts of humanity with eternal demands, all great things have first to wander the earth as monstrous and fear-inspiring grotesques: dogmatic philosophy [...] was a grotesque of this kind. Let us not be ungrateful to it, even though it certainly has to be admitted that the worst, the most wearisomely protracted and most dan-gerous of all errors hitherto has been a dogmatist's error, namely Plato's invention of pure spirit and the good in itself.
>
> (*Beyond Good and Evil*, Preface)

Some things immediately suggest themselves here. *First*, we gain some additional knowledge about dogmatism: Plato exemplifies the dog-matic approach. Second, the bodily and seductive imagery Nietzsche deploys takes on a deeper meaning. The use of this kind of metaphor to discuss dogmatic philosophy is significant. The language Nietzsche is using does not merely proclaim or argue against dogmatism; it *enacts his rejection of it* in its deliberate employment of imagery that relies on bodily desire and passion to be meaningful. The discussion of truth, it follows, is operating not simply at the level of philosophical argument ('if...then', etc.); it is actively constructing meaning through images that themselves involve a rejection of platonic dogmatism. Third, something 'great' lurks behind the monstrosity of dogmatism. The monstrosity was a means to an end: a means to *inscribing* something on humanity's character. In short, the implication is that to fashion humankind by monstrous means is the only way it gets fashioned at all. This is a theme that Nietzsche will take up in greater detail with the notion of genealogy.

'To be sure, to speak of spirit and the good as Plato did meant standing truth on her head and denying *perspective* itself, the basic condition of all life' (*Beyond Good and Evil,* Preface). *Life,* for Nietzsche, consists of a multitude of viewpoints (perspectives). This is its truth. Without the possibility of a plurality of views, life would not be possible. (This is a possibility, one should add, that finds its most forceful expression in individual experience: each of us, according to Nietzsche, is capable of seeing the world differently – one does not have to embark on the impossible project of stepping out of one's head into the world of another in order for this to happen; we all do it all the time. We are each of us a plurality of selves – *see* **self**). Dogmatism has not, it turns out, been all bad: it has helped produce something of world historical significance:

[T]he struggle against Plato, or, to express it more plainly and for 'the people', the struggle against the Christian-ecclesiastical pressure of millennia – for Christianity is Platonism for 'the people' – has created in Europe a magnificent tension of the spirit such as has never existed on earth before: with so tense a bow one can now shoot for the most distant targets.

(*Beyond Good and Evil,* Preface)

Truth talk, it follows, has consequences that are concrete, consequences that serve to constitute lived cultural experience: the intellectual possibilities of modern humanity have arisen in the form of the struggle against Platonism. As a self-proclaimed free spirit, Nietzsche is a product of the very way of thinking that he now (and with gratitude) attacks: the notion of 'pure spirit'. Spirituality, the view that there is something about humans the significance of which cannot be reduced to the body, is valued by Nietzsche. The value of spirituality is that it proclaims an essential difference between humans and the animal world. Nietzsche does not wish to sacrifice this. He, however, wishes to reintegrate the spiritual into the bodily, to play upon the tension between embodied existence (the fact that we are collections of drives, passions and other organic functions) and reflective existence (the fact that we can think and reflect, that we are conscious). The mistake of dogmatism was that it took human consciousness to signify an ultimate reality, the domain of absolute truth. It does not. We are also unconscious, driven beings. Indeed, we are *both* conscious and unconscious, multiple beings not merely capable of but actively *driven* to interpret the world from one perspective and then another and so on, acting on the basis of beliefs and impulses (which are two sides of the same coin). Truth, it follows, cannot be divorced from the notion of perspective (*see* **perspectivism**). What, then, does the desire for truth signify? '*What* really is it in us that wants "the truth"?' (*Beyond Good and Evil*, §1). Philosophers are driven by a 'will to truth'. Where does this come from (the question of its *origins*)? There is also 'an even more fundamental question. We asked after the *value* of this will. Granted we want truth: *why not rather* untruth? And uncertainty? Even ignorance?' (*Beyond Good and Evil*, §1). To pose the question of the value of truth requires that the issue of perspective be invoked. The positive value of *wanting* truth cannot be taken for granted. The will to truth must itself be interrogated.

Nietzsche's notebooks also offer a stunning range of reflections on the nature of truth. Often, his comments in these continue themes first mooted in 'On Truth and Lie'. Thus, for example, he dwells upon the inherently errant nature of truth and its relationship to language: '*We cease to think when we do so under the constraint of language; we barely reach the doubt that sees this limitation as a limitation. Rational thought is interpretation according to a scheme that we cannot throw off*' (*Will to Power*, §522). To think, in other words, is to act in a manner that accords with constraints imposed by our linguistic constitution. In this sense, our ability to engage in truth talk is a product of environmental, biological and cultural factors. Likewise, the notes also reflect Nietzsche's more or less constant concern with questioning oppositions and antitheses. The opening pages of *Human, All Too Human, Beyond Good and Evil* and *Twilight of the Idols* all question in much the same way the philosophical obsession with understanding meaning and truth in terms of predetermined and immutable logical structures. Logic, for Nietzsche, is a cultural achievement. The problem with metaphysical philosophy is that it has always taken this achievement to be an eternal given. Truth, on this view, 'does not necessarily denote the antithesis of error, but in the most fundamental cases only the posture of various errors in relation to one another' (*Will to Power*, §535). Consequently, it 'is the kind of error without which a certain *species* of life could not live. The value for life is ultimately decisive' (*Will to Power*, §498). Thus, the demands of life trump those of our rational abilities. Truth nevertheless remains an inescapable and hence important notion for Nietzsche, for the *demand* for truth has become part of human nature. More specifically, this demand has given rise to the notion of *truthfulness* (*see* **will to truth**).

Further reading: Clark 1990; Conway and Groff 1998; Danto 2005 [1965]; De Man 1979; Dews 1988; Fink 2003; Grimm 1977; Havas 1995; Heidegger 1979–82 [1936–9]; May 1993; Poellner 1995; Rorty 1991; Sadler 1995; Welshon 2004; Wilcox 1974.

WILL TO POWER

Even in his so-called 'middle period' writings of the early 1880s, the question of power is on Nietzsche's mind:

> Not necessity, not desire – no, the love of power is the demon of men. Let them have everything – health, food, a place to live, entertainment – they are and remain unhappy and low-spirited: for the demon waits and waits and will be satisfied. Take everything from them and satisfy this, and they are almost happy – as happy as men and demons can be.
>
> (*Daybreak*, §262)

It is in *Thus Spoke Zarathustra*, however, that the notion of the will to power is announced. Zarathustra holds there to be an inextricable connection between values and will to power:

> A tablet of the good hangs over every people. Behold, it is the tablet of their overcomings; behold, it is the voice of their will to power [...] Whatever makes them rule and triumph and shine, to the awe and envy of their neighbors, that is to them the high, the first, the measure, the meaning of all things.
>
> (*Zarathustra*, Part I, 'On the Thousand and One Goals')

What is celebrated by any nation as denoting the highest, the first, the most valued is esteemed because it separates that culture from others by expressing a feeling of superiority over them. The desire for power that is present as a characteristic of all peoples *expresses itself as values.*

Zarathustra goes on to announce the principle of will to power and says that this desire is the evaluative drive, the dominant feature of all living things (see *Zarathustra*, Part II, 'On Self-Overcoming').

One can consider in this connection the second essay of the *Genealogy*, where Nietzsche argues that *anything* that exists can always be:

> interpreted anew, requisitioned anew, transformed and redirected to a new purpose by a power superior to it [...] everything that occurs in the organic world consists of *overpowering, dominating*, and in their turn, overpowering and dominating consist of re-interpretation, adjustment, in the process of which their former 'meaning' [*Sinn*] and 'purpose' must necessarily be obscured or completely obliterated.
>
> (*Genealogy*, Essay II, §12)

The discussion here centres on the nature of purposes. On the one hand, one must not confuse the current purpose of a thing with 'the reason for its existence' (do not be fooled into thinking that 'the eye is made to see, the hand to grasp') (*Genealogy*, Essay II, §12). Purposes need to be reinterpreted. Purposes are *signs* (i.e. they are symptomatic of something else). Every purpose reveals that 'the will to power has achieved mastery over something less powerful, and has impressed upon it its own idea [*Sinn*] of a use function' (*Genealogy*, Essay II, §12). Purposes, in other words, always concern relations of power. In turn, Nietzsche claims that 'the essence of life, [is] its *will to power*' (*Genealogy*, Essay II, §12). Here, 'will to power' means the 'spontaneous, aggressive, expansive, re-interpreting, re-directing and formative powers' (*Genealogy*, Essay II, §12). Will to power denotes the priority of *affirmation* and hence *activity:* it is the 'life-will' made manifest.

How is one to make sense of these claims? What does Nietzsche mean by 'power' and by 'will'? Consider the following notebook entry from 1885:

> And do you know what 'the world' is to me? Shall I show it to you in my mirror? This world: a monster of energy, without beginning, without end; a firm, iron magnitude of force that does not grow bigger or smaller, that does not expend itself but only transforms itself; as a whole, of unalterable size, a household without expenses or losses, but likewise without increase or income; enclosed by 'nothingness' as by a boundary; not something blurry or wasted, not something endlessly extended, but set in a definite space as a definite force, and not a space that might

be 'empty' here or there, but rather as force throughout, as a play of forces and waves of forces, at the same time one and many, increasing here and at the same time decreasing there [...] as a becoming that knows no satiety, no disgust, no weariness: this, my *Dionysian* world of the eternally self-creating, the eternally self-destroying [...] my 'beyond good and evil', without goal, unless the joy of the circle is itself a goal; without will, unless a ring feels good will toward itself – do you want a *name* for this world? A *solution* for all its riddles? A *light* for you, too, you best-concealed, strongest, most intrepid, most midnightly men? – *This world is the will to power – and nothing else besides!* And you yourselves are also this will to power – and nothing else besides!

(*Will to Power*, §1067)

Other notebook entries from the late 1880s continue the theme: 'Life is only a *means* to something; it is the expression of the forms of the growth of power' (*Will to Power*, §706). Will to power is 'the ultimate ground and character of all change' (*Will to Power*, §685). It is the underlying principle of organic activity: 'For what do trees in a jungle fight each other? For "happiness"? – *For power!*' (*Will to Power*, §704). Consider also *Beyond Good and Evil*, §36:

Granted that nothing is 'given' as real except our world of desires and passions, that we can rise or sink to no other 'reality' than the reality of our drives – for thinking is only the relationship of these drives to one another –: is it not permissible to make the experiment and ask the question whether this which is given does not *suffice* for an understanding even of the so-called mechanical (or 'material') world? I do not mean as a deception, an 'appearance', an 'idea' (in the Berkeleyan and Schopenhaueran sense), but as possessing the same degree of reality as our emotions themselves – as a more primitive form of the emotions in which everything still lies locked in mighty unity and then branches out and develops in the organic process [...] as a kind of instinctual life in which all organic functions, together with self-regulation, assimilation, nourishment, excretion, metabolism, are still synthetically bound together – as an *antecedent form of life?* – [...] In the end, the question is whether we really recognize will as *efficient*, whether we believe in the causality of the will: if we do so – and fundamentally *this* is precisely our belief in causality itself – we *have* to make the experiment of positing causality of will hypothetically as the only one. 'Will' can of course only operate on 'will' – and not on matter (not on 'nerves', for example): enough, one must venture the hypothesis that wherever 'effects' are recognized, will is operating upon will – and that all mechanical occurrences, in so far as a force is active in them, are force of will, effects of will. Granted finally that one succeeded in explaining our entire instinctual life as the development and ramification of *one* basic form of will – as will to power, as is *my* theory –; granted that one could trace all organic functions back to this will to power and could also find in it the solution to the problem of procreation and nourishment – they are *one* problem – one would have acquired the right to define *all* efficient force unequivocally as: *will to power*. The world seen from within, the world defined and described according to its 'intelligible character' – it would be 'will to power' and nothing else.

(Beyond Good and Evil, §36)

These passages make it plain enough why a great deal of critical discussion has been devoted to Nietzsche's conception of will to power. Strong claims are made with regard to the nature of power, and how one interprets them has important ramifications for the interpretation both of different aspects of Nietzsche's thought and of his philosophy generally. By way of example: critics often concur with the view that Nietzsche is an anti-metaphysical thinker. Introduce the notion of will to power, however, and Nietzsche's attack on metaphysics begins to look unstable. The notion of power is itself all too susceptible to being interpreted as a metaphysical principle, leaving Nietzsche open to charges of inconsistency or contradiction. Thus, Heidegger argues that the will to power compromises Nietzsche's criticism of the philosophical concept of truth. For Heidegger, the notion of the will to power represents an attempt to overcome metaphysics. Through the will to power, the supposed universality of truth is shattered and replaced by questions about the interests of subjects speaking from particular perspectives. However, by asserting the constitutive nature of will to power as the essence of all that lives, Nietzsche invokes the very universality he apparently rejects and thereby fails to escape from metaphysics since will to power itself becomes a metaphysical principle. It is for this reason that Heidegger labels Nietzsche as the last metaphysical thinker: he articulates the limits of metaphysics but is nevertheless unable to overcome it.

The notion of will to power has also been taken to initiate an undercutting of the grounds of rational critique and, hence, Enlightenment thought and with these the aspirations of science and modernity itself. The great Frankfurt School thinker Jürgen Habermas has consistently identified this aspect of Nietzsche's philosophy. Habermas argues that Nietzsche turns to the will to power as a means of unmasking and thereby challenging the Enlightenment project of rational critique. In this way, the kind of philosophy exemplified by Kant's epistemological scepticism is rendered prey to being exposed as 'a veiled dogmatism' (Habermas 1971, p. 290). One should note in this context Nietzsche's famous assertion that philosophy is an 'involuntary and unconscious memoir' (*Beyond Good and Evil*, §6). Considered in this way, philosophy is rendered incapable of independent critique. Instead it becomes prey to interests, which are simultaneously concealed and acted out within it. For Habermas, Nietzsche thereby renders the transcendental aspirations of Kant's philosophy a mere ruse behind which are concealed prejudices about morality. (Kant, Nietzsche says in *Twilight of the Idols*, is really little more than a deceitful old Christian in epistemological garb ['"Reason" in Philosophy', §6]), Habermas sees Nietzsche as enacting the nemesis of critical reason: Nietzsche transforms reason into 'absolute purposive rationality' that renders it 'a form of depersonalized exercise of power' (Habermas 1988, p. 44). Habermas argues that this aspect of Nietzsche's philosophy reaches its culmination in the conservative 'New Nietzsche' of postmodernism (Habermas 1981). Such an approach threatens the legitimacy of the democratic liberal state (see Habermas 2004). On Habermas's conception, the liberal state is legitimate in so far as it spurns brute power. Thus, modern liberal–democratic states cannot permit a pre-constitutional notion of sovereignty (exemplified by the 'decisionism' of Nazi philosopher Carl Schmit). Likewise, such states cannot sanction the subjugation of individuals that such despotism demands. In contrast, Habermas regards the Nietzschean postmodernist as turning to the thought of power rather than law and validity in order to explain the historical crises of legitimacy that have marked the modern era and threaten to undo the project of Enlightenment. Nietzschean regards what the Enlightenment takes as legitimate forms of political authority as veiled articulations of interest. This Nietzschean response to questions of political legitimacy, Habermas argues, is chronically insufficient, for all it encapsulates is the rootless and directionless potential of secular modernity run riot. Nietzsche becomes here a destructive thinker. Truth claims are rendered mere assertions of will to power and thereby rendered psychoaesthetic questions of individual taste. In turn, what becomes important is the demand for mastery that is revealed in the battle between competing evaluative frameworks (e.g. the psychological opposition of master and slave).

One can contrast Habermas's approach with those of Kaufmann and Clark. For both, Nietzsche's power talk is rather distasteful. Kaufmann regards the will to power as being 'first and foremost the key concept of a psychological hypothesis' (Kaufmann 1974, p. 204). Nietzsche's theory of power is a combination of philosophical and psychological elements governed by the demands of scientific method and hence 'evidently offered in an empirical spirit' (Kaufmann 1974, p. 204; see also pp. 422, 178, 206). Nietzsche is thereby rendered akin to an empirical scientist following the stipulations of methodological rationality. The universal and metaphysical aspect of Nietzsche's will to power talk is thereby rendered a consequence of (rather poor) inductive empirical psychology. Likewise, where Habermas sees Nietzsche as a counter-Enlightenment thinker of will to power, Kaufmann proffers an image of Nietzsche as Enlightenment thinker (Kaufmann 1974, pp. 125, 137–8, 287, 295, 350, 400, 407). Clark also wishes to preserve the integrity of Nietzsche's rejection of meta-physics and to stress the positive aspect of his relationship to the Enlightenment. Thus, she holds that Nietzsche's mature works 'exhibit a uniform and unambiguous respect for facts, the senses, and science' (Clark 1990, p. 105). In order to defend this claim, Clark must give persuasive reasons for holding will to power to be of mar-ginal importance to Nietzsche's philosophy. She admits that many of Nietzsche's notebook comments support a metaphysical interpretation of will to power. However, Nietzsche's published works, according to her, do not. Even §36 of *Beyond Good and Evil* (cited above) is interpreted as being inconsistent with other comments Nietzsche makes in his books. How is one to explain this inconsistency? Clark's answer is simple enough: Nietzsche is here enacting an argument that he does *not* endorse. The view put forward in *Beyond Good and Evil* is framed by irony. On this view, will to power is simply a shorthand for something Nietzsche himself favours but is not regarded by him as something one can argue for with good warrant. *Beyond Good and Evil* §36 is thus really criticising rather than endorsing a metaphysical account of the will to power. The will to power is thereby rendered 'a second order drive' that 'belongs to psychology rather than to metaphysics or cosmology' (Clark 1990, p. 227). Clark's position is problematic. One could, for example, challenge the central claim she makes, which is that *Beyond Good and Evil* §36 asserts notions that Nietzsche elsewhere rejects (the effective power of consciousness and belief in the causality of the will) to be indisputable givens. It is instincts and drives that serve as a starting point here, and neither of them are for Nietzsche determined by consciousness any more than thought itself is. Second, there is little reason to hold, as Clark implies, that Nietzsche considers willing to be an adjunct of consciousness. Nietzsche's holding the kind of causal willing we usually attribute to consciousness to be illusory does not commit him to holding all other kinds of willing to be illusory or incapable of causal efficacy. Finally, in propounding her argument, Clark is driven to invoke the very thing she denies: the effective power of consciousness. She holds that Nietzsche's notebooks ought to be relegated to secondary status compared with the texts that Nietzsche published or completed before his mental collapse because such texts bear the imprimatur of Nietzsche's intentions; they reveal 'a development to a defensible and consistent position' (Clark 1990, p. 27). However, such an argument presupposes an agency that is both *self-correcting* and *self-interpreting*. A subject understood in these terms is endowed with abilities that amount to an expression of will – although it does not follow from this that the will expressed is equivalent to consciousness. That Clark in fact herself presupposes some kind of effective volition along these lines is also evident when she claims that the notion of will to power 'reflects' Nietzsche's 'will, that is, his values' (1990, p. 131), which presupposes the very causality of the will she denies. The attribution of irony Clark makes to Nietzsche's position compounds the mystery: irony is itself dependent upon a mode of subjectivity that is able to exercise power over meaning.

There are clearly stark differences between Habermas's view of Nietzsche and the view of him cultivated by Kaufmann and Clark. For Habermas, since Nietzsche is a thinker of power he is also a figure of the counter-Enlightenment. Kaufmann and Clark's commitment to rendering Nietzsche an Enlightenment thinker rules out of court the possibility that he may have interesting things to say about power. What both approaches share is the presupposition that Nietzsche's conception of will to power is something that can be properly addressed only in psychological terms. An alternative view, which is suggested by the interpretations of Deleuze and Müller-Lauter, is that Nietzsche's understanding of power is not psychological. Rather it is normative. In other words, Nietzsche's conception of power is rooted in his analysis of what he takes to be the defining feature of human existence: the domain of community, society and hence values (*see* **morality of custom**) (see Sedgwick 2007b). On this account, 'will to power' is derived not from psychology but from the forces of organisation (the realm of command) at work in any social order. Will to power in this way does not denote a metaphysical state but is, in Müller-Lauter's words, 'the multiplicity of forces locked in struggle with one another. Force in Nietzsche's sense can only be called a unity in the sense of organization' (Müller-Lauter 1999, p. 131). In other words, 'will to power' is a term Nietzsche uses to describe the organisation of plurality and heterogeneity that flows from command. As such, the phrase 'will to power' denotes the condition of normativity itself in terms of its structural determinations and the affects of these determinations. To be a normative being is to act in accordance with procedures and to recognise the legitimacy of those procedures in doing so. Normative beings are creatures (us) that act within the recognition of authority and discover themselves thereby. For Nietzsche, that they can do so is the case only in virtue of the fact that they have a history. This is the history of the formation of the human will through normative com-pulsion (*see* **genealogy**). The will, in this sense, is the great reason of the self that Zarathustra elaborates. It is the affect of the command structure in virtue of which there is a human world consisting of subjects endowed with interests and values. This structure, in so far as it is a structure of command, is always already permeated by power. As a structure it is regulative, organising and hence in its affective essence willing.

Further reading: Clark 1990; Deleuze 1987; Golomb 1989; Habermas 1971, 1981, 2004; Heidegger 1979–82 [1939–9]; Hillard 2002; Janaway 1998; Kaufmann 1974; Owen and Ridley 2000; Richardson 2000; Schacht 1983; Sedgwick 2007b.

WILL TO TRUTH

Nietzsche holds us to be animals whose conceptual abilities, while pragmatically useful, are subject to profound errors. The concept of truth, as thought by metaphysics, epitomises this tendency to error, for it seeks reality in the stable realms of idea and substance – in short, it believes all too willingly in the concept of being. Such a view asks too much of truth. It is our unconditional desire for truth (our will to truth) run amok. Truth, when sought in this unselfcritical manner, is the worst of delusions. Nietzsche does not seek to step outside the will to truth which drives us to such possible excesses. Given the degree to which it has become constitutive of our nature such an attempt would represent a delusory and parodic re-enactment of the errors of metaphysics. What he proposes, rather, is a critique of the will to truth that is to be performed within its horizon. The will to truth can no more be casually abandoned than Christianity's moralisation of the concept of guilt in the form of 'sin'. We must remain beings who live within the ambit of the realm delineated by the will to truth. 'The will to truth [...] is still going to tempt us on many a hazardous enterprise in the same way as it has in fact raised many dangerous questions so far. It is already a long story – yet does it not seem as if it has only just begun?' (*Beyond Good and Evil*, §1). We are, in other words, not at the conclusion but at the beginning of a journey that requires we question the concept of truth in ever more rigorous ways. Nietzsche, then, refuses us the right to transcend the problematic in simplistic fashion. We must remain pious, in so far as we seek to be rigorous with regard to our conception of knowledge. The expression of such piety is surprising given Nietzsche's often critical denunciations of Christian pious attitudes. All knowledge, he tells us (*Gay Science*, §344), requires presuppositions. No form of knowing would be possible without the satisfaction of this requirement. Wishing to know means affirming *beforehand* the value of knowing and the truths that such knowing will yield. This demand, which is an 'unconditional will to truth', is capable of being interpreted in a self-reflexive manner. 'Will to truth' need not mean wishing not to be deceived when it comes to the world of matters of fact but can signify a desire to affirm above all else the value of *truthfulness:* it is an active wishing not to deceive, not even oneself. Two possible senses thus arise with regard to the meaning of the will to truth. The first concerns prudential considerations (one does not want to be deceived because deception has bad consequences). However, need this be the case? Might it not be, Nietzsche muses, that being deceived is actually rather good for us? The 'truths' we often adhere to are errors that facilitate existence (belief in things, substances, etc.). Utility, in other words, cannot fully explain the will to truth. 'Consequently, "will to truth" does *not* mean "I will not allow myself to be deceived" but – there is no alternative – "I will not deceive, not even myself"; *and with that we stand on moral ground*' (*Gay Science*, §344). The affirmation of the demand for truth and morality go together. In so far as we are creatures who are driven by the desire not to deceive, we are creatures of the virtues, the greatest of which is honesty. Nietzsche envisages a humanity that stands against the fundamental conditions of existence, which is a plurality of simulacra. Might it be the case, he ponders, that because of this the will to truth is in fact a masked form of death drive? However that may be, one thing becomes clear from Nietzsche's late writings: the will to truth and the discipline of the sciences that rest upon it can never wholly escape from the domain of metaphysics. God himself, it may turn out, is our 'most enduring lie'. Rendered explicit in this way, the will to truth is revealed as something that needs to be subject to 'critique' (*Genealogy*, Essay III, §24). By this, Nietzsche does not mean that it is something that must be relentlessly criticised. Rather, a critique in the Kantian sense of the word is intended. As has already been mentioned, this is a critique which, in Nietzsche's case, aims at exploring the domain of the will to truth with a view to establishing its value and limits. We must, in brief, address the question of the value of truth from within its own domain – which is the domain of thought that it has fashioned for us. In the era of modernity, this means beginning from the position of an honest atheism (*Genealogy*, Essay III, §27).

Further reading: Havas 1995; Poellner 1995; Wilcox 1974.

WOMAN/WOMEN

Nietzsche is often tempted to resort to feminine metaphors in his writings. Thus, bad conscience is a sickness, but akin to the feminine sickness that accompanies pregnancy (*Genealogy*, Essay II, §19), truth can be construed as a 'woman' (and philosophers bad seducers) (*Beyond Good and Evil*, §1). Generally, however, Nietzsche does not have many things to say about women and femininity that could be considered to be complimentary. Sometimes what he says is, and not just by modern standards, outrageous: 'When a woman has scholarly inclinations there is usually something wrong with her sexuality' (*Beyond Good and Evil*, §144). Sections 231 ff. of the same text reveal a similar tendency. The desire of women to be independent is something to be discouraged, for within them women generally conceal pedantry, 'superficiality, schoolmarmishness, petty presumption, petty unbridledness and petty immodesty [...] Woe when the "eternal-boring in woman" – she has plenty of that! – is allowed to venture forth' (§232). The reference here is to Goethe's *Faust*, which concludes with the lines 'the eternal feminine pulls us ever upward'. In spite of his adoration of Goethe (*see* **Dionysus**), Nietzsche did not agree. Such comments have not, however, prevented some interpreters seeing in Nietzsche's construction of the feminine something more subversive and positive. Impetus to this kind of approach has been given by the writings of Jacques Derrida, who holds that a post-feminist reading can be made of Nietzsche's vehement comments about women. Truth, Derrida claims, rendered in feminine terms is also rendered as illusion. Like truth, then, the feminine as such ('in itself') does not exist. Constructions of femininity, it follows, can be challenged in a Nietzschean style destabilisation of the concepts of truth and knowledge. Derrida's approach is, however, questionable. For one thing, it suppresses the instrumental nature of Nietzsche's use of metaphor, i.e. the fact that when employed in a text for a specific purpose the question of the identity of, in this case, the feminine is not so much the issue as what is being attacked by way of the metaphor's deployment. One might, in other words, equally claim that what is central to the image of woman as truth in *Beyond Good and Evil* is the delusory, petty and clumsy vanity that Nietzsche sees at work in the writings of metaphysicians.

Further reading: Ainley 1988; Burgard 1994; Derrida 1979; Irigaray 1991; Krell and Wood 1988; Oliver and Pearsall 1998; Patton 1993.

ZARATHUSTRA

The central character of Nietzsche's *Thus Spoke Zarathustra* (written in four parts between 1883 and 1885), Zarathustra is first introduced in what was the concluding section of the first (1882) edition of *The Gay Science* (§342 – the book was substantially expanded in 1887). This concluding section in large part resembles the opening of *Thus Spoke Zarathustra*. Zarathustra (or Zoroaster, as the Greeks called him) was a sixth-century BC Persian religious teacher and prophet. The central feature of the historical Zarathustra's teachings was a mono-theistic view of the world, in which the forces of good/light are locked in conflict with those of bad/darkness. Nietzsche's Zarathustra teaches the path of overcoming this opposition, of going 'beyond good and evil' (a privilege granted him since he was its inventor). The text of *Zarathustra* is a dizzying blend of biblical parody, philosophical speculation, psychological rumination and irony. The text consists of a prologue and speeches or discourses, framed within the narration of Zarathustra's self-appointed mission to proclaim that humanity must be overcome. Elsewhere, many other issues are explored (commentaries are offered on the nature of values, women, the self, the body, modernity, politics and the State). Also proclaimed are the philosophies of eternal recurrence and will to power. Some points of debate clearly warrant less patience than others: God is dead, Zarathustra notes bluntly near the text's beginning. In fact, the death of God shapes the central question that Zarathustra wishes to address, which concerns what we can envisage and commend as the highest possible goal of human existence in the absence of a transcendent, God-given purpose. Nietzsche's answer is the Overman. The figure of Zarathustra himself remains mysterious. In Nietzsche's hands he is a historical personage become fictive philosophical and rhapsodic instrument, a visionary who has gone beyond mere prophecy; a moral voice that purports to stand beyond morality as it is generally understood; a philosophical voice that argues for an as yet unacknowledged mode of philosophical practice. It would be easy, in consequence, to succumb to the temptation to see in Zarathustra a prophetic figure or poetic soothsayer seeking to convey some mystical insight into the fundamental nature of reality, as many early readers did (see Sedgwick 1997). This, however, would be to take the text of *Thus Spoke Zarathustra* so seriously as to underplay its playful, ironic and parodic elements. Nietzsche never wants 'disciples', in the sense of mere passive consumers of his supposed wisdom (see *Gay Science,* §§106, 359). Zarathustra clearly urges a kind of transcendence in the form of the perfectionism that seeks the overcoming of humanity: its foibles and weaknesses ought to be mastered by its potential for greatness. Such greatness, however, is not for all – Nietzsche is no egalitarian. Rather, we should offer ourselves up as means to the end of achieving the Overman. Zarathustra also teaches love of the earth and corporeal embodiment in a manner that stands in stark contrast to traditional Christian teachings, which revile the body in favour of the supposed purity of the spirit. He seeks to offer us a radical new view of humanity as being the only animal whose evaluative abilities characterise it in such a manner that it becomes endowed with the ability to fashion itself (freedom). Nietzsche's Zarathustra may be a teacher (see Schacht 1995b), but his is a teaching that does not require religious 'faith'. To use Nietzsche's own terminology, Zarathustra teaches a philosophy of attempting or experimenting. It is a teaching that does not seek to communicate procedures or methods so much as an attitude toward life of affirmation.

Further reading: Foster 2000; Hollingdale 1973; Lampert 1986, 1987; Rosen 1995; Schacht 1995b; Thiele 1991.

BIBLIOGRAPHY

Acampora, C. D. (2003) '*Agonistes* Redux: Reflections of the Streit of Political Antagonism', *Nietzsche-Studien*, 32.

—— (ed.) (2006) *Nietzsche's 'On the Genealogy of Morals': Critical Essays,* Lanham, Md.: Rowman & Littlefield.

Adorno, T.W. and Horkheimer, M. (1973) *Dialectic of Enlightenment,* London: Allen Lane.

Ainley, A. (1988) '"Ideal Selfishness": Nietzsche's Metaphor of Maternity', in D. F. Krell and D. Wood (eds), *Exceedingly Nietzsche: Aspects of Contemporary Nietzsche Interpretation,* London and New York: Routledge.

Allison, D. B. (ed.) (1985) *The New Nietzsche: Contemporary Styles of Interpretation,* Cambridge, Mass.: MIT Press.

—— (2001) *Reading the New Nietzsche,* Lanham, Md.: Rowman & Littlefield.

Ansell-Pearson, K. (1991) *Nietzsche contra Rousseau: A Study of Nietzsche's Moral and Political Thought,* Cambridge: Cambridge University Press.

Babich, B. E. (1994) *Nietzsche's Philosophy of Science,* Albany, NY: State University of New York Press.

Babich, B. and Cohen, S. (eds) (1999) *Nietzsche and the Sciences,* 2 vols., Dordrecht: Kluwer.

Bataille, G. (1992) *On Nietzsche,* trans. Bruce Boone, London: Athlone Press. First published 1945.

Behler, E. (1991) *Confrontations: Derrida, Heidegger, Nietzsche,* trans. S. Taubeneck, Stanford, Calif.: Stanford University Press.

Bennett, J. (1966) *Kant's Analytic,* Cambridge: Cambridge University Press.

—— (1974) *Kant's Dialectic,* Cambridge: Cambridge University Press.

Bergmann, P. (1987) *Nietzsche: 'The Last Antipolitical German',* Bloomington, Ind.: Indiana University Press.

Berkowitz, P. (1995) *Nietzsche: The Ethics of an Immoralist,* Cambridge, Mass.: Harvard University Press.

Berlin, I. (ed.) (1979) *The Age of Enlightenment,* Oxford: Oxford University Press.

Bernstein, J. (1987) *Nietzsche's Moral Philosophy,* London: Associated University Press.

Blondel, E. (1991) *Nietzsche: The Body and Culture: Philosophy as a Philological Genealogy,* trans. S. Hand, London: Athlone Press.

Bowie, A. (1990) *Aesthetics and Subjectivity: From Kant to Nietzsche,* Manchester: Manchester University Press.

Burgard, P. J. (ed.) (1994) *Nietzsche and the Feminine*, Charlottesville, Va.: University of Virginia Press.

Butler, J. (2000) 'Circuits of Bad Conscience: Nietzsche and Freud', in A. Schrift (ed.), *Why Nietzsche Still? Reflections on Drama, Culture, and Politics*, Berkeley, Calif.: University of California Press.

Chadwick, R.F. and Cazeaux, C. eds. (1992) *Kant: Critical Assessments*, 4 vols, London: Routledge.

Clark, M. (1990) *Nietzsche on Truth and Philosophy*, Cambridge: Cambridge University Press.

Connolly, W. E. (1988) *Political Theory and Modernity*, Oxford: Blackwell.

Conway, D. W. (1995) 'Returning to Nature: Nietzsche's *Götterdämmerung*', in P. Sedgwick (ed.) *Nietzsche: A Critical Reader*, Oxford: Blackwell.

—— (1997) *Nietzsche's Dangerous Game: Philosophy in the Twilight of the Idols*, Cambridge: Cambridge University Press.

Conway, D. W. and Groff, P. S. (eds) (1998) *Nietzsche: Critical Assessments*, 4 vols., London and New York: Routledge.

Cottingham, J. (ed.) (1992) *The Cambridge Companion to Descartes*, Cambridge: Cambridge University Press.

Cox, C. (1999) *Nietzsche: Naturalism and Interpretation*, Berkeley, Calif.: University of California Press.

Crawford, C. (1988) *The Beginnings of Nietzsche's Theory of Language*, Berlin: Walter de Gruyter.

Dannhauser, W. J. (1974) *Nietzsche's View of Socrates*, Ithaca, NY: Cornell University Press.

Danto, A. C. (2005) *Nietzsche as Philosopher*, New York: Columbia University Press. First published 1965.

De Man, P. (1979) *Allegories of Reading: Figural Language in Rousseau, Nietzsche, Rilke, and Proust*, New Haven, Conn.: Yale University Press.

Del Caro, A. (1981) *Dionysian Aesthetics: The Role of Destruction in Creation as Reflected in the Life and Works of Friedrich Nietzsche*, Frankfurt: Lang.

Deleuze, G. (1983) *Nietzsche and Philosophy*, trans. Hugh Tomlinson, London: Athlone Press.

—— (1987) *Dialogues*, trans. B. Habberjam, New York: Columbia University Press.

—— (1990) *The Logic of Sense*, trans. M. Lester with C. Stivale, London: Athlone Press.

—— (2001) *Empiricism and Subjectivity: An Essay on Hume's Theory of Human Nature*, trans. C. V. Boundas, New York: Columbia University Press.

Deleuze, G. and Guattari, F. (1988) *A Thousand Plateaus*, trans. B. Massumi, Minneapolis, Minn.: University of Minnesota Press.

—— (1994) *What is Philosophy?* trans. G. Burchell and H. Tomlinson, London and New York: Verso.

Derrida, J. (1979) *Spurs: Nietzsche's Styles*, trans. Barbara Harlow, Chicago, Ill.: University of Chicago Press.

Descartes, R. (1986) [1641] *Meditations on First Philosophy*, trans. J. Cottingham, Cambridge: Cambridge University Press.

Detwiler, B. (1990) *Nietzsche and the Politics of Aristocratic Radicalism*, Chicago, Ill.: University of Chicago Press.

Dews, P. (1988) 'Nietzsche and the Critique of *Ursprungsphilosophie*', in D. F. Krell and D. Wood (eds), *Exceedingly Nietzsche: Aspects of Contemporary Nietzsche Interpretation*, London and New York: Routledge.

Diethe, C. (2003) 'Nietzsche Emasculated: Postmodern Readings', in D. Large and R. Görner (eds) *Ecce Opus: Nietzsche-Revisionen im 20. Jahrhundert*, Göttingen, Vandenhoeck & Ruprecht.

Dombowsky, D. (2002) 'A Response to Alan D. Schrift's "Nietzsche *for* Democracy?"', *Nietzsche-Studien*, 31.

Dombowsky, D. and Cameron, F. (2008) *Political Writings of Friedrich Nietzsche*, Basingstoke: Palgrave Macmillan.

Eagleton, T. (2009) *Trouble with Strangers: A Study of Ethics*, Oxford: Wiley-Blackwell.

Fink, E. (2003) *Nietzsche's Philosophy*, trans. G. Richter, New York: Continuum.

Foster, J. B. (2000) 'Zarathustrian Millennialism before the Millennium', in A. D. Schrift (ed.), *Why Nietzsche Still? Reflections on Drama, Culture, and Politics*, Berkeley, Calif.: University of California Press.

Foucault, M. (1977) 'Nietzsche, Genealogy, History', in D. F. Bouchard (ed.), *Language, Counter-Memory, Practice*, Oxford: Blackwell.

Fraser, G. (2002) *Redeeming Nietzsche: On the Pity of Unbelief*, London and New York: Routledge.

Gay, P. (1988) *The Enlightenment: An Interpretation*, 2 vols., London: Weidenfeld & Nicolson.

Géffre, C., Jossua, J. P. and Lefébure, M. (eds) (1981) *Nietzsche and Christianity*, New York: Seabury Press.

Geuss, R. (1999) *Morality, Culture and History: Essays on German Philosophy*, Cambridge: Cambridge University Press.

Giddens, A. (1990) *The Consequences of Modernity*, Cambridge: Polity Press.

Gillespie, M. (1996) *Nihilism Before Nietzsche*, Chicago, Ill.: University of Chicago Press.

Gillespie, M. A. and Strong, T. B. (1988) *Nietzsche's New Seas: Explorations in Philosophy, Aesthetics and Politics*, Chicago, Ill.: University of Chicago Press.

Golomb, J. (1989) *Nietzsche's Enticing Psychology of Power*, Ames, Iowa: Iowa State University Press.

—— (ed.) (1997) *Nietzsche and Jewish Culture*, London and New York: Routledge.

Golomb, J. and Wistrich, R. S. (eds) (2002) *Nietzsche, Godfather of Fascism? On the Uses and Abuses of a Philosophy*, Princeton, NJ: Princeton University Press.

Grimm, R. H. (1977) *Nietzsche's Theory of Knowledge*, Berlin: Walter de Gruyter.

Haar, M. (1996) *Nietzsche and Metaphysics*, Albany, NY: State University of New York Press.

Habermas, J. (1971) *Knowledge and Human Interests*, trans. J. J. Shapiro, Boston, Mass.: Beacon Press.

—— (1981) 'Modernity versus Postmodernity', trans. S. Benhabib, *New German Critique*, 22.

—— (1988) *The Philosophical Discourse of Modernity*, Cambridge, Mass.: MIT Press. First published 1985.

—— (2004) '*Stellungnahme*: Professor Dr. Jürgen Habermas', in *Zur Debatte*, 1: '*Gesprächsabend mit Joseph Kardinal Raztinger und Prof. Dr. Jürgen Habermas*'.

Hales, S. D. and Welshon, R. (2000) *Nietzsche's Perspectivism*, Chicago, Ill.: University of Illinois Press.

Hartman, G. (ed.) (1979) *Deconstruction and Criticism*, New Haven, Conn.: Yale University Press.

Harvey, D. (1989) *The Condition of Postmodernity: An Enquiry into the Conditions of Cultural Change*, Oxford: Blackwell.

Hassan, I. (1987) *The Postmodern Turn: Essays in Postmodern Theory and Culture*, Columbus, Ohio: Ohio State University Press.

Hatab, L. J. (1978) *Nietzsche and Eternal Recurrence: The Redemption of Time and Becoming*, Washington, DC: University Press of America.

—— (1995) *A Nietzschean Defense of Democracy: An Experiment in Postmodern Politics*, Chicago Ill.: Open Court.

—— (2005) *Nietzsche's Life Sentence: Coming to Terms with Eternal Recurrence*, London and New York: Routledge.

Havas, R. (1995) *Nietzsche's Genealogy: Nihilism and the Will to Knowledge*, Ithaca, NY: Cornell University Press.

Heidegger, M. (1979–82) *Nietzsche*, 4 vols., trans. D. F. Krell et al., New York: Harper & Row. First published 1936–9.

Heller, E. (1988) *The Importance of Nietzsche: Ten Essays*, Chicago, Ill.: University of Chicago Press.

Higgins, K. M. (1987) *Nietzsche's 'Zarathustra'*, Philadelphia, Pa.: Temple University Press.

Hillard, D. (2002) 'History as Dual Process: Nietzsche on Exchange and Power', *Nietzsche-Studien*, 31.

Hollingdale, R. J. (1973) *Nietzsche*, London: Routledge & Kegan Paul.

Houlgate, S. (1986) *Hegel, Nietzsche and the Criticism of Metaphysics*, Cambridge: Cambridge University Press.

Hunt, L. H. (1991) *Nietzsche and the Origin of Virtue*, London and New York: Routledge.

Irigaray, L. (1991) *Marine Lover of Friedrich Nietzsche*, New York: Columbia University Press. First published 1980.

Janaway, C. (ed.) (1998) *Willing and Nothingness: Schopenhauer as Nietzsche's Educator*, Oxford: Oxford University Press.

Jaspers, K. (1961) *Nietzsche and Christianity*, Chicago, Ill.: Regnery.

—— (1997) *Nietzsche: An Introduction to the Understanding of his Philosophical Activity*, trans. C. F. Walraff and F. J. Schmitz, Baltimore, Md.: Johns Hopkins University Press. First published 1936.

Jenks, C. (1991) *The Language of Postmodern Architecture*, 6th edn, London: Academy Editions.

Jones, B., Darby, T. and Egyed, B. (eds) (1989) *Nietzsche and the Rhetoric of Nihilism: Language and Politics*, Ottawa: Carleton University Press.

Kant, I. (1970) *Political Writings*, ed. H. Reiss, Cambridge: Cambridge University Press.

——(1976) *Critique of Practical Reason, and Other Writings in Moral Philosophy*; tr. and ed. Lewis White Beck, New York: Garland.

——(1983) 'Speculative Beginning of Human History', in *Perpetual Peace and Other Essays*, tr. T. Humphrey, Indianapolis, Ind.: Hackett.

——(1987) *The Critique of Judgement*, tr. W.S.Pluhar, Indianapolis, Ind.: Hackett.

Katsafanas, P. (2005) 'Nietzsche's Theory of Mind: Consciousness and Conceptualization', *European Journal of Philosophy*, 13.

Kaufmann, W. (1974) *Nietzsche: Philosopher, Psychologist, Antichrist*, Princeton, NJ: Princeton University Press.

Kemal, S., Gaskell, I. and Conway, D. W. (eds) (1998) *Nietzsche, Philosophy and the Arts,* Cambridge: Cambridge University Press.

Klossowski, P. (1997) *Nietzsche and the Vicious Circle,* London: Athlone. First published 1969.

Koelb, C. (ed.) (1990) *Nietzsche as Postmodernist: Essays Pro and Contra,* Albany, NY: State University of New York Press.

Kofman, S. (1993) *Nietzsche and Metaphor,* ed. and trans. D. Large, London: Athlone Press. First published 1972.

Köhler, J. (2002) *Zarathustra's Secret: The Interior Life of Friedrich Nietzsche,* trans. R. Taylor, New Haven, Conn.: Yale University Press.

Körner, S. (1955) *Kant,* Harmondsworth: Penguin.

Krell, D. F. and Bates, D. L. (1997) *The Good European: Nietzsche's Work Sites in Word and Image,* Chicago, Ill.: University of Chicago Press.

Krell, D. F. and Wood, D. (eds) (1988) *Exceedingly Nietzsche: Aspects of Contemporary Nietzsche Interpretation,* London and New York: Routledge.

Lampert, L. (1986) *Nietzsche's Teaching: An Interpretation of 'Thus Spoke Zarathustra',* New Haven, Conn.: Yale University Press.

——(1987) *Nietzsche's Teaching: An Interpretation of Thus Spoke Zarathustra,* New Haven, Conn.: Yale University Press.

—— (1993) *Nietzsche and Modern Times: A Study of Bacon, Descartes, and Nietzsche,* New Haven, Conn.: Yale University Press.

—— (2001) *Nietzsche's Task: An Interpretation of 'Beyond Good and Evil',* New Haven, Conn.: Yale University Press.

Leiter, B. (2002) *Routledge Guidebook to Nietzsche on Morality,* London and New York: Routledge.

Lemm, V. (2007) 'Animality, Creativity and Historicity: A Reading of Friedrich Nietzsche's *Vom Nutzen und Nachteil der Historie für das Leben'*, *Nietzsche-Studien,* 36.

Liebert, G. (2004) *Nietzsche and Music,* trans. D. Pellauer and G. Parkes, Chicago, Ill.: University of Chicago Press.

Lippitt, J. and Urpeth, J. (eds) (2000) *Nietzsche and the Divine,* Manchester: Clinamen.

Love, F. R. (1981) *Nietzsche's Saint Peter: Genesis and Cultivation of an Illusion,* Berlin: Walter de Gruyter.

Löwith, K. (1997) *Nietzsche's Philosophy of the Eternal Recurrence of the Same,* trans. J. Lomax, Berkeley, Calif.: University of California Press. First published 1956.

Lyotard, J.-F. (1988) *The Differend: Phrases in Dispute,* trans. G. Van Den Abeele, Manchester: Manchester University Press. First published 1983.

—— (1989) *The Postmodern Condition: A Report on Knowledge,* trans. G. Bennington, Manchester: Manchester University Press. First published 1979.

—— (1991) *The Inhuman: Reflections on Time,* trans. G. Bennington and R. Bowlby, Cambridge: Polity Press.

MacIntyre, A. (1981) *After Virtue: A Study of Moral Theory,* Notre Dame, Ind.: Notre Dame University Press.

Magnus, B., Stewart, S. and Mileur, J.-P. (1993) *Nietzsche's Case: Philosophy as/and Literature,* London and New York: Routledge.

Mandel, S. (1998) *Nietzsche and the Jews,* New York: Prometheus Books.

May, K. M. (1993) *Nietzsche on the Struggle between Wisdom and Knowledge,* Basingstoke: Macmillan.

May, S. (1999) *Nietzsche's Ethics and his War on 'Morality',* Oxford: Clarendon.

Minson, G. (1985) *Genealogies of Morals: Nietzsche, Foucault, Donzelot and the Eccentricity of Ethics,* Basingstoke: Macmillan.

Moore, G. (2002) *Nietzsche, Biology and Metaphor,* Cambridge: Cambridge University Press.

Moore, G. and Brobjer, T. (eds) (2004) *Nietzsche and Science,* Aldershot: Ashgate.

Müller-Lauter, W. (1999) *Nietzsche: His Philosophy of Contradictions and the Contradictions of His Philosophy,* trans. D. J. Parent, Urbana, Ill.: University of Illinois Press.

Natoli, C. M. (1985) *Nietzsche and Pascal on Christianity,* New York: Lang.

Nehamas, A. (1985) *Nietzsche: Life as Literature,* Cambridge, Mass.: Harvard University Press.

Nietzsche, F. W. (1968) *The Birth of Tragedy* in *Basic Writings of Nietzsche,* ed. and trans. Walter Kaufmann, New York: Basic Books. First published 1872.

—— (1968) *The Will to Power,* trans. Walter Kaufmann and R. J. Hollingdale, New York: Viking. First published 1901.

—— (1968) *Twilight of the Idols* and *The Antichrist,* trans. R. J. Hollingdale, Harmondsworth: Penguin. First published 1889.

——(1968) *Basic Writings of Nietzsche* (including *The Birth of Tragedy,* 1972; *Beyond Good and Evil,* 1885; *On the Genealogy of Morals,* 1887; *The Case of Wagner,* 1888; *Ecce Homo,* 1888/1908) ed. and trans. W. Kaufman, New York: Basic Books.

——(1968) *The Case of Wagner,* in *Basic Writings of Nietzsche,* ed. and trans. W. Kaufmann, New York: Basic Books.

—— (1973) *Beyond Good and Evil,* trans. R. J. Hollingdale, Harmondsworth: Penguin. First published 1885.

—— (1974) *The Gay Science,* trans. Walter Kaufmann, New York: Vintage. First published 1882/1887.

——(1979) 'On Truth and Lie in a Non-Moral Sense', in *Philosophy and Truth: Selections from Nietzsche's Notebooks of the Early 1870s,* ed. and trans. D. Breazeale, Sussex: Harvester Press.

—— (1980) *Sämtliche Werke: Kritische Studienausgabe,* 15 vols., eds. G. Colli & M. Montinari, Berlin: Walter de Gruyter.

—— (1982) *Daybreak,* trans. R. J. Hollingdale, Cambridge: Cambridge University Press. First published 1881.

—— (1983) *Untimely Meditations,* trans. R. J. Hollingdale, Cambridge: Cambridge University Press. First published 1873–6.

—— (1986) *Human, All Too Human,* (including *Assorted Opinions and Maxims* and *The Wanderer and His Shadow*) trans. R. J. Hollingdale, Cambridge: Cambridge University Press.

—— (1992) *Ecce Homo*, trans. R. J. Hollingdale, Harmondsworth: Penguin. First published 1908.

—— (1994) *On the Genealogy of Morality*, ed. K. Ansell-Pearson, trans. C. Diethe, Cambridge: Cambridge University Press. First published 1887.

—— (1995) *The Portable Nietzsche*, ed. and trans. Walter Kaufmann, (including *Thus Spoke Zarathustra*; *Twilight of the Idols*; *The Antichrist*; *Nietzsche contra Wagner*) New York: Penguin.

—— (1998) *Twilight of the Idols*, trans. D. Large, Oxford: Oxford University Press. First published 1889.

—— (2001) *Beyond Good and Evil*, ed. R.-P. Horstmann and trans. J. Norman, Cambridge: Cambridge University Press. First published 1885.

—— (2001) *The Birth of Tragedy and Other Writings*, ed. R. Geuss and R. Spears, trans. R. Spears, Cambridge: Cambridge University Press.

—— (2001) *The Gay Science*, ed. B. Williams and trans. J. Nauckhoff and A. Del Caro, Cambridge: Cambridge University Press. First published 1882/ 1887.

—— (2005) *Ecce Homo, Twilight of the Idols and Other Writings*, ed. A. Ridley, and trans. J. Norman, Cambridge: Cambridge University Press.

—— (2006) *Ecce Homo*, trans. Duncan Large, Oxford: Oxford University Press. First published 1908.

—— *Säntliche Werke: Kritische Studienausgabe* (1980) eds G. Coli and M. Montinari, 15 vols, Berlin: Walter de Gruyter.

Norris, C. (1986) *Deconstruction: Theory and Practice*, rev. edn, London and New York: Routledge.

—— (1987) *Derrida*, London: Fontana.

—— (1988) *Paul de Man: Deconstruction and the Critique of Aesthetic Ideology*, London and New York: Routledge.

Oliver, K. and Pearsall, M. (eds) (1998) *Feminist Interpretations of Friedrich Nietzsche (Re-reading the Canon)*, University Park, Pa.: Pennsylvania State University Press.

Owen, D. and Ridley, A. (2000) 'Dramatis Personae: Nietzsche, Culture and Human Types', in A. Schrift (ed.), *Why Nietzsche Still? Reflections on Drama, Culture, and Politics*, Berkeley, Calif.: University of California Press.

Parkes, G. (ed.) (1991) *Nietzsche and Asian Thought*, Chicago, Ill.: University of Chicago Press.

—— (1994) *Composing the Soul: Reaches of Nietzsche's Psychology*, Chicago, Ill.: University of Chicago Press.

Pasley, M. (ed.) (1978) *Nietzsche: Imagery and Thought*, London: Methuen.

Patton, P. (ed.) (1993) *Nietzsche, Feminism and Political Theory*, London and New York: Routledge.

Pickus, D. (2003) 'The Walter Kaufmann Myth: A Study in Academic Judgment', *Nietzsche-Studien*, 32.

Poellner, P. (1995) *Nietzsche and Metaphysics*, Oxford: Clarendon Press.

Pollard, D. (1988) 'Self-Annihilation and Self-Overcoming: Blake and Nietzsche', in D. F. Krell and D. Wood (eds), *Exceedingly Nietzsche: Aspects of Contemporary Nietzsche Interpretation*, London and New York: Routledge.

Pothen, P. (2002) *Nietzsche and the Fate of Art*, Aldershot: Ashgate.

Rampley, M. (2000) *Nietzsche, Aesthetics and Modernity*, Cambridge: Cambridge University Press.

Reginster, B. (2006) *The Affirmation of Life: Nietzsche on Overcoming Nihilism*, Cambridge, Mass.: Harvard University Press.

Richardson, J. (1996) *Nietzsche's System*, Oxford: Oxford University Press.

—— (2000) 'Clark on Will to Power', *International Studies in Philosophy*, 32 (3).

—— (2004) *Nietzsche's New Darwinism*, Oxford: Oxford University Press.

Ridley, A. (1998) *Nietzsche's Conscience: Six Studies from the 'Genealogy'*, Ithaca, NY: Cornell University Press.

Rorty, R. (1978) 'Philosophy as a Kind of Writing: An Essay on Derrida', *New Literary History*, 10 (1).

—— (1991) *Objectivity, Relativism and Truth: Philosophical Papers*, Cambridge: Cambridge University Press.

Rosen, S. (1995) *The Mask of Enlightenment: Nietzsche's Zarathustra*, Cambridge: Cambridge University Press.

Sadler, T. (1995) *Nietzsche: Truth and Redemption: Critique of the Postmodernist Nietzsche*, London: Athlone Press.

Schacht, R. (1983) *Nietzsche*, London and New York: Routledge.

—— (ed.) (1994) *Nietzsche, Genealogy, Morality: Essays on Nietzsche's On the Genealogy of Morals*, Berkeley, Calif.: University of California Press.

—— (1995a) *Making Sense of Nietzsche: Reflections Timely and Untimely*, Urbana, Ill.: University of Illinois Press.

—— (1995b) 'Zarathustra/*Zarathustra* as Educator', in P. R. Sedgwick (ed.) *Nietzsche: A Critical Reader*, Oxford: Blackwell.

—— (ed.) (2001) *Nietzsche's Postmoralism: Essays on Nietzsche's Prelude to Philosophy's Future*, Cambridge: Cambridge University Press.

Schrift, A. D. (1990) *Nietzsche and the Question of Interpretation: Between Hermeneutics and Deconstruction*, London and New York: Routledge.

—— (2000) *Why Nietzsche Still? Reflections on Drama, Culture, and Politics*, Berkeley, Calif.: University of California Press.

Schutte, O. (1984) *Nietzsche Without Masks*, Chicago, Ill.: University of Chicago Press.

Scott, J. (1998) 'Nietzsche and Decadence: the Revaluation of Morality', *Continental Philosophy Review*, 31.

Sedgwick, P. R. (1997) 'Nietzsche as Literature/Nietzsche as "German" Literature', *Journal of Nietzsche Studies*, No. 13, Spring.

—— (2001) *Descartes to Derrida: An Introduction to European Philosophy*, Oxford: Blackwell.

—— (2005) 'Violence, Economy and Temporality: Plotting the Political Terrain of *On the Genealogy of Morality*', *Nietzsche-Studien*, 34.

—— (2007a) 'Nietzsche, Normativity and Will to Power', *Nietzsche-Studien*, 36.

—— (2007b) *Nietzsche's Economy: Modernity, Normativity and Futurity*, Basingstoke: Macmillan.

Siemens, H. (ed.) (2001a) 'Nietzsche's Language and Use of Language', *Journal of Nietzsche Studies*, 22 (autumn).

—— (2001b) 'Nietzsche's Political Philosophy: A Review of Recent Literature', *Nietzsche-Studien*, 30.

Simmel, G. (1991) *Schopenhauer and Nietzsche,* trans. H. Loiskandle, D. Weinstein and M. Weinstein, Urbana, Ill.: University of Illinois Press. First published 1907.

Small, R. (1987) 'Nietzsche and the Platonist Tradition of the Cosmos: Center Everywhere, Circumference Nowhere', *Journal of the History of Ideas,* 44.

Solomon, R. C. (ed.) (1973) *Nietzsche: A Collection of Critical Essays,* Garden City, NY: Anchor Books.

—— (2003) *Living With Nietzsche: What the Great 'Immoralist' Has to Teach Us,* Oxford: Oxford University Press.

Spinks, L. (2003) *Friedrich Nietzsche,* London and New York: Routledge.

Stambaugh, J. (1972) *Nietzsche's Thought of Eternal Return,* Baltimore, Md.: Johns Hopkins University Press.

—— (1987) *The Problem of Time in Nietzsche,* trans. J. F. Humphrey, Philadelphia, Pa.: Bucknell University Press.

Stegmaier, W. (2001) 'God, Faith and Justice', *New Nietzsche Studies,* 4.

Stern, J. P. (1979) *A Study of Nietzsche,* Cambridge: Cambridge University Press.

Strong, T. (1975) *Friedrich Nietzsche and the Politics of Transfiguration,* Berkeley, Calif.: University of California Press.

Tejera, V. (1987) *Nietzsche and Greek Thought,* Dordrecht: Nijhoff.

Thiele, L. P. (1990) *Friedrich Nietzsche and the Politics of the Soul: A Study of Heroic Individualism,* Princeton, NJ: Princeton University Press.

Vattimo, G. (1988) *The End of Modernity: Nihilism and Hermeneutics in Postmodern Culture,* trans. J. R. Snyder, Cambridge: Polity Press.

—— (2002) *Nietzsche: An Introduction,* trans. N. Martin, London: Continuum.

Warren, M. (1988) *Nietzsche and Political Thought,* Cambridge, Mass.: MIT Press.

Welshon, R. (2004) *The Philosophy of Nietzsche,* Chesham: Acumen.

Wilcox, J. (1974) *Truth and Value in Nietzsche,* Ann Arbor, Mich.: University of Michigan Press.

Winchester, J. (1994) *Nietzsche's Aesthetic Turn: Reading Nietzsche after Heidegger, Deleuze, and Derrida,* Albany, NY: State University of New York Press.

Young, J. (1992) *Nietzsche's Philosophy of Art,* Cambridge: Cambridge University Press.

—— (2006) *Nietzsche's Philosophy of Religion,* Cambridge: Cambridge University Press.

Yovel, Y. (ed.) (1986) *Nietzsche as Affirmative Thinker,* Dordrecht: Nihoff.

INDEX

The Index does not contain main entries.

After Empire

What is the future for multiculturalism? Can we move beyond the melancholic celebration of past glories embodied in the cry "two world wars and one World Cup" to imagine a modern, multicultural British identity? In this important new book, Paul Gilroy addresses the plight of a beleaguered multiculture, and defends it against accusations of failure. He examines the invention of the hierarchical category of "race," and its terrible consequences in colonialism and fascism, and considers how the work of thinkers including George Orwell, Frantz Fanon and W. E. B. DuBois can shed light on contemporary debates about nationalism, postcolonialism, and race. Finally, citing examples ranging from Mike Skinner of *The Streets* to Ali G, Gilroy explores aspects of Britain's spontaneous, convivial culture—a culture that is flourishing in Britain's urban areas and in postcolonial cities around the world—to discover a new value in our ability to live with difference without becoming anxious, fearful, or violent.

Paul Gilroy is the Charlotte Marian Saden Professor of Sociology and African American Studies at Yale University. He is the author of *There Ain't No Black in the Union Jack* (Routledge Classics edition, 2002), *The Black Atlantic* (1993), and *Small Acts* (1994). A revised edition of his recent book, *Between Camps: Nations, Cultures, and the Allure of Race*, is also published by Routledge.

PAUL GILROY

After Empire
Melancholia or convivial culture?

Routledge
Taylor & Francis Group

LONDON AND NEW YORK

First published 2004
by Routledge
2 Park Square, Milton Park, Abingdon, Oxon, OX14 4RN

Routledge is an imprint of the Taylor & Francis Group

Transferred to Digital Printing 2010

© 2004 Paul Gilroy

Typeset in Sabon by RefineCatch Limited, Bungay, Suffolk

British Library Cataloguing in Publication Data
A catalogue record for this book is available from the British Library

ISBN 0-415-34307-0 (hbk)
ISBN 0-415-34308-9 (pbk)